WATER
FOR A
THIRSTY LAND

FORTRESS CLASSICS
in
BIBLICAL STUDIES

Forthcoming Titles

The Spirit and the Word
Prophecy and Tradition in Ancient Israel
Sigmund Mowinckel

Jesus and the Message of the New Testament
Joachim Jeremias

WATER
FOR A
THIRSTY LAND

Israelite Literature and Religion

HERMANN GUNKEL

Edited by K. C. Hanson

FORTRESS PRESS
MINNEAPOLIS

WATER FOR A THIRSTY LAND
Israelite Literature and Religion

Scripture is from the Revised Standard Version of the Bible, copyright © 1946, 1952, 1971 by the Division of Christian Education of the National Council of the Churches of Christ in the U.S.A. Used by permission.

Cover image: *Crescent Moon over the Southwest* by Sherri Silverman (20th century, American). Pastel. Private collection. Courtesy of Sherri Silverman/Superstock, Inc. Used by permission.
Cover and book design: Zan Ceeley

Library of Congress Cataloging-in-Publication Data

Gunkel, Hermann, 1862–1932.
　　　[Essays. English. Selections]
　　　Water for a thirsty land : Israelite literature and religion / Hermann Gunkel ; edited by K. C. Hanson ; translated by A. K. Dallas and James Schaaf.
　　　　　p. cm. — (Fortress classics in biblical studies)
　　　Includes bibliographical references (p.) and index.
　　　Contents: Why engage the Old Testament? — Israelite literary history — The Jacob traditions — The Hagar traditions — The prophets, oral and written — The religion of the Psalms.
　　　ISBN 0-8006-3438-1 (alk. paper)
　　　　　1. Bible. O.T.—Criticism, interpretation, etc. I. Hanson, K. C. (Kenneth C.) II. Title. III. Series.

　　　BS1171.3 .G86 2001
　　　221.6—dc21   2001040714

Manufactured in the U.S.A.   AF 1–3438
05   04   03   02   01   1   2   3   4   5   6   7   8   9   10

Contents

Acknowledgments

Chapter 1 was first published as "Was bleibt vom Alten Testament?" *Deutsche Rundschau* 41 (1914). This translation is a modification of the one done by A. K. Dallas as "What Is Left of the Old Testament?" in *What Remains of the Old Testament and Other Essays* (London: George Allen & Unwin; New York: Macmillan, 1928) 13–56.

Chapter 2 was first published as "Die Grundprobleme der israelitischen Literaturgeschichte," *Deutsche Literaturzeitung* 27 (1906) cols. 1797–1800 and 1861–66; it was reprinted in Gunkel's *Reden und Aufsätze* (Göttingen: Vandenhoeck & Ruprecht, 1913) 29–38. This translation is a modification of the one done by A. K. Dallas as "Fundamental Problems of Hebrew Literary History," in *What Remains of the Old Testament and Other Essays* (London: George Allen & Unwin; New York: Macmillan, 1928) 57–68.

Chapter 3 was first published as "Jakob," *Preussische Jahrbücher* 176 (1919). This translation is a modification of the one done by A. K. Dallas as "Jacob," in *What Remains of the Old Testament and Other Essays* (London: George Allen & Unwin; New York: Macmillan, 1928) 150–86.

Chapter 4 was first published as "Two Accounts of Hagar," *The Monist* 10 (1900) 321–42. This translation is a modification of the one done by W. H. Carruth for that journal.

Chapter 5 was first published as "Die Propheten als Schriftsteller und Dichter," in *Die Propheten* (Göttingen: Vandenhoeck & Ruprecht, 1923) 34–70. This translation is a modification of the one done by James Schaaf, which first appeared in *Prophecy in Israel*, edited by David L. Peterson, Issues in Religion and Theology 10 (Philadelphia: Fortress Press, 1987) 22–73.

Chapter 6 was first published in sections in *Die Christliche Welt* 36 (1922) nos. 1, 2, 5, 6, and 7. This translation is a modification of the one done by A. K. Dallas as "The Religion of the Psalms," in *What Remains of the Old Testament and Other Essays* (London: George Allen & Unwin; New York: Macmillan, 1928) 69–114.

Abbreviations

HTIBS	Historic Texts and Interpreters in Biblical Scholarship
HUCA	*Hebrew Union College Annual*
IDB	*Interpreter's Dictionary of the Bible*
IDBSup	*Interpreter's Dictionary of the Bible Supplementary Volume*
Int	*Interpretation*
IRT	Issues in Religion and Theology
JBL	*Journal of Biblical Literature*
JJS	*Journal of Jewish Studies*
JNES	*Journal of Near Eastern Studies*
JQR	*Jewish Quarterly Review*
JSOT	*Journal for the Study of the Old Testament*
JSOTSup	JSOT Supplement Series
JSS	*Journal of Semitic Studies*
KAT	Kommentar zum Alten Testament
MLBS	Mercer Library of Biblical Studies
Mon	*The Monist*
NVBS	New Voices in Biblical Studies
OBT	Overtures to Biblical Theology
OTL	Old Testament Library
OTP	*Old Testament Pseudepigrapha*, Ed. J. H. Charlesworth. 2 vols. Garden City, N.Y.: Doubleday, 1983–85.
OTWP	*De Ou Testamentiese Werkgemeenskap in Suid-Afrika*
PJ	*Preussische Jahrbücher*
ResQ	*Restoration Quarterly*
RGG²	*Die Religion in Geschichte und Gegenwart*, 2nd ed. (1927–30)
SBLDS	Society of Biblical Literature Dissertation Series
SBT	Studies in Biblical Theology
SBTS	Sources for Biblical Theological Study
SemeiaSup	Semeia Supplements
SHANE	Studies in the History of the Ancient Near East
SWBA	The Social World of Biblical Antiquity Series
TBl	*Theologische Blätter*
TDOT	*Theological Dictionary of the Old Testament*
ThBü	Theologische Bücherei
TRu	*Theologische Rundschau*
TUMSR	Trinity University Monograph Series in Religion
VT	*Vetus Testamentum*
VTSup	VT Supplements
ZAW	*Zeitschrift für die alttestamentliche Wissenschaft*
ZDMG	*Zeitschrift für die deutsche morgenländische Gesellschaft*
ZS	*Zeitschrift für Semitistik und verwandte Gebiete*
ZTK	*Zeitschrift für Theologie und Kirche*

Editor's Foreword

The importance of Hermann Gunkel's contributions to biblical studies can hardly be overestimated. His breadth of knowledge, his innovations of methodology, and his sensitivity to the ancient literatures put him on the cutting edge of research, influencing both Old Testament and New Testament scholars.

Born in Springe, Germany, in 1862, Gunkel taught Old Testament at the universities of Halle, Berlin, and Giessen. He retired from Halle in 1927 and died in 1932 after being ill for several years.

What began as a career in New Testament scholarship was sidetracked into Old Testament studies. Gunkel's publication in 1888 of *Die Wirkungen des heiligen Geistes* (*The Influence of the Holy Spirit*; trans. 1979), when he was only twenty-six, created difficulty in his getting a university position in Germany, where theological faculties were influenced by church concerns. But his probing mind and skillful control of the ancient sources allowed him to move on to Old Testament research.

Gunkel was a pioneer among the scholars who became identified as the *Die religionsgeschichtliche Schule* ("the History of Religion School"). Their concern was to get at the essence of religion itself. They were interested in studying the histories of the variety of religions, but also what was fundamental to religion itself—that is, the history of *religion*. They went about this task by exploring religious traditions as widely as possible; and they were interested in tracing the histories of religious ideas, traditions, and practices—in short, the whole development of religion. Led by the older Albert Eichhorn (history of Christianity), other members in this movement were all approximately the same age as Gunkel: Hugo Gressmann (Old Testament), William Wrede (New Testament), Wilhelm Bousset (New Testament and history of Judaism), and Ernst Troeltsch (history of theology).

Because of his religio-historical method, one of the things that makes Gunkel's work of continuing interest is that he always paid close attention to literary, historical, and cultural parallels from Egypt, Babylon, and even later Arab cultures. He unfortunately died too soon to benefit from the enormous explosion of textual discoveries from Ugarit, Mari, Nuzi, and Bogazköy, to say nothing of the Dead Sea Scrolls and the Nag Hammadi Library. But he was especially cognizant of the importance of the Babylonian discoveries made in the late nineteenth century. This was first shown in his *Schöpfung und Chaos in Urzeit und Endzeit* (Creation and Chaos in Primeval-time and End-time) in 1895, the first systematic use of the religio-historical method on biblical texts.

Beyond his groundbreaking religio-historical work, he was the father of form criticism. Building on the insights of German folklorists (especially Wilhelm Wundt and the Grimm brothers), he clearly saw the relationship of genres, setting in life, and intention in texts. Integral to this methodology was paying attention to oral traditions that eventually took shape in written documents. This was particularly evident in his major commentaries on Genesis (1st ed. 1901) and the Psalms (1929), and also *Das Märchen im Alten Testament* (1921; *The Folktale in the Old Testament*, trans. 1987). But his posthumously completed work *Einleitung in die Psalmen* (1933; *An Introduction to the Psalms*, trans. 1998), completed by his son-in-law and student, Joachim Begrich, demonstrates his remarkable attention to detail, sense of traditio-historical development, and wide-ranging coverage of ancient sources: Hebrew Bible, New Testament, Apocrypha, Pseudepigrapha, and ancient Near Eastern texts. This form-critical method had further impact on New Testament studies because of his influence on Rudolf Bultmann and Martin Dibelius.

Gunkel is one of those handful of biblical scholars whose work has not faded with time. Not only did he open new doors for research, his insights have maintained their importance for more than a century.

The reader should be aware that I have edited Gunkel's essays in a number of ways. Most importantly, I have provided numerous corrections to the earlier English translations. In addition, I have: (1) moved some citations from the essays to the footnotes, adding all the relevant data; (2) deleted some side comments (especially about German schooling and church catechetical practices) that are not germane to the topic; (3) added footnotes (marked by square brackets) and bibliographies in order to bring the reader up-to-date in the discussion; (4) employed the RSV for biblical translations in most cases; and (5) added biblical citations for some of Gunkel's biblical allusions. I have also made occasional modifications in the RSV quotations by changing RSV's "LORD" to "Yahweh" and changing words such as "thou" to "you."

K. C. Hanson

1

Why Engage the Old Testament?

The question posed by this essay takes for granted that much of the Old Testament, which was foundational for faith in earlier generations, has ceased to hold that position in our minds, and that we are neither able nor anxious to retain all that our ancestors thought they possessed in the Old Testament. Let us begin by asking how this change has occurred. How has it come about that the Old Testament appears to the present generation in a different light than that in which it appeared to our ancestors?

When the Christian Church came into existence it accepted not only the Old Testament writings but also the doctrine that that book was a work of God, given and inspired by the Holy Spirit. Although in the course of the first Christian centuries the New Testament came to occupy a place alongside the Old, the esteem in which the Old Testament was held continued as before, and both collections were handed down over almost two thousand years, both equally accepted as the Word of God and as the source of true doctrine. Every sentence—even every letter—was received as divine and infallible. This unqualified estimate of the Old Testament continued almost unchanged down to the middle of the eighteenth century; and, although it has lost some of its uncompromising definiteness, it has by no means disappeared even now. But biblical research, which came into existence about the middle of the eighteenth century and gradually gathered strength and confidence, first challenged that view, then attacked it, and finally shook it to its foundations, if it has not completely destroyed it.

Many of the positions that Old Testament research has examined have gradually become familiar to everyone, but a few of them may be briefly indicated here.

THE DIFFICULTIES

Many of the traditions with regard to the authors of the Old Testament writings that have come down to us—either in the Bible itself, in the form of titles and superscriptions, or from sources outside the Bible—have proved to be erroneous. Thus, only certain passages in the Book of Isaiah derive from that ancient prophet. The Book of Daniel does not derive from the period of the Babylonian exile (sixth century B.C.E.), but from a much later period. The Book of Proverbs was not written by Solomon, and neither was Ecclesiastes nor the Song of Songs. The Psalms that are called by David's name were not all written by that king; indeed, it is questionable whether one single Psalm is Davidic. Again, the idea that the first five books of the Bible are the work of Moses was a mistake of tradition. As a matter of fact, these books were not written by any one single author but are a collection of ancient writings gradually put together. These ancient writings themselves belong to various periods, and the mere raising of the question whether they are Mosaic is conceivable only in the case of very few of them. These positions are currently regarded as common ground by all practitioners of Old Testament research and accepted even by conservative scholars.

Doubt has therefore been cast on the credibility of many of the biblical narratives. The natural sciences have long recognized that the sequence of the works of creation as given in the opening chapters of Genesis is entirely out of keeping with modern views. For example, the biblical account places the creation of plant life before that of the heavenly bodies. To us it seems childish to believe that Elisha on one occasion caused an iron axe-head to float on the water. A modern reader smiles when he or she finds it recorded as a historical fact that a she-ass opened its mouth and spoke, or that a man spent three days in the belly of a great fish and then emerged alive, or that the first humans lived for centuries.

Moreover, there are numerous contradictory statements in the Old Testament. How, for example, could Cain marry a wife and build a city at a time when there were no other human beings in the world?

As soon as observations of this kind had shaken the esteem in which the Old Testament was held, people gained courage to go further and give expression to criticisms regarding the religion and morality of the Old Testament. And, indeed, there is much in it that cannot but offend—sometimes very gravely—a pure, moral sensibility. Jacob, by lies and deception, obtains the divine blessing. Some have tried to read into this narrative the idea of divine discipline and a conversion of the deceiver; but the narrative itself does not contain one single word that indicates disapproval of the deception he practiced on Isaac. In Egypt, Abraham passes his wife off as his sister, and it is only by divine interposition that the matter ends without evil result. Again, one feels surprise at the exclusive nature of the relation in which Israel's religion stands to Israel's interests. Yahweh is the God of Israel and of no other people. Israel's wars are (neither more nor less) Yahweh's wars. The pious Israelite hurls fearful curses against the enemy of his people without any feeling of the injustice and wrong involved in such conduct:

> How honorable is the one who takes and dashes
> your children against the rocks. (Ps 137:9) [Ed. trans.]

Thus the opinion that the Old Testament is a safe guide to true religion and morality can no longer be maintained.

In view of all this, it is not surprising that during the nineteenth century a vigorous discussion was carried on with reference to these and numerous similar "causes of offense" in the Old Testament. The opponents of religion and of the Bible seized on them as subjects of mockery. Stalwart supporters of the Bible, on the other hand, also often saw in the criticisms urged by Bible-loving scholars nothing but the results of unbelief.

Another serious hindrance to a proper understanding of the Old Testament was the fact that many unthinking people have identified ancient Israel with the Jews of our own day, leaving out of account the long interval between the ancient past and the present time, and forgetting that the great changes that have passed upon Israel in the course of three thousand years cannot possibly have been without effect on the national character of that people. This is just as intelligent as seeing a German business traveler of today as a typical representative of the ancient Germans.

As a result, many half-informed people, unable to forget their former estimate of the Old Testament, find themselves unable to read its writings simply as human works. Their historical education is in many cases good enough to enable them to appreciate the differences between the Old Testament and the New; but it is not comprehensive enough to enable them to study such an ancient book simply and without prejudice. People of this sort take offense at incidents narrated in the Old Testament that would be quite inoffensive if they occurred, say, in Homer. They are offended when they read about Jacob's deceit; but they can read with pleasure about the constant lying of Odysseus. If they could only bring themselves to understand the Hebrew narrative simply as a roguish piece of folklore—that is to say, if they would read it in the sense in which it was originally meant—they would see it in an entirely different light.

The Babel-Bible controversy[1] has revealed how many people have felt the force of the criticisms that have been directed against the Old Testament and who, when they learn that parts of the Old Testament are of Babylonian origin, are ready to throw the whole book overboard. Whoever pays attention to what is being thought and said in our day cannot fail to hear the eagerness with which the question is asked, "What is left to us of the Old Testament?"

CONTEMPORARY OLD TESTAMENT RESEARCH

To this question Old Testament research is prepared to give a frank and clear reply. For a century and a half scholars have been busy: first groping uncertainly, then progressing with increasing confidence, until they have now worked out a clear conception of what the Old Testament is. Among the scholars who have helped to achieve this result, Julius Wellhausen will always be named with honor. Old Testament scholarship, by means of great acumen, patient detailed investigation, and a power of intuition amounting to genius, has sketched a splendid picture of the history of the people of Israel, its religion, and its literature. To Old Testament research, the Bible is in the first instance a book produced by human means in human ways, thus definitively giving up the old conception of inspiration. Research has brought it down from heaven and set it up in the midst of the earth. It treats the Old Testament and the people of Israel with the same methods as would be applied to any other book and any other people. And by doing so, Old Testament research justly claims to be a fully qualified member of the historical disciplines. A university that gives no place to this research cannot claim to be in a full sense an institution of higher learning (*universitas literarum*). Because we have dealt with the Old Testament in this manner, we have rediscovered its true significance for world history. To the question "What do we have in the Old Testament?" we reply soberly and definitely: "We have a great treasure, a very great treasure, in the Old Testament."

To begin with, we have in the Old Testament an almost unlimited wealth of artistic stimulation. It was one of the German classical authors, Johann Gottfried Herder (1744–1803), who discovered the beauty of the Old Testament, and Johann Wolfgang von Goethe (1749–1832), who, like Francis Bacon (1561–1626), "took all knowledge for his province," followed that discovery with sympathy and interest. Goethe writes: "When we recall the time when Herder and Eichhorn pointed this out to us, we are reminded of a great delight comparable to a veritable oriental sunrise."[2] In the Prologue to his greatest poem (*Faust*, 1808), Goethe had in mind the Prologue to the Book of Job; and in the concluding act of the second part of the same poem, where angels and devils fight for Faust's soul, we have an echo of a Judean legend, in which a similar fight takes place for the dead body of Moses, so that a brilliant writer of the modern era has even called Moses both the prototype and anti-type of Faust.[3] Everyone knows also how devotedly Goethe read the Old Testament from his early youth; how greedily he drank in Martin Luther's glorious translation; and how, by making the powerful German of Luther's Bible his own, he invigorated the German literary style of his time, which had degenerated to insipidity.

Our educated people, even our lovers of aesthetics, seem to have forgotten what living streams of poetical beauty are found in the Old Testament. Our pious people say that the Bible walks around in the guise of a slave, wearing the humble garments of a beggar. To be sure, by no means everything in the Old Testament is of equal aesthetic value; much of it from this point of view is arid and desolate enough. But looking at it as a whole we may nevertheless say that the Old Testament wears no beggar's garment, but the royal robe that befits it.

NARRATIVES

In the first place, among the best-known aesthetic creations of the Bible are those glorious poetic narratives of marvelous insight and unique feeling for beauty of form, composed with a truly classic sense of style. They are therefore the delight of artists down through the ages and the theme of ever new creations, imitated again and again, in poetry and on canvas. These narratives bring the life of antiquity vividly before our eyes, a well of rejuvenation for a civilization grown old, immediately recognizable to our children, loved by them, and embodying for them lofty and eternal ideas.

Think of the force with which murder is set forth as a base crime in the story of Cain; the charm of the Joseph story, eloquent with fraternal envy and love, and full of faith in an overarching Providence; the attractiveness of the Ruth story, exhibiting a widow's love lasting beyond death and the grave; the magnificent solemnity of the creation narrative; the wondrous story of paradise, naïve yet profound. Old Testament research has only begun to apply itself to the study of this aesthetic side of the narratives. One should imagine that linguists, historians of civilization, and everyone interested in aesthetics would vie with us in holding up to view these golden treasures, and that even our poets would study these ancient narratives and learn from them the secret of compact power, unity of construction, and graphic clarity.

We hope this will be the case before long. In the meantime, however, we would say to teachers: realize what valuable material you have in these narratives. How much poorer in poetical materials our schools would be if these were absent from them! It would mean the ruin of our aesthetic civilization if adults, not having learned the Old Testament at school, should be unable to understand at once allusions to those Old Testament narratives that former times have bequeathed to us in lavish abundance.

THE PROPHETS

There are the prophets—many of them also poets of the first rank, using a language full of power and energy and majestic elevation—trumpets of God, uttering notes of such strength that our ears can hardly bear them. They are filled with overwhelming anger and overflowing with rapture, or at other times melting into pity, torn by grief and sorrow, and rising to defiant faith. Here too is a marvelously varied world—only partially, it is true, intelligible to our children—unlike any modern literature, but just because of its strangeness, its bizarre, rugged greatness, full of attractiveness to our older students. In this unforgettable poetical style, we have the highest thoughts of humanity. Above all, the imperishable power of the moral idea is expressed.

Let us look at a few passages in order to gain some idea of the prophets' poetic power. Take first the famous passage of Isaiah, in which he describes the approach of dread Assyria (Isa 5:26-30). Summoned by Yahweh himself— a thought both sublime and terrifying to the ancient Israelite—Assyria advances from the end of the earth, marching with unstoppable haste. No obstacle, such as usually delays an army's advance, stalls its progress. With his terrible war-cry, like the roar of a lion making his adversary quake, he springs upon Israel and then stands shrieking over his prey. An obscure image, borrowed from the ancient creation-myth, concludes the dreadful description—darkness covers heaven and earth, and through the darkness sounds the roar of the enemy, like the roaring of the raging sea. Primeval chaos—darkness and great waters—again prevails. The last fight and end of the gods has arrived:

> He will raise a signal for a nation afar off,
>   and whistle for it from the ends of the earth;
> and lo, swiftly, speedily it comes!
> None is weary, none stumbles,
>   none slumbers or sleeps,
> not a waistcloth is loose,
>   not a sandal-thong broken
> their arrows are sharp,
>   all their bows are bent,
> their horses' hoofs seem like flint
>   and their wheels like the whirlwind.
> Their roaring is like a lion,
>   like young lions they roar;
> they growl and seize their prey,
>   they carry it off, and none can rescue.

They will growl over it on that day
    like the roaring of the sea.
And if one look to the land,
    behold darkness and distress;
and the light is darkened by its clouds. (Isa 5:26-30)

Among all the battle scenes the Assyrians and Egyptians have left us, not one can compare in vivid grandeur with this Old Testament picture.

Another passage from the same prophet describes the end of the Assyrian dominion and the coming of the messiah (Isa 9:2-7). In a time of misery, due to foreign oppression, the prophet sees his people walking in "the land of darkness," that is, in the land where the sun is unknown—a legendary idea that also appears elsewhere. But he also sees the hour of deliverance, when the sheen of the glorious light pierces this awesome land. That will be a day of rejoicing, such as at harvesttime or when the people divide the booty brought home at the end of a war. What does this light mean? Why this joy? The prophet explains it in a parable. Until now Israel was like a beast of burden, sighing under the heavy oppression of Assyria. Now Yahweh has broken the yoke and destroyed the oppressor's rods. Then a new image rises before the prophet's eye: the enemy's army is destroyed; the battlefield is strewn with the enemy's weapons, cast aside in sudden flight. These are all gathered into a great heap, and what till now was Israel's terror is burned in the fire—the war boots in which the enemy had once marched with the noise of thunder and the military cloaks stained with the blood of the slain. Then the prophet's eye passes from the deliverance to the deliverer. A new ruler appears in Israel, a mysterious child, bearing the rod of a prince on his shoulder. And by means of a series of divine epithets, the prophet announces what the characteristics of this new ruler will be. Wise in counsel, never at a loss, he will be "wonderful"; and in his strength he will be like a god. Like a father, he will guard his people forever and give them the peace for which they long. Thus on David's ancient throne—for the wonderful one is from David's line—there will arise the dominion of righteousness and peace forever. But all this is due to the "zeal" of Yahweh Sabaoth (Yahweh of the Armies), who will not allow his people to be robbed or harmed by foreigners.

The people who walked in darkness
    have seen a great light;
those who dwelt in a land of deep darkness,
    on them has light shined.
You have multiplied the nation,
    you have increased its joy;

They rejoice before you
    as with joy at the harvest,
    as men rejoice when they divide the spoil.
For the yoke of his burden,
    and the staff for his shoulder,
    the rod of his oppressor,
    thou hast broken as on the day of Midian.
For every boot of the tramping warrior in battle tumult
    and every garment rolled in blood
    will be burned as fuel for the fire.
For to us a child is born,
    to us a son is given;
and the government will be upon his shoulder,
    and his name will be called
    Wonderful Counselor, Mighty God,
    Everlasting Father, Prince of Peace.
Of the increase of his government and of peace
    there will be no end,
upon the throne of David, and over his kingdom,
    to establish it, and to uphold it
with justice and with righteousness
    from this time forth and for evermore.
The zeal of Yahweh of hosts will do this. (Isa 9:2-7)

No one who looks at such pictures can ever lose the impression made by these strong colors. Surely it is high time that people awake from their neglect of the prophetic writings.

LYRIC POETRY

In the third place is the whole realm of Old Testament lyric poetry, containing secular and spiritual poems of the most varied kind. Like the prophetic writings, these are not all of equal worth, but they include many of the most fascinating and delightful creations in all literature, some with a deep organ tone and some undulating and rippling like the sea. A few examples will be better than any descriptions.

In imperishable words, full of deep sadness, the psalmist sings of the brevity and misery of human life: he does not, however, in his sorrow, sink into despair, but sets over against this human fate the eternity of God, immeasurable by any human gauge: people pass away, but God abides.

Lord, you have been our dwelling place in all generations.
Before the mountains were brought forth,
> or before you had formed the earth and the world,
> from everlasting to everlasting you are God.
You turn a person back to the dust,
> and say, "Turn back, O children of humanity!"
For a thousand years in your sight
> are but as yesterday when it is past,
> or as a watch in the night.
You sweep people away; they are like a dream,
> like grass which is renewed in the morning.
in the morning it flourishes and is renewed;
> in the evening it fades and withers.
For we are consumed by your anger;
> by your wrath we are overwhelmed. (Ps 90:1-7)

Or take the following passage from another profound psalm:

Whither shall I go from your Spirit?
> Or whither shall I flee from your presence?
If I ascend to heaven, you are there!
> If I make my bed in Sheol, you are there!
If I take the wings of the morning
> and dwell in the uttermost parts of the sea,
even there your hand shall lead me,
> and your right hand shall hold me.
If I say, "Let only darkness cover me,
> and the light about me be night,"
even the darkness is not dark to you,
> the night is bright as the day;
> for darkness is as light with you. (Ps 139:7-12)

Or consider a poem full of pain and homesickness with a savage ending:

By the waters of Babylon,
> there we sat down and wept,
> when we remembered Zion.
On the willows there
> we hung up our lyres.
For there our captors
> required of us songs,

> And our tormentors, mirth, saying,
>   "Sing us one of the songs of Zion!"
> How shall we sing Yahweh's song
>   in a foreign land?
> If I forget you, O Jerusalem,
>   let my right hand wither!
> Let my tongue stick to the roof of my mouth,
>   if I do not remember you,
> if I do not set Jerusalem
>   above my highest joy!
> Remember, O Yahweh, against the Edomites
>   the day of Jerusalem,
> how they said, "Burn it, burn it,
>   Down to its foundations!"
> O daughter of Babylon, you devastator!
>   How honorable is the one who requites you
>   with what you have done to us!
> How honored shall be the one who takes your little ones
>   and dashes them against the rocks! (Ps 137:1-9) [Ed. trans.]

This poem tells us how keen foreigners were to enjoy the strains of a Hebrew melody. We may infer that even in antiquity Hebrew music was renowned throughout the world. This inference is supported by the fact that King Hezekiah was compelled to deliver his musical instruments to the Assyrians along with other valuables. In the modern era, we are now beginning to know the poetry of Babylon, Assyria, and Egypt and can heartily confirm this verdict of the ancient world. Taken as a whole, all the poetry of the ancient Near East is much inferior to that the Israelites, and the highest praise that can be given to a Babylonian or Egyptian song is that it is not altogether unworthy of being compared with the poems of the Bible.

And what a wealth of varied forms is set before us here! The Israelite poets describe the majesty of Yahweh in triumphant strains. They celebrate his glory in creation: "The heavens are telling the glory of God" (Ps 19:1); his forgiving grace to Israel: "As a father pities his children, so Yahweh pities those that fear him" (Ps 103:13). Or they lament with hearts broken by their personal sorrow or by national misfortune, or from their tears they look up confidently to God. Perhaps the most arresting and most genuine of all their poems are those in which in liturgical fashion alternate voices are heard: first, with bell-like tones, expressing the confidence of their faith, and then with the note of pain of the burdened heart—the burdened heart that yearns for those heights of bliss.

Take for example Psalm 85. In the lofty tone of prophetic vision, the first part announces as actual fact the deliverance that is still to come:

> You, O Yahweh, were favorable to your land;
>> you restored the fortunes of Jacob.
>
> You forgave the iniquity of your people;
>> you pardoned all their sin.
>
> You withdrew all your wrath;
>> you turned from your hot anger. (vv. 1-3)

The second part contains a prayer, expressing the yearning of the people for this deliverance:

> Restore us again, O God of our salvation,
>> and put away your indignation toward us!
>
> Will you be angry with us forever?
>> Will you prolong your anger to all generations?
>
> Will you not revive us again,
>> that your people may rejoice in you?
>
> Show us your steadfast love, O Yahweh,
>> and grant us your deliverance. (vv. 4-7)

The third stanza reverts to the opening note. Out of the circle of singers rises a man accustomed to hear the divine voice. And he is able to announce that what the downcast hearts so ardently desire is at hand! Deliverance is near!

> Let me hear what Yahweh will speak,
>> for he will speak peace to his people,
>> to his saints, to those who turn to him in their hearts.
>
> Surely his deliverance is at hand for those who fear him,
>> that glory may dwell in our land.
>
> Steadfast love and faithfulness will meet;
>> righteousness and peace will kiss each other.
>
> Faithfulness will spring up from the ground,
>> and righteousness will look down from the sky.
>
> Yea, Yahweh will give what is good,
>> and our land will yield its increase.
>
> Righteousness will go before him,
>> and make his footsteps a way. (vv. 8-13)

Thus ends the poem in a tone of ecstatic vision: deliverance and grace on all sides, above and below, and everywhere.

Songs such as these cry out for a composer. They were once meant to be sung; they ought to be set to music once more. Would Bach not have known how to do justice to the varied religious moods of these songs if he had known them in their new, more vivid interpretation?

Speaking generally, the Israelite mind did not excel at lengthy productions, and so the shorter the pieces the more beautiful they are.[4] The Israelite had a special gift for painting a richly colored picture in very small compass. But the Israelite mind succeeded in producing one great poem that is also long: the Book of Job. Here the author is bold enough to impugn, and even to attack, the strongest base of the whole Israelite religion, that is the doctrine of divine retribution. Heartsick and afflicted by a horrible and incurable disease—a fate that flatly contradicted the doctrine ardently believed by all good people—Job still refuses to give up his conviction of his own innocence. He enters upon a bitter contest with his pious friends, who find their whole religion in this doctrine, and even ventures to call into question the very justice of God. Three friends argue with him, but Job overthrows all three and remains alone on the field. Then he rises, and his words sound like an accusation addressed to heaven in the name of all humanity: Why? Why? Now the Eternal One comes forth in person, revealing his divine majesty in sublime words to this son of earth. All questioning is hushed: "I lay my hand upon my mouth" (Job 40:4). The Book of Job is like a titanic structure towering up to heaven; but by the end, all that is human fades and only God's greatness remains.

It is significant that the orthodoxy of past centuries revealed no understanding of this pearl of Old Testament poetry, just as in some ecclesiastical circles today aesthetic considerations are treated with disdain or even with displeasure. The false halo surrounding everything in the Old Testament prevented its natural beauties from being enjoyed. But we are deliberately emphasizing this aesthetic side in the hope that the reader who has learned to appreciate the beauty of so many of the biblical poems will also come to love the ideas they enshrine.

HISTORY

But it is not only the poetry of the Old Testament that still has a message for us; its history is also of great importance. The people of Israel produced not only poetical narratives but also a highly developed historical literature. Portions of this are preserved for us in 2 Samuel and in scattered passages of the other narrative books. This literature has an amazing objectivity.[5] Owing to this astounding objectivity, the work of the Israelite historian far surpasses anything produced elsewhere in the ancient Near East—and is exceeded only by the great historians among the Greeks. "Hebrew civilization," says Eduard

Meyer, "alone of all the other (ancient Eastern) civilizations, really stands on the same intellectual level as the Greek."[6] The pictures have been painted in such true colors that Israelite history, incomplete as our knowledge of it is, is more familiar to us than the history of any other people of the ancient Near East. Everywhere else in the East the annals of history were written in the service of despots, whereas in Israel there prevailed a spirit of freedom that refused to fall slavishly in the dust before the king but depicted faithfully both him and his deeds.[7] Even the legends provide us with an abundance of historical information, clearly revealing the internal conditions of Israel: its religion, its customs, its laws, and its social relationships.

RELIGION

All the things that we have mentioned are but trifles when compared with the greatest treasure of the Old Testament: its religious value. Israelite religion, it is true, is not simply to be identified with the Christian religion. Indeed, in numerous details and in its profoundest thoughts Israelite religion is much inferior to it. And the type of exposition that is still to be found in many schools, an exposition that seeks to obliterate these differences, is open to many objections and involves many dangers. In these numerous points where this inferiority of Old Testament religion and morality is most apparent, the teacher who has not appreciated these differences is forced either to resort to all sorts of artificial interpretation or to present to students the religion of ancient Israel as a perfect divine revelation. Under such circumstances, either truth is sinned against or religion and morality are degraded. That this latter result is sometimes produced is, unfortunately, a sad fact.

All the same, a close connection between the two testaments does exist. The religion of the New Testament arose on the foundation of Old Testament religion, and it cannot be adequately understood without an understanding of the latter.[8] It is now acknowledged that other religions also have influenced both pre-Christian Judaic religion and the Christianity that arose from it. Old Testament research is just beginning to understand these relations—in particular, the syncretistic mystery religions of that time, in which, under the cover of Hellenism, many Near Eastern elements became intermingled with it—and to get at the real nature of earliest Christianity.[9]

But although these investigations are still far from having reached their goal, it can already be said that Christianity is historically inconceivable without the Old Testament. Jesus was born and educated as a Judean and nourished in spirit on the Old Testament. No trace of Hellenistic influence can be found in him. And although such influence was undoubtedly present in Paul and John, they too remained Judeans in all essential elements. It was within the walls of the synagogue that Christianity spent its earliest days. Christianity only left the synagogue when it was forcibly expelled from it, and through the centuries it has clung to the inheritance that it brought with it from its ancestral home, the Old Testament.

In its early days the Christian church did meet one captivating tempter, gnosticism, which suggested that it should abandon the Old Testament as the charter of an inferior religion.[10] With good reason, the church resisted this temptation and clung to its Old Testament, in spite of the serious difficulties presented by the task of interpreting it. This position of the Old Testament in the Christian church is a historical fact, against which it would be foolish to grumble. It is extremely improbable that history will ever retrace its steps in this regard. The interpretation of the Old Testament may change, but the right of the Old Testament to its place in the church is indisputable. It will be read as holy scripture as long as the church endures, and it is simply a result of unhistorical thinking when the proposal is made that the church should let the Old Testament go. To the most basic reader of the Bible, it can be made clear that one must not overlook the Old Testament if one desires to understand the New Testament. In numerous passages, the New Testament refers to the Old and develops the thoughts contained in it. Who can hope to grasp Paul's thought if one knows nothing of the Law from which Christ has delivered us? Or of Adam, through whom sin came into the world? Or of Abraham, whose faith made him the father of all who believe? No, the very name Christianity is a reminder that the first disciples of Jesus transferred to their master the greatest name in the Old Testament, the name *Christos,* the messiah.

It is, to be sure, undeniable that in Paul's writings there are numerous survivals from the Judean past that we are fully entitled to lay aside. It is clear, too, that both Jesus and Paul, in their contest with the Judean legalism of their day, opposed that spirit that is found here and there in the legal sections of the Old Testament, especially in the so-called Priestly work (a post-exilic source in the Pentateuch); but it is also clear that in the main content of their thinking—up to a certain point—they are descendants of the Old Testament. Thus the reader of the Bible always returns to the Old Testament, and as long as our schools provide religious instruction, they cannot help dealing with the Old for the sake of the New. It is pointless to discuss the matter. History has spoken and the case is decided. The Christian church—a mighty structure—will unfold its nature in the course of its growth, but it will only change it at the cost of serious convulsions; and one of the foundations of the church is the Old Testament.

But completely apart from its connection with the New Testament and the Christian church, the Old Testament possesses many features that give it an outstanding religious value for the present day. Here again we must draw distinctions. Much of the Old Testament has no religious value—such as the lists of names and genealogical trees and compositions like the Song of Songs, a collection of poems dealing with love and marriage, which is interesting on account of their poetic beauty but of entirely secular value. Other things, in the course of the history of religion, have also lost their position, despite the fact that they were understood to have religious value. We have already spoken of some of these at the beginning of this chapter. The close connection of religion with the states of Israel and Judah has no meaning for us. The creation story, valuable for religious thought, is for us not actual history. The morality of early Israel differs to a large extent from ours. The intolerance of Israelite religion towards all other religions has become impossible for people who have learned to attach some value to other religions. This intolerance is axiomatic to Israelite religion, as articulated in such words as "heathen" and "idols"; and it has unfortunately penetrated via Judaism into Christianity and has long held a prominent position in it. An unbiased person will admit differences like these. Christian orthodoxy and Jewish interests do no service to the cause of the Bible when they claim that everything in the Old Testament is equally great and valuable.

Enduring Value

But just because we frankly give up what cannot be defended, we hope to obtain a hearing when we point out what is of lasting value in the Old Testament. For the Old Testament has a wealth of ideas and conceptions that form the imperishable achievements of the Israelite spirit. These are not, and never can become, obsolete, for they lie at the root of all modern thinking, whatever attitude people may take up toward church and religion. In addition, the Old Testament contains conceptions that, although they have now been outgrown in the history of ideas, can never be forgotten, because they are necessary stages in the path of evolution; and again, the Old Testament has, among its distinctive ideas, some which form a valuable counterposition to certain injurious tendencies of our own time.

The Decalogue

A few of the numerous examples may be mentioned here. We have already spoken of the simplicity of Israelite thought as mirrored in the ancient sages. This simplicity is a fundamental feature of Israelite religion. Thoughts that are at the root of all religious and moral civilization have been rammed like posts into its soil. For example, take the principles of morality as expressed in the Ten Commandments or Decalogue,[11] with their majestic and inviolable "Thou shalt. . . ." Words like these, with the breath of the primeval world upon them, tower like giant mountain peaks. Empires disappear, kingdoms pass away, and even modern nations and states have no promise of permanence; all external civilization is in constant movement, but foundations like these moral principles abide. Who would dare to take them from our children, just because for us they are no longer complete as they stand, but require to be extended and applied?

Monotheism

Again, take the great tenet of monotheism—a tenet that seems so simple that any child should be able to understand it.[12] The deity is to be conceived as a unity; but the Israelite conception is far simpler than that. Yahweh, God of Israel, is the one living and true God; beside this figure, concretely conceived, there is no other. This also is an absolutely inviolable tenet, the root of all higher moral and spiritual religion, and finds an echo in every idealistic view of the world down to the present day.

Retribution

Another tenet of the Old Testament, equally simple, appearing and reappearing in countless variations, addresses the divine retribution of good and evil.[13] This great thought finds a place even among the Ten Commandments. Although it was all too often externalized in ancient Israel, with the result that retribution was looked for and found to an undue extent in the outward lot of people, it still remains one of the most important principles of every moral religion and of every higher view of the world. Namely, this is the belief that the natural and the moral governance of the world, however often they seem to be at variance, are not at bottom mutually exclusive; that the course of events in its final purpose serves good and not evil ends; that it is constructive and not destructive; and that retribution is a reality. To be sure, Christianity knows a higher relation between God and humanity than that of retributive law; but Christianity merely shifts the thought of retribution into the second place—it by no means suspends it. "Do not be deceived; God is not mocked, for whatever a man sows, that he will also reap" (Gal 6:7). Our children understand the message of retribution far better than they understand that of redemption; for the latter can only be understood when a person has by long and painful experience learned one's own powerlessness. It is therefore wise to lead our children by the same path that history has trod.

True Worship

The prophets carried on a controversy with the people of their time with regard to the question, "In what does true service to God consist?" The view that they struggled against was the view common to all antiquity: that the deity should be worshiped by all manner of holy acts, by sacrifice and cere-monies. But the prophets achieved a fundamentally new conception of reli-gion. God does not require people to obey certain holy customs; he demands the entire life, a piety that is shown in action—moral behavior. A maid sweep-ing a room can, as Luther expressed it, be leading a holy life, holier than that lived by the monk in his cell. This great principle, which does away with all action that is merely formal—a principle that is also fundamental in the Protestant tradition—finds perfect expression in the prophets: "For I desire steadfast love and not sacrifice, the knowledge of God, rather than burnt offer-ings" (Hos 6:6). Here religion and morality have formed an alliance that shall never be dissolved. We cannot conceive a type of piety that is not at the same time moral. Today all views of the world lead up to morality, even those in which it is not easy to see any relation to morality at all. But in this inward necessity, to which even the modern spirit pays homage, we have an achieve-ment of the Israelite prophets.

Morality

The manner in which these people conceived of morality was also of great importance for the history of the world. With trenchant power they ham-mered into the hearts of their people, and through their writings, into the heart of all humanity, the truth that the essence of sin is oppression of the lowly, and that righteousness consists in worthy treatment of the poor and the oppressed. When, some decades ago, the economic conditions among mod-ern nations had become intolerable to the masses, this message of the prophets was laid anew on people's consciences. All modern social legislation is an outcome of the prophetic spirit, and the spirit of these Israelite teachers will continue to urge the nations to ever fresh reform.

Eschatology

Further, we hit upon the eschatology of the prophets, their teaching on the last things. Here, too, Israel's prophets gave an impulse to the world, the effect of which continues down to our own day. These ardent souls, driven nearly to despair amid the sin and wretchedness of their time, lived on the faith that this world of misery and forgetfulness of God must be followed by a new world in which the ideal will be victorious. This unswerving hope in a better day was characteristic of Israel and distinguishes that people from a people like the Greeks, who knew nothing of such a future hope. This attitude of mind, how-ever, is a fundamental feature of present-day nations; all peoples today, how-ever they differ in their ways of thinking, agree in the conviction that the history of humanity is not yet ended. Religious minds are sighing, "It does not yet appear what we shall be" (1 John 3:2).

Nature

When we try to understand any religion that has appeared, it is of fundamental importance to discover the sphere in which it traces the peculiar workings of God. It is characteristic of the religion of the New Testament that it lays supreme emphasis on the relation of God to humanity, and that, in comparison with that relation, God's activity in nature recedes into the background. Life in and with nature, such as had existed in earlier eras, had receded into the background, even though it was not completely lost. Thus, although the belief that God is at work in nature was never abandoned in the teaching of the Christian church—that would have been impossible—it was not especially dynamic or powerful. Since the days of Rousseau and Goethe, the deep feeling for nature has reawakened among modern nations and grown to a degree that was previously undreamed of.

If it is correctly guided, this communion with nature can become an antechamber to the temple of religion. In this regard, therefore, the modern world is conscious of a need that cannot be completely satisfied by the New Testament. The Old Testament fills this gap. In the hymns of nature contained in the Old Testament, notes are struck that awaken an echo in the hearts of contemporary people. Our churches and schools should not, as they so often do, continue to ignore these hymns of nature. We should not be deflected from the study of these poems by the fact that many of them still contain traces of mythological color; for it is just this peculiar mythological feature, bringing phenomena like the storm, the volcanic eruption, the earthquake, into the special and immediate relation to the deity, that supplies conceptions of outstanding poetic and religious power. The light is "the garment of God"; the heavens are his "tent"; the hills "smoke" when they are "touched by his hand"; to the sea, rushing towards the shore, he sets a limit and says, "Thus far and no further"; the lions roar to him for their food, and he gives their nourishment to the young ravens.

Political Religion

We can identify another aspect in which the Old Testament can supplement the New. In the New Testament, the actual point where God and humanity meet is the human heart. The decisive question is: "What must I do to be saved?" The salvation meant here is the salvation of the individual soul, and it is a supramundane, heavenly salvation. Compared with this, the Old Testament is on a lower level, for in its pages religion deals in the first instance with political life, although it was out of this political religion that the higher religion of the individual arose. But at this level of political religion, ideas were born that are still of great value for our time. Chief among these is the thought of the direct interest of religion in political affairs. The New Testament developed at a time when the gigantic Roman Empire was endeavoring to wean its provinces from all independent political action and was just about to break the last remnant of Judean political existence; the only message of the New Testament is subjection to the state. It makes no mention of the duty of positive cooperation in the tasks of the state.

There is a different message in the Old Testament, which dates from the time when the Israelite state was still at its full strength. In the Old Testament we find a magnificent combination of piety and patriotism: "If I forget you, O Jerusalem, let my right hand wither!" (Ps 137:5). Yahweh's faithful servants did not by any means withdraw from political affairs as if these were unclean or concerned the authorities only, or were things with which subjects had nothing to do. They felt most deeply the fate of their nation and took part with all their might in public affairs in the name of their God. The prophets in particular endeavored with passionate ardor to guide the affairs of the state toward their own goal. Today, we cannot imitate these endeavors in detail, but we may learn that an interest in politics and patriotism, on the one hand, and piety, on the other, still belong together.

Yahweh and History

Furthermore, it was on the basis of Israel's state religion that the great idea of Yahweh's sovereignty in history arose. We repeatedly read in the Old Testament that a comprehensive purpose of God runs through the entire history of Israel. That thought never loses its meaning, although it occasionally employs imperfect means and works with unhistorical or legendary materials. To express it in abstract terms, revelation takes place in history.[14] And the Old Testament even reached the idea that the heathen world is also included in God's purpose. In Daniel 6, the whole course of world history is summed up into a unity—four world empires are to succeed each other on the stage. Here we have the conception of world history, and it is no mere accident that, almost down to the present day, our great historians have divided the history of the world in accordance with the four empires of Daniel.

Doctrine

Other countries besides Israel have possessed the gift of reflection on religious subjects. They have given forth difficult and complicated doctrines concerning what goes on within the godhead or concerning the salvation of humanity. There is, for example, the doctrine of the Greek Orthodox Church and the scholasticism of the Middle Ages. We find nothing but faint hints of all that in the Old Testament. Israelite religion never developed lengthy doctrines. It was content with the statement of a few great principles. Compared with the truths set forth in the Old Testament, even the epistles of the New Testament are difficult, where the subtlety and acuteness of Hellenistic thought are manifested. That is why it is so difficult to introduce contemporary youth to the thought of these epistles. It is not our concern, however, to deny that this is a weakness of Israelite thinking. As long as it remained pure and untouched by outside influence, the Israelite mind was hardly capable of philosophic thought. But to see this sheer simplicity is good for us, a generation whose spiritual world has come to be as complex as our social conditions.

Religious Emotion

Combined with this simplicity of Israelite mentality is a magnificent religious emotion. By nature the Israelite was more temperamental than a cold Northerner. No Greek ideal of moderation curbs the Israelite mind and heart. Unlike Christianity, the Israelite religion did not exhort one to gentleness, and a hot temperament impels the Israelite to deeds of passionate energy, sometimes even of violence and fanaticism.

And as was the people, so was its history. This history is full of tragedies, even great tragedy. The Greek people fight against the Persians, conquer them, and then enjoy its period of greatest glory; but the Israelite people, once the equal of the Greeks in nobility and power of spirit, are repeatedly crushed mercilessly by colossal world powers.

THE GOD OF ISRAEL

The one who revealed himself to Moses at Sinai was originally a volcanic deity. It was in the grandest but most awesome thing that earth has to show—that is, in a volcanic eruption, that Moses found his God. The thunder crashes like the blare of trumpets. A heavy, dark cloud, pierced by the thunderbolts, covers the mountain. The whole mountain quakes. Flames shoot forth from the midst of the heavens. Moving with incredible speed, the smoke cloud rises, changing into ever new forms, lit up by the internal glow of the mountain. This is the "pillar of fire and smoke," "the glory of Yahweh," in which Yahweh reveals himself. Yahweh was originally a volcanic deity, and this characteristic of suddenness and unexpectedness is always retained. He may control himself—the volcano does not erupt every day—but suddenly he rises to his sublime greatness and destroys in one blow all his surrounding enemies.

In keeping with this idea of the deity, Israel conceived war as a special revelation of God; and with what terrible realism was Yahweh pictured as the God of war! Gentler natures may be filled with dismay at the thought of such a God spattered with blood, but stronger natures will recognize in this conception the revelation of a mighty, tremendous power.

The deeds performed for this God were dreadful. In the wild fury of war, ancient Israel sacrificed to its God entire cities with all their inhabitants as an awful whole-offering. Elijah with his own hand cut down the prophets of Baal at the Kishon spring. At the word of Elisha, Jehu swept Baal out of Israel in a sea of blood. But these are only the excesses of the power of the faith that produced in Israel the grandest figures and ultimately led moral religion to victory through many difficulties and storms.

Moses

It is in the Old Testament that we find the two greatest figures in Israelite narrative. The first is Moses, just as Michelangelo (a kindred spirit) has depicted him.[15] He sits high on Mount Sinai, holding in his hands the tablets of the Law, which he has received from God. From the valley at the foot of the mountain he hears a distant noise—it a sound of war in the camp! No, it is not the shout of victory, nor the shout of vanquished troops. He hears notes of melody. The people have fallen away from Yahweh, have cast a golden calf, and are now celebrating a festival in its honor. Then the anger of Moses flares up; he hurls the tables, inscribed as they are by God's own hand, and smashes them to pieces on the ground. The saga that relates this deed imputes no blame to Moses in is fury. It understands full well that the extreme of passion befits the extreme of delinquency, and that a rage so fierce cannot but destroy.

Elijah

The second great figure in the Old Testament is Elijah on the same mountain.[16] He is in the twilight of his life. Throughout his long life he has wrestled for the soul of his people and failed to win it. All have fallen away, except "seven thousand in Israel, all the knees that have not bowed to Baal" (1 Kings 19:18). Wearied, the prophet flees to the distant hill of God in order to lay his complaint before Yahweh, who appears to him and speaks consoling words. The dread judgment, so Yahweh tells him, is at hand. Three bloody "swords of Yahweh" are to cut down the faithless Israelites. These swords are the cruel king of their enemy Aram, who will not even spare the child in the womb; the king of Israel itself, the savage Jehu, who will root out the royal dynasty and all other followers of Baal; and finally Elisha the prophet, Elijah's successor, who will slay "by the words of his mouth." In this manner Israel will be swept away and only the faithful seven thousand will be left alive. What about that? In all that horror of blood, it is Yahweh's judgment that is being accomplished. Yahweh's cause triumphs, and that is all that matters.

Classical Prophets

Moses and Elijah are succeeded by the writing prophets—Amos, Hosea, Isaiah, Jeremiah, Ezekiel—a great series of heroic figures, all "intoxicated with God," and upheld by the sublime thought that evil must have no place on earth, that a kingdom like Israel, so given over to sin, so faithless towards God, cannot continue to exist. Unlike the great men of former days, they do not appeal to the sword. Their sole weapon is the word: in the meantime, the times have become softer. But in true greatness these representatives of God are not inferior to the ancients.

For example, in Mic 6:1-6, the man of God rises and stands, as it were, between heaven and earth. God has a dispute with his people, and the prophet is God's spokesman. The judges are the surrounding hills.

> Hear what Yahweh says:
> Arise, plead your case before the mountains,
> and let the hills hear your voice.
> Hear, you mountains, the controversy of Yahweh
> and you enduring foundations of the earth;
> for Yahweh has a controversy with his people,
> and he will contend with Israel. (vv. 1-2)

This exordium is followed by Yahweh's charge—not, as we might expect, in anger and wrath but in love and with gentle reproach:

> O my people, what have I done to you?
> In what have I wearied you? Answer me!
> For I brought you up from the land of Egypt
> and redeemed you from the house of bondage;
> and I sent before you Moses,
> Aaron, and Miriam.
> O my people, remember what Balak . . . devised
> and what Balaam . . . answered him . . . (vv. 3-5a)

Balak, king of Moab, desired Balaam to curse Israel, but Balaam, under Yahweh's constraint, opened his mouth in blessing.

> From Shittim to Gilgal,
> that you may know the saving acts of Yahweh. (v. 5b)

These last words refer to the marvelous passage of Israel through the Jordan River.

And now we are to suppose that Israel's heart is broken by those pleading words of love. Israel draws near to God in penitence, asking how it may atone for its sins:

> With what shall I come before Yahweh,
>   and bow myself before God on high?
> Shall I come before him with burnt offerings,
>   with calves a year old?
> Will Yahweh be pleased with thousands of rams,
>   with ten thousands of rivers of oil? (vv. 6-7a)

The sacrifices are increasingly great until ultimately they cannot be measured; but the last is the greatest:

> Shall I give my first-born for my transgression,
>   the fruit of my body for the sin of my soul? (v. 7b)

The penitent sinner thus outbids himself, offering ever greater sacrifices, and finally reaches the most awful of all. But now it is as when the sun rises. Nothing of all that.

> He has showed you, O man, what is good;
>   and what does Yahweh require of you
> but to do justice and to love kindness,
>   and to walk humbly with your God? (v. 8)

This example shows better than many words the greatness of prophecy and the power of moral passion that resided in the prophets. Here we see how gloriously the power of Old Testament religion can work.

Creation

The grandeur of this image of God is shown with special clarity in the sublime conception of creation.[17] In other religions, the deity may enter into the world, wrestle with its powers and finally reduce them to order. Yahweh is too great for that! He stands outside of the world and works on it from the outside by his will. "And God said, 'Let there be light'; and there was light" (Gen 1:3).

It is also in keeping with the greatness of this notion of God that Israelite religion disdained every image of the deity. This was not the result of intelligent reflection or illumination, but a profound fear of God that made them forbid every image and almost every symbol. To make an image is to make a comparison, but "To whom then will you liken God, or what likeness compare with him?" (Isa 40:18; compare 40:25; 46:5).

Hymns

This profound feeling of the greatness of God explains the important part played by the hymn in practical religion.[18] Of course, in Israelite religion the universal human motive drives the pious one to seek from God the deliverance of his people, his own deliverance, and the fulfillment of earthly desires—a thought that undeniably appears repeatedly in the New Testament with many marks of human limitation. But right alongside it we find the nobler idea that people must have something outside themselves that they can look up to and worship, and to which they can devote themselves to wholeheartedly. This deep need was profoundly felt by the people of the Old Testament—hence the richness and variety of the moving hymns in which God's praise is sung.

Holiness

In addition to the warmth of these songs of praise, in the Old Testament we find expressions of the fear of the holy God. Israelite religion is essentially a religion of holiness.[19] "Woe is me! For I am lost; for I am a man of unclean lips, . . . for my eyes have seen the King, Yahweh Sabaoth" (Isa 6:5). We could desire for our own people and religion something of this depth of feeling that is so manifest in the Israelite people and in their religion. The Old Testament, in its rugged strength, would be as iron in the blood of our time, which has become so soft, so irresolute, and so "out of joint."

To be sure, not everything in the Old Testament bears in equal degree this mark of sternness. The softer and more tender notes of religion also find expression in it. Even genial and cheerful features are found, especially in the later writings. We find numerous touching narratives and arresting psalms. But common to all these is one feature our generation sorely needs, and for which the profoundest minds of our day are hungering: certainty in religion. For the Israelite people, religion was something quite different from a worldview, although the two are not completely distinct. To them, God is not an "auxiliary conception" or a pale abstraction but a real figure, close to the heart. They walk "before him" and they live with him, just as we commune with a friend whom we saw yesterday and will see again tomorrow, who is thinking of us, although we do not see him at the moment. But this idea must not be misunderstood.

The living God is just as close to the heart today as he was yesterday and as he will be tomorrow. Through this nearness of God and this certainty of faith, the religious life gained in depth and warmth, and the religious personality received an inward strength that seems to us, with our weaker faith, like a distant goal far beyond us. We look up, therefore, full of reverence and longing to the prophets, to whom it was given to feel the reality of God. That is why the religious heart of all the ages has loved the Psalms so much and responded more readily to their appeal than to that of those earlier heroic figures, who are great but overly vehement. It is in this spiritual lyric poetry of the Psalms that the natural notes of piety are heard.

> As a hart longs for flowing streams,
> so longs my soul for you, O God. (Ps 42:1)

> Whom have I in heaven but you?
>   And there is nothing upon earth that I desire besides you.
> My flesh and my heart may fail,
>   but God is the strength of my heart and my portion for ever.
>   (Ps 73:25-26)

These are the basic words of religion in which generations still unborn will express their deepest feelings. The religion of the Psalms lives amongst us still; in our hearts it is more effective than many of the Christian dogmas. How many pious hearts articulate their real religion in the words, "Yahweh is my shepherd, I shall not want" (Ps 23:1). Let us also keep in mind the simple exhortation of the pious Tobias, "Remember the Lord our God all your days, my son, and refuse to sin or to transgress his commandments" (Tob 4:5a).

Personalities

We must refer to one more feature of the Old Testament: its rich and varied gallery of personalities. We have already mentioned many of them in this brief outline: prophets, singers, thinkers, heroes, poets, and sages. This wealth of religious personalities is the real greatness of Israelite religion. For this reason alone it is an insult to the historical spirit even to name Babylonians and Egyptians in the same breath with Israel. These civilizations are great because of things achieved by great masses of people under the domination of despots and priests: gigantic world empires, great walls and canals, huge structures. But these civilizations, especially that of Babylon, are entirely destitute of personal life. With regard to Egypt, an exception must be made in the Amarna Period, when that country was affected by Semitic influence. Israel, on the other hand, was poor in technical achievements; apart from its temporary greatness under David, the state had little importance. The kingdom was never great in works of external civilization. In the sphere of spiritual things, however, it produced the highest that was achieved anywhere throughout the East—human personality living in the presence of God. *That* is the achievement of Israelite prophecy. Because of that achievement, Israel is "the chosen people" and "salvation is of the Jews." There can be no dispute about the matter. Our own day, with its marvelous technical achievements and its comprehensive organization of labor, may bear comparison with the civilizations of Egypt and Babylon, but the complaint is heard more and more loudly that the personalities that the idealistic age produced so abundantly are beginning to die out. It is becoming more and more difficult for independent people to maintain their ground in the face of the mighty machine that reduces everyone to the same pattern. Would not a dash of the spirit of ancient Israel be good for our spiritual life today? If the prophets would only awaken!

CONCLUSION

The Old Testament reveals its true greatness only when we have made up our minds to surrender unreservedly the ancient doctrine of inspiration. We have brought it down from heaven to earth, and now it rises majestically before our eyes from earth to heaven. We have also seen that it contains much that appears to us far from admirable, and many things that would be dangerous and destructive to our religion and morality if they were carried over unintelligently into our time. Scientific integrity demands that we do not lay emphasis only on the one side like a bad advocate, but that like a just judge, we frankly set forth both sides.

Those who have undergone historical training see not only beautiful incidents but history. To them it is clear that in every human effort and attainment there is and must be both "great" and "small," the sublime beside the ordinary. The inferior elements do not repel historians; indeed, they love history because, as a faithful picture of human nature, it contains, and must contain, these features. We see in history lofty and worthy life; but we see it not only as consolidated achievements but also in the process of becoming, wrestling with lower elements and slowly freeing itself from these. It was only at the end of its history that Israel fully attained the monotheism toward which it was steering from the very beginning. In fact, in many utterances, especially the poetical ones, we find it still entangled with remnants of polytheism. To students with a historical turn of mind such a picture of struggling growth seems more attractive than that of a finished achievement. Even Christian faith will not be offended by this thought. The Old Testament is not the perfect revelation of the Christian view: it is only the revelation taking place in history.

The course taken by world history has made the spiritual life of Israel one of the foundations of the civilization of the Christian nations of Europe. Our civilization rests on two bases—the Bible (the Old Testament and the New Testament) and the civilization of Greece. We have become what we are by virtue of the combination of these two worlds. It would be a revolution, the magnitude of which no one living can estimate, if either of these foundations were to be moved. Everyone with a historical mind will consider it their duty to understand the mind that is revealed in all history and that has set these two pillars as a foundation. With this conviction comes the realization that while the process of building goes on, its foundation stones will abide.

Notes

[1.] The Babel-Bible controversy concerned the question of the influence of Babylonian literature on the Bible. The controversy, begun by lectures first given in 1902 by Friedrich Delitzsch (*Babel and Bible: Three Lectures on the Significance of Assyriological Research for Religion, Embodying the Most Important Criticisms and the Author's Replies*, trans. J. McCormack et al. [Chicago: Open Court, 1906]), aroused a conservative backlash. For a historical discussion of this controversy, see Mogens Trolle Larsen, "The 'Babel/Bible' Controversy and Its Aftermath," in *Civilizations of the Ancient Near East*, ed. J. M. Sasson (New York: Scribners, 1995) 1.95–106. For later views of the issues involved, see Herbert B. Huffmon, "Babel und Bibel: The Encounter between Babylon and the Bible," in *Backgrounds for the Bible*, ed. M. P. O'Connor and D. N. Freedman (Winona Lake, Ind.: Eisenbrauns, 1987); and Mogens Trolle Larsen, "Orientalism and the Ancient Near East," *Culture and History* 2 (1987).

2. Goethe, in his notes to the *Westöstlichen Divan;* see the English translation in *Poetical Works of J. W. von Goethe*, ed. N. H. Dole (Boston: Niccolls, 1902).

3. Konrad Burdach, *Faust und Moses*, 3 vols. (Berlin: Sitzungsberichte d. Kg. Preuss. Akademie der Wissenschaften, 1912), numbers 22, 35, 38.

[4.] On the controversial notion of an "Israelite mind" or mentality see J. R. Porter, "Biblical Classics III: Johs. Pedersen: *Israel*," *ExpT* 90 (1978) 36–40.

[5.] On the "objectivity" of Israelite historical literature, it would be difficult to find many who agree with Gunkel's perspective today. For more nuanced notions of history and its attendant problems in the current discussion, see the diverse views expressed by Baruch Halpern, *The First Historians: The Hebrew Bible and History* (San Francisco: Harper & Row, 1988); Thomas L. Thompson, *Early History of the Israelite People from the Written and Archaeological Sources*, SHANE 4 (New York: Brill, 1992); Gösta Ahlström, *The History of Ancient Palestine* (Minneapolis: Fortress Press, 1993) 19–55; and Mark Zvi Brettler, *The Creation of History in Ancient Israel* (London: Routledge, 1995).

6. Eduard Meyer, *Die Israeliten und ihre Nachbarstämme* (Halle: Niemeyer, 1906) 486; reprinted Darmstadt: Wissenschaftliche Buchgesellschaft, 1967.

[7.] On the relation of the Old Testament to other literatures of the ancient

Near East, see Morton Smith, "The Common Theology of the Ancient Near East," *JBL* 71 (1952) 135–48; Frank Moore Cross, *Canaanite Myth and Hebrew Epic: Essays in the History of the Religion of Israel* (Cambridge: Harvard Univ. Press, 1973); Helmer Ringgren, "The Impact of the Ancient Near East on Israelite Tradition," in *Tradition and Theology in the Old Testament,* ed. D. A. Knight (Philadelphia: Fortress Press, 1977) 31–46; and Cyrus H. Gordon and Gary A. Rendsburg, *The Bible and the Ancient Near East,* 4th ed. (New York: Norton, 1999).

[8.] On the relation of the Old Testament and New Testament, see Gerhard von Rad, *Old Testament Theology,* Vol. 2: *The Theology of Israel's Prophetic Traditions,* trans. D. Stalker (New York: Harper & Row, 1967) 318–409; Rolf Knierim, *The Task of Old Testament Theology: Substance, Method, and Cases* (Grand Rapids: Eerdmans, 1995) 123–38; the twenty-eight essays in two collections: Claus Westermann, ed., *Essays on Old Testament Hermeneutics,* trans. J. L. Mays (Richmond: John Knox, 1963), and Bernhard W. Anderson, ed., *The Old Testament and Christian Faith: A Theological Discussion* (New York: Harper & Row, 1963); and Walter Brueggemann, *Theology of the Old Testament: Testimony, Dispute, Advocacy* (Minneapolis: Fortress Press, 1997) 729–33.

[9.] On the development of the earliest churches, see Gerd Theissen, *The Religion of the Earliest Churches,* trans. J. Bowden (Minneapolis: Fortress Press, 1999); Ekkehard W. Stegemann and Wolfgang Stegemann, *The Jesus Movement: A Social History of Its First Century,* trans. O. C. Dean Jr. (Minneapolis: Fortress Press, 1999).

On Greco-Roman mystery religions, see Walter Burkert, *Greek Religion,* trans. J. Raffan (Cambridge: Harvard Univ. Press, 1985); Luther H. Martin, *Hellenistic Religion: An Introduction* (New York: Oxford Univ. Press, 1987); Robert Turcan, *The Cults of the Roman Empire,* trans. A. Nevill, The Ancient World (Oxford: Blackwell, 1996); and Hans-Josef Klauck, *The Religious Context of Early Christianity: A Guide to Graeco-Roman Religions,* trans. B. McNeil (Edinburgh: T. & T. Clark, 2000).

[10.] On gnosticism, see Kurt Rudolph, *Gnosis: The Nature and History of Gnosticism,* trans. R. McL. Wilson (San Francisco: Harper & Row, 1983); Bentley Layton, *The Gnostic Scriptures* (Garden City, N.Y.: Doubleday, 1987); Pheme Perkins, *Gnosticism and the New Testament* (Minneapolis: Fortress Press, 1993); and Gregory J. Riley, *Fortress Introduction to Gnosticism* (Minneapolis: Fortress Press, forthcoming).

[11.] On the Decalogue, see Albrecht Alt, "The Origins of Israelite Law," in *Essays on Old Testament History and Religion,* trans. R. A. Wilson (Oxford: Blackwell, 1966) 79–132 (esp. 117–32); Eduard Nielsen, *The Ten Commandments in New Perspective: A Traditio-Historical Approach,* trans. D. J. Bourke, SBT 2/7

(Naperville, Ill.: Allenson, 1970); Anthony Phillips, *Ancient Israel's Criminal Law: A New Approach to the Decalogue* (Oxford: Blackwell, 1970); Hans Jochen Boecker, *Law and the Administration of Justice in the Old Testament and the Ancient Near East*, trans. J. Moiser (Minneapolis: Augsburg, 1980); Walter Harrelson, *The Ten Commandments and Human Rights*, OBT (Philadelphia: Fortress Press, 1980); and Dale Patrick, *Old Testament Law* (Atlanta: John Knox, 1985).

[12.] On monotheism in historical perspective, see Mark S. Smith, *The Early History of God: Yahweh and the Other Deities in Ancient Israel* (San Francisco: Harper & Row, 1990); *idem, The Origins of Biblical Monotheism: Israel's Polytheistic Background and the Ugaritic Texts* (New York: Oxford Univ. Press, 2000); the seven essays in Diana Vikander Edelman, editor, *The Triumph of Elohim: From Yahwisms to Judaisms* (Grand Rapids: Eerdmans, 1995); and Robert Karl Gnuse, *No Other Gods: Emergent Monotheism in Israel*, JSOTSup 241 (Sheffield: JSOT Press, 1997).

[13.] On retribution, see Klaus Koch, "Is There a Doctrine of Retribution in the Old Testament?" in *Theodicy in the Old Testament*, trans. T. H. Trapp, ed. J. L. Crenshaw, IRT 4 (Philadelphia: Fortress Press, 1983) 57–87.

[14.] On revelation in history, see Rolf Rendtorff, "The Concept of Revelation in Ancient Israel," in *Revelation as History*, ed. W. Pannenberg, trans. D. Granskou (New York: Macmillan, 1968) 25–53; and Knierim, *The Task of Old Testament Theology*, 149–70.

[15.] On Moses, see Martin Noth, *The History of Pentateuchal Traditions*, trans. B. W. Anderson (Englewood Cliffs, N.J.: Prentice Hall, 1972; German ed. 1948) 156–75; Dewey M. Beegle, *Moses: Servant of Yahweh* (Grand Rapids: Eerdmans, 1972); *idem*, "Moses," in *ABD* 4.909–18; George W. Coats, *Moses: Heroic Man, Man of God*, JSOTSup 57 (Sheffield: JSOT Press, 1988); and Knierim, *The Task of Old Testament Theology*, 351–79.

[16.] On Elijah, see Robert R. Wilson, *Prophecy and Society in Ancient Israel* (Philadelphia: Fortress Press, 1980) 192–201; and Robert B. Coote, editor, *Elijah and Elisha in Socioliterary Perspective*, Semeia Studies (Atlanta: Scholars, 1992).

[17.] On creation, see Gerhard von Rad, "The Theological Problem of the Old Testament Doctrine of Creation," in *The Problem of the Hexateuch and Other Essays*, trans. E. W. T. Dicken (New York: McGraw-Hill, 1966) 131–43; Claus Westermann, *Creation*, trans. J. J. Scullion (Philadelphia: Fortress Press, 1974); Knierim, *The Task of Old Testament Theology*, 171–224; and Brueggemann, *Theology of the Old Testament*, 528–51.

[18.] On Israelite hymns, see Hermann Gunkel and Joachim Begrich, *An Introduction to the Psalms*, trans. J. D. Nogalski, MLBS (Macon, Ga.: Mercer Univ. Press, 1998) 22–65; Walter Brueggemann, *Israel's Praise: Doxology against*

Idolatry and Ideology (Philadelphia: Fortress Press, 1988); and Patrick D. Miller, Jr., *Interpreting the Psalms* (Philadelphia: Fortress Press, 1988) 64–78.

[19.] On holiness, see John G. Gammie, *Holiness in Israel*, OBT (Minneapolis: Fortress Press, 1989); and David P. Wright, "Holiness (OT)," in *ABD* 3.237–49.

A SELECT BIBLIOGRAPHY OF INTRODUCTORY WORKS ON THE OLD TESTAMENT

Coote, Robert B., and Mary P. Coote. *Power, Politics, and the Making of the Bible: An Introduction.* Minneapolis: Fortress Press, 1990.

Gottwald, Norman K. *The Hebrew Bible: A Socio-Literary Introduction.* Philadelphia: Fortress Press, 1985.

Koch, Klaus. *The Growth of the Biblical Tradition: The Form-Critical Method,* translated by S. M. Cupitt. New York: Scribner, 1969.

Rendtorff, Rolf. *The Old Testament: An Introduction,* translated by J. Bowden. Philadelphia: Fortress Press, 1986.

Rogerson, John, editor. *Beginning Old Testament Study.* Rev. ed. St. Louis: Chalice, 1998.

2

Israelite Literary History

Down to the present time there has been nothing, properly speaking, that can be called a "history of Israelite literature," although much valuable preliminary work has been done. There is, of course, a branch of study, usually called "Old Testament Introduction," that deals mainly with the critical questions that concern the literature. For many years these critical problems have occupied the most prominent place in Old Testament study. That was just and right, and criticism will always remain an important, even a fundamental, branch of Old Testament scholarship. Some of the Old Testament writings have come down to us without any statement regarding the date when they were composed. In the case of others, traditional statements on that subject have proved to be erroneous. We have learned that many of the Old Testament books have a very complicated history. They have been compiled from older oral or written traditions and have been subjected to frequent redaction. The first duty of scholarship was to clear away this jungle before undertaking any constructive work. Even if some of the results reached can only be called tentative, this task has now been practically accomplished, and it is now possible to build on this foundation and make an attempt toward constructing the history of Israelite literature.

Many scholars will at once raise the objection that no such history can be established. To begin with, the chronology of the writings is quite uncertain. In many cases the most that can be done is to assign the writing in question to a period. To arrange all the books and their constituent parts in anything like a fixed chronological order is quite impossible since we have no knowledge of the writers. In many cases we do not even know their names, and there is hardly a single case where we have reliable information regarding the personal circumstances and career of the writer. It is clear then that a history of Israelite literature, meaning an indication of the chronological order of the Old Testament writings and an exposition of each writing in the light of the personality of the author of it, cannot possibly be written.

But now the question arises whether, despite this situation, there cannot be a history of Israelite literature in a different sense. The lack of a definite chronology would not be an insuperable obstacle. We would have to be content with indicating the periods of literary activity and dispense with more definite statements. In the case of such ancient literature the personalities of the writers are far less important than in the literature of later ages. In the great periods of later literatures, literary history must necessarily take the form of biographies of the great writers, and their works must be interpreted through their personal experiences. But in ancient Israel, personality, even in the case of an author, was far less developed. In the Psalms, for example, we find an extraordinary sameness of content—in different psalms we find the same thoughts, moods, forms of expression, metaphors, rhetorical figures, and phrases. Even the very greatest writers in Israel, the prophets, frequently exhibit the most striking uniformity. This is due to the fact that in antiquity the power of custom was far greater than it is in the modern world. Besides, like everything else connected with religion, religious literature—and the writings contained in the Old Testament are almost exclusively religious—is very conservative.

A history of Israelite literature, therefore, if it is to do justice to its subject matter, has comparatively little concern with personalities of the writers. That has, of course, a place of its own, but Israelite literary history should occupy itself more with the literary genre (German: *Gattung*) that lies deeper than any individual effort. Israelite literary history is therefore the history of the literary genres employed in Israel, and it is perfectly possible to produce such a history from the sources that are available.[1]

The prime task of a history of Israelite literature must consequently be to determine the genres represented in the Old Testament. We must take the writings of the Old Testament, and, since many of these are collections of writings, we must take their constituent parts out of the order in which they happen to appear in the canon and in which Old Testament Introduction usually studies them, and then rearrange them according to the genres to which they belong.

We may briefly mention some of the main genres. There are first the broad classifications of prose and poetry. Narrative is usually found in prose form, and the following different kinds of narrative can be distinguished: stories about deities (namely myths); primitive folktales—of these first two, only fragments are found in Israel; the popular saga; the developed novella; the spiritual legend; and lastly, historical narrative in the stricter sense.[2] The poetic genres include: wisdom saying, the prophetic saying, the lyric poem—the last two being particularly frequent. Lyric poetry is again subdivided into secular lyrics and spiritual lyrics.[3] Secular lyrics include the dirge, love song, ridiculing song, drinking song, wedding song, victory song, and royal song. Spiritual lyrics include the hymn, thanksgiving song, complaint song of the individual and the community, and the eschatological song. Numerous genres are found within the prophetic writings: the vision in narrative form, prophetic word, and discourse (in many forms). Among these last mentioned, the most ancient is that which foretells the future, and may either be a threat or a promise; the invective, upbraiding sin; the exhortation, calling to positive behavior; and many others.

Most of these genres have long been recognized, and it is the task of literary history to raise this recognition to the level of research—that is, to undertake a systematic investigation. Each genre must be studied in order to show the materials with which it deals and the forms that it necessarily assumes. It will be found that a particular literary type is distinguished by a certain form of exordium. Just as the more modern fairytale usually opens with "Once upon a time," a letter with "Dear Sir/Madam," a sermon with "O beloved in the Lord," so the Israelite hymn frequently opens with "Sing to Yahweh," the dirge with, "Ah! How," the prophetic invective with "Ho, you." It is possible that students who are still unfamiliar with these ancient genres will at first find it difficult to recognize them, definite and distinct as they are; but we must remember that this difficulty did not exist for the ancient audiences. To the people of Israel, the rules of literary form were as familiar as the rules of Hebrew grammar. They obeyed them unconsciously and lived in them; it is only we who have to learn to understand them. Karl Budde was the first to describe one ancient Israelite genre: the dirge.[4] It was also Budde who recognized the wedding song and thus encouraged others to undertake similar studies.[5]

It goes without saying that a task of this kind calls for an artistic sense that until now has not been very prominent in Old Testament Introduction. But this aesthetic sense must not be content to express delight over the beauty of ancient Israelite compositions. It must endeavor to analyze with understanding the beauty that is there, and scholars will then perhaps abandon the view that the aesthetic treatment of the Old Testament writings is unscientific and should be left to "popular" writers.

This study of the genres, however, will only merit the name of literary history when it attempts to get at the history through which these genres have passed.

Every ancient genre originally belonged to a quite definite aspect of Israel's life. Just as among ourselves the sermon belongs to the pulpit, while the fairytale has its home in the nursery, so in ancient Israel the victory song was sung by maidens greeting the returning army; the lament was chanted by hired female mourners by the corpse; the torah was announced by the priest in the sanctuary; the judgment (*mišpaṭ*) was given by the judge in his seat; the prophet uttered his oracle in the outer court of the temple; and the elders at the gate pronounced the wisdom saying. To understand the genres we must in each case have the whole situation clearly before us and ask ourselves: Who is speaking? Who is the audience? What is the setting in life? What is the intention? In many cases a particular class of speaker employs a genre and its use reveals the speaker's class. Just as today a sermon implies a professional preacher, so in ancient times the torah and the hymn of praise were given through the priest, the wisdom saying was uttered by the sage, and the song was performed by the singer. There may even have been a professional class of popular storytellers.

Only a brief study of these genres is needed to demonstrate that, almost without exception, they were originally not written but spoken. It is another of the profound differences between ancient Israelite life and modern life that writing dominated life and even "literature" to a far less extent than it does with us. This explains the extreme brevity and small compass of the ancient compositions. This deserves to be strongly emphasized, because modern students, accustomed to much longer compositions, find it difficult to understand such brevity, and because the delimitation of the literary units is an essential postulate of any literary history. It is a familiar fact that a listener is able to grasp much longer literary units than a reader, who can, of course, suspend and resume reading at will. This is especially true of the ancient listener, whose receptive power was very limited. Therefore, the units of ancient times, both spoken and sung, are much shorter than the written ones with which we are more familiar today. The most ancient Israelite ballad is contained in one or perhaps two long lines—that was all the average listener of the day could grasp at one time.[6] The wisdom literature existed originally as single proverbs or sayings, only one being put forth at a time. And even the most ancient legal judgments, prophetic utterances, and torah statutes are not much longer. In the legends we can make out an ancient style in which the narrative originally consisted of not more than two or three of our modern Bible "verses."

It is still possible, in the case of many of these genres, to trace how they gradually became longer. Compare, for instance, the lengthy utterances of Ezekiel with the much briefer ones from which the Book of Amos is composed. Or note how much more detailed the Joseph novella (Genesis 37–50) is compared with the brief legend of the tower of Babel (Gen 11:1-9). Just as we see the development of our children's minds in the gradually increasing amount that they can take in at one time, so we can trace one feature of the growth of civilization in the gradual increase of the literary units in Israel. Finally, it is true that in contrast to the ancient brevity of style, an entirely new tendency arose, a tendency that resulted in tediousness, such as we find in the extended speeches in Deuteronomy, in some passages of Jeremiah, in the previously mentioned Joseph novella, in a psalm like Psalm 119. Without a doubt, this drift towards length indicates that the times had grown more literary.

But it is one of the critical moments in the life of an ancient literature when some of the types that originally belonged to the life of the people appear in definitive written form. Then, as a rule, collections of writings appear. Almost all that we have in the "books" of the Old Testament comes under this category. It is among the common people that the single proverb, single song, and single narrative emerges; but when these are reduced to writing, naturally several of them are put together. Thus arise collections of legends, poems, and proverbs.

Such collections are of various kinds. Sometimes the original brief units are simply put together without any connection between the items, as in the case of our modern hymnbooks, or Grimm's tales, the Old Testament Psalter, Proverbs, and many of the prophetic books. In that case the chief literary interest lies not so much in the "books" as in the shorter units that were afterwards gathered into "books." In other cases, the compilers have united shorter units to form longer units, and these together constitute a new separate entity, that is, a "book." Thus most of the so-called historical books of the Old Testament are composed of oral traditions that have been woven—sometimes by a complicated process—into some degree of unity by professional writers and infused with their spirit. Here again literary history is particularly interested in these collectors, who did more than merely collect the material. Then, lastly, there emerged great creative personalities who followed up the artificial work of less gifted people and produced new, more comprehensive units. Thus, in the days when the author of Job lived, there must have been an abundant literature of songs and sayings. But that genius proceeded to create complete cycles of long speeches and worked them up into one splendid comprehensive poem.

There is another line of the history of these genres that runs parallel to that which has been described above. Originally the ancient genres had their setting in the life of the people (German: *Sitz im Volksleben*) and were part of their ethnic heritage. Eventually, professional writers arose—poets, storytellers, prophets—who employed the styles that had been perfected by the people and applied them for their own purposes. Thus artistic poetry arose out of the people's poetry. Less gifted people adopted a style as they found it; more skilled ones added here and there something of their own; geniuses transformed it. Each genre had its classical period; then came the mere imitators. In many parts of the Old Testament we have examples of the oldest popular composition, classical creations, and fainter imitations (more than a few) juxtaposed. Our research has the task of describing the mentality and the work of these writers, and the exposition of Israel's great writers is the keystone of Israelite literary history. It will be clear from what has been said that a true appreciation of these people is only possible when the genres have been studied. We must also keep in view that writers who employ genres that they have borrowed may use them in various ways. There is no foundation for the fear that such a study of the genres will push into the background the more important study of the writers; the two lines of study in no way exclude one another, but scholars should meantime devote attention first to what is really the primary task—the study of genres.

The oldest genres, which are still part of the people's life, always have a pure style. But in later periods, when people and relationships were more complex, when authors took hold of the genre, one finds deviations and mixtures of styles. The dirge, for example, which was originally sung at the grave of the individual, was used metaphorically in connection with the downfall of a people or a city. At a still later stage it was employed to express scornful exultation over a fallen enemy. Religious songs, originally used in worship services, were sometimes divorced from such public use and were sung by an individual in his own house. It was in this way that the psalmic poetry arose. Or again, we find a combination of song and proverb or song connected with narrative. All types of mixed styles are especially frequent in the prophets. In their eagerness to reach their people they adopted a large number of genres used by other writers, combined them, and filled them with prophetic content. This is how the prophets became poets, historians, and legislators, and the genres that they thus used and developed were continued by their disciples as independent genres. Such mixing of styles is frequently found when the history of a literature is nearing its close.

Occasionally it is even possible to see the same material passing through different genres and being transformed on each occasion in the spirit of a new age. For instance, the legend can be seen transforming into the novella or saga.

Finally we come to the tragedy of Israelite literature. The spirit loses power. The genres are exhausted; imitations begin to abound. Redactions take the place of original creations. Hebrew ceases to be the living language of the people. By this time the collections are grouped together into larger collections. Finally, the canon took shape.

It need hardly be stated that the literary history of Israel, having such tasks to perform, must necessarily take the shape of historical narrative. Old Testament Introduction may consider it sufficient to treat its problems separately, following the accidental order in which the books have come down to us. Some attempts have been made, even from that standpoint, to produce something to which the label "literary history" has been given. But a genuine history of the literature can only be founded on a thorough study of the genres. Its character must be determined by a consideration of the genres and of the periods into which the history of the country and its civilization falls. It will only merit the title it claims when it can show how the literature emerged from Israel's history and was the expression of its spiritual life. Professor Reuss has done much to prepare the way for a real literary history of Israel.[7]

One more point of great importance remains. The history of Israel has very close connections with the history of the other Near Eastern peoples, and therefore, in the study of its literature, constant attention must be paid to the cognate genres that were current among these people, especially in Babylonia and Egypt.[8] In this regard, Old Testament scholars still have a large debt to pay. The time is now surely past when people will try to interpret the oracles of the Old Testament without regard to the similar literature of Egypt, or to understand the religious songs of Israel apart from those of Babylonia. This study is still in its infancy, and a rich harvest awaits the student who endeavors to collect all the narratives, including those of distant countries, that exhibit any likeness to those of Israel and compare them with each other. Very curious affinities will be recognized, but on the other hand, the peculiar character of the Israelite spirit will be seen all the more clearly. Such a task is, to be sure, far beyond the power of any one person. Is there no German academy that feels the importance of the subject and is willing to follow it up?

Although literary history presupposes the settlement of the main problems of "introduction," it will doubtless also have a reflex influence on that branch of study. It will save scholars from giving exclusive interest to mere details and direct their attention to larger problems. It will also shed new light on many aspects of Israelite life. When we have seen how genres arise and understand that they are not the creations of individuals but are produced by the cooperation of many generations, we shall not be likely to claim that one person— say Jeremiah—wrote the Psalms. Furthermore, one must take the oral tradition more into account in the assessment of literary phenomena.[9] One will, for example, have to be more careful about accepting hypotheses of literary dependence.

NOTES

[Note: Gunkel included no footnotes to this essay. Notes 4, 5, and 7 below are based on comments within the text of the essay.]

[1.] For overviews of the method Gunkel was articulating (form criticism), see Klaus Koch, *The Growth of the Biblical Tradition: The Form-Critical Method,* trans. S. M. Cupitt (New York: Scribner, 1969); Rolf Knierim, "Old Testament Form Criticism Reconsidered," *Int* 27 (1973) 435–68; Gene M. Tucker, *Form Criticism of the Old Testament,* GBS (Philadelphia: Fortress Press, 1971);

and John H. Hayes, ed., *Old Testament Form Criticism*, TUMSR 2 (San Antonio: Trinity Univ. Press, 1974). The team of scholars who is working out the method on the entire Old Testament is publishing in: Rolf Knierim and Gene M. Tucker, eds., The Forms of the Old Testament Literature (Grand Rapids: Eerdmans, 1981–).

[2.] For the author's detailed analysis of Israel's narrative forms and traditions, see Hermann Gunkel, *The Stories of Genesis,* trans. J. J. Scullion, ed. W. R. Scott (Vallejo, Calif.: BIBAL, 1994; German orig. 1910); and *idem, The Folktale in the Old Testament,* trans. M. D. Rutter, HTIBS (Sheffield: Almond, 1987; German orig. 1921).

For more recent treatments, see J. A. Wilcoxen, "Narrative," in *Old Testament Form Criticism,* 57–98; Robert Alter, *The Art of Biblical Narrative* (New York: Basic, 1981); George W. Coats, *Genesis, with an Introduction to Narrative Literature,* FOTL 1 (Grand Rapids: Eerdmans, 1983) esp. 1–10; Rolf Knierim, "Criticism of Literary Features, Form, Tradition, and Redaction," in *The Hebrew Bible and Its Modern Interpreters,* ed. D. A. Knight and G. M. Tucker (Philadelphia: Fortress Press; Chico, Calif.: Scholars Press, 1985) 123–65; George W. Coats, ed., *Saga, Legend, Tale, Novella, Fable: Narrative Forms in Old Testament Literature,* JSOTSup 35 (Sheffield: JSOT Press, 1985); and Yairah Amit, *Reading Biblical Narratives: Literary Criticism and the Hebrew Bible* (Minneapolis: Fortress Press, 2001).

[3.] For Gunkel's detailed analysis of Israel's poetic forms and traditions, see Hermann Gunkel and Joachim Begrich, *An Introduction to the Psalms,* trans. J. D. Nogalski (Macon, Ga.: Mercer Univ. Press, 1998; German orig. 1933). For key essays by Gunkel's contemporaries, see D. C. Simpson, ed., *The Psalmists: Essays on Their Religious Experience and Teaching, Their Social Background, and Their Place in the Development of Hebrew Psalmody* (London: Oxford Univ. Press, 1926).

For more recent treatments, see Claus Westermann, *Praise and Lament in the Psalms,* trans. K. Crim and R. N. Soulen (Atlanta: John Knox, 1981); Walter Brueggemann, *The Message of the Psalms: A Theological Commentary* (Minneapolis: Augsburg, 1984); Robert Alter, *The Art of Biblical Poetry* (New York: Basic, 1985); Erhard S. Gerstenberger, "The Lyrical Literature," in *The Hebrew Bible and Its Modern Interpreters,* 409–44; Patrick D. Miller, Jr., *Interpreting the Psalms* (Philadelphia: Fortress Press, 1986); Erhard S. Gerstenberger, *Psalms; Part 1, with an Introduction to Cultic Poetry,* FOTL 14 (Grand Rapids: Eerdmans, 1988); David L. Petersen and Kent H. Richards, *Interpreting Hebrew Poetry,* GBS (Minneapolis: Fortress Press, 1992); David J. A. Clines, ed., *The Poetical Books: A Sheffield Reader,* Biblical Seminar 41 (Sheffield: Sheffield Academic, 1997); and Gerstenberger, *Psalms, Part 2; and Lamentations,* FOTL 15 (Grand Rapids, Eerdmans, 2001).

4. Karl Budde, "Das hebräische Klagelied," ZAW 2 (1882) 1–52; and *idem,* "Ein althebräisches Klagelied," *ZAW* 3 (1883) 299–306.

5. Karl Budde, *Geschichte der althebräischen Litteratur,* 2nd ed. (Leipzig: Amelangs, 1909). [Ed.] See also Aage Bentzen, *Introduction to the Old Testament,* 2 vols. (Copenhagen: Gad, 1948) 1.128–34.

[6.] This judgment by Gunkel about the inability of the ancients to deal with longer oral performances is certainly wrong. Everything we have learned since the mid-twentieth century—through comparative studies by anthropologists and folklorists—indicates that oral cultures can compose, perform, and listen to very extensive oral performances. See Alfred Bates Lord, *Singer of Tales,* HSCL 24 (Cambridge: Harvard Univ. Press, 1960); Burke O. Long, "Recent Field Studies in Oral Literature and Their Bearing on Old Testament Criticism," *VT* 26 (1976) 187–98; Susan Niditch, *Folklore and the Hebrew Bible,* GBS (Minneapolis: Fortress Press, 1993); *idem, The Oral and Written Word: Ancient Israelite Literature,* Library of Ancient Israel (Louisville: Westminster John Knox, 1996). See also Antony F. Campbell, "The Reported Story: Midway between Oral Performance and Literary Art," *Semeia* 46 (1989) 77–85.

7. Eduard Reuss, *Geschichte der Heiligen Schriften des Alten Testaments* (Braunschweig: Schwetschke, 1881).

[8.] Keep in mind that Gunkel published this essay in 1906. Many of the Aramaic papyri from Elephantine were being acquired and discovered at just this time (1905–1907) but were still largely unpublished. The Hittite tablets, while discovered in the nineteenth century, were not deciphered until after 1915. The first tablets from Ugarit were not discovered until the late 1920s. The Dead Sea Scrolls were discovered primarily in the late 1940s and early 1950s. And the tablets from Ebla were not discovered until the 1970s.

In the wake of these discoveries, collections of translations of writings from the ancient Near East have had a deep impact on biblical research, for example: Robert William Rogers, ed., *Cuneiform Parallels to the Old Testament* (New York: Eaton & Mains, 1912); D. Winton Thomas, ed., *Documents from Old Testament Times* (London: Thomas Nelson, 1958); James B. Pritchard, ed., *Ancient Near Eastern Texts Relating to the Old Testament,* 3rd ed. (Princeton: Princeton Univ. Press, 1969); Walter Beyerlin, ed., *Near Eastern Religious Texts Relating to the Old Testament,* trans. J. Bowden, OTL (Philadelphia: Westminster, 1978); Benjamin R. Foster, *Before the Muses: An Anthology of Akkadian Literature,* 2 vols. (Bethesda, Md.: CDL, 1993); Florentino García Martínez, *The Dead Sea Scrolls Translated: The Qumran Texts in English,* trans. W. G. E. Watson, 2nd ed. (Leiden: Brill; Grand Rapids: Eerdmans, 1996); Bezalel Porten, ed., *The Elephantine Papyri in English: Three Millennia of Cross-Cultural Continuity and Change* (Leiden: Brill, 1996); and Victor H. Matthews and Don C. Benjamin,

Old Testament Parallels: Laws and Stories from the Ancient Near East, 2nd ed. (New York: Paulist, 1997).

[9.] An extensive literature on the issues of orality has developed in the generations following Gunkel. Some examples include: Eduard Nielsen, *Oral Tradition: A Modern Problem in Old Testament Introduction,* SBT 1/11 (Chicago: Allenson, 1954); Sigmund Mowinckel, "Tradition, Oral," in *IDB* 4.683–85; David M. Gunn, "Narrative Patterns and Oral Tradition in Judges and Samuel," *VT* 24 (1974) 286–317; Douglas A. Knight, *Rediscovering the Traditions of Israel,* rev. ed., SBLDS 9 (Missoula, Mont.: Scholars, 1975); Robert B. Coote, "Tradition, Oral, OT," in *IDBSup,* 914–16; Burke O. Long, "Recent Field Studies in Oral Literature and Their Bearing on Old Testament Criticism," *VT* 26 (1976) 187–98; Walter J. Ong, *Orality and Literacy: The Technologizing of the Word* (New York: Methuen, 1982; reprinted New York: Routledge, 1988); Robert C. Culley, "Oral Tradition and Biblical Studies," *Oral Traditions* 1 (1986) 30–65; Ruth Finnegan, *Literacy and Orality* (Oxford: Blackwell, 1988); John Miles Foley, *The Theory of Oral Composition: History and Methodology* (Bloomington: Indiana Univ. Press, 1988); Bendt Alster, "Interaction of Oral and Written Poetry in Early Mesopotamian Literature," in *Mesopotamian Epic Literature: Oral or Aural?* ed. M. E. Vogelzang and H. I. J. Vanstiphout (Lewiston, N.Y.: Edwin Mellen, 1992) 23–55; Douglas A. Knight, "Tradition History," in *ABD* 6.633–38; and Susan Niditch, *The Oral and Written Word.*

A SELECT BIBLIOGRAPHY ON ISRAEL'S LITERARY FORMS AND HISTORY

Barton, John. "Form Criticism (OT)." In *ABD* 2.838–41.

———. *Reading the Old Testament: Method in Biblical Study,* 30–44. Philadelphia: Westminster, 1984.

Gunkel, Hermann. *Introduction to Psalms: The Genres of the Religious Lyric of Israel,* completed by Joachim Begrich, translated by J. D. Nogalski. MLBS. Macon, Ga.: Mercer Univ. Press, 1998.

Hayes, John H., editor. *Old Testament Form Criticism.* TUMSR 2. San Antonio: Trinity Univ. Press, 1974.

Knierim, Rolf. "Criticism of Literary Features, Form, Tradition, and Redaction." In *The Hebrew Bible and Its Modern Interpreters,* edited by D. A. Knight and G. M. Tucker, 123–65. Philadelphia: Fortress Press, 1985.

Koch, Klaus. *The Growth of the Biblical Tradition: The Form-Critical Method,* translated by S. M. Cupitt. New York: Scribner, 1969.

————. "Old Testament Form Criticism Reconsidered." *Int* 27 (1973) 435–68.

Mowinckel, Sigmund. *The Psalms in Israel's Worship.* 2 vols., translated by D. R. Ap-Thomas. Nashville: Abingdon, 1962.

Ohler, Annemarie. *Studying the Old Testament: From Tradition to Canon,* translated by D. Cairns. Edinburgh: T. & T. Clark, 1985.

3

The Jacob Traditions

THE PATRIARCHS

The source and original meaning of the patriarchal figures in the Bible still generate a great diversity of opinion among scholars. For a long time the discussion of this, the most important of all the questions raised by the latter part of Genesis, seemed to remain unresolved. The lengthy task of separating the documentary sources of this book pushed all the other problems connected with Genesis into the background. Of course this separation of the sources had to be carried through, or at least surveyed, before the deeper questions could be addressed with any prospect of success. It is therefore perhaps not surprising that although the original meaning of the patriarchal figures has in recent years been the subject of detailed discussion, no one view has yet been generally accepted as satisfactory.

Although the view contained in the tradition itself—that the patriarchs were really and literally historical persons—has by no means been universally surrendered, it is not now held with the same sure confidence as before. There can be no doubt that the narratives that deal with the patriarchs are legends and not strict history; and if many scholars are still reluctant to give up the figure of Abraham, surely the historicity of Jacob cannot rouse anyone to enthusiasm. For what is there that should be historical about him? That on one occasion he deceived his blind father? Or that he fought hand to hand with a god? Or is it his journeys? This essay is intended to show that these do not belong to the original elements of the legend.

But if these patriarchal figures are not historical, what shall one make of them? One perspective, widely held for some time, explained them as "degraded deities." At that time, it was an accepted principle that legends had their origin in myths, and scholars searched these narratives for mythical features. Hugo Winckler and the so-called "Pan-Babylonian School" claimed to

42

have found such features.[1] It is not overbold to say that this claim cannot be maintained. In the patriarchal narratives one finds few echoes of myth, perhaps none at all. In connection with Jacob, one finds no trace of his ever having been a god or heroic figure. Even his contest with a demon is no indication of this, for similar tales are frequent in folklore. Nor is there any mythic indication in the fact that the locality of his grave is mentioned, for he must be buried somewhere according to tradition. Nor is there any basis for the suggestion that he was a giant, and the statement that along with Laban he piled up a mountain as a boundary rampart is derived from later expositors and does not belong to the original source.

There seemed to be a better scientific basis for another view, according to which the narratives are to be understood as describing events in the life of nations. This view, which prevailed for a long time among Julius Wellhausen's followers, can claim some support in the ancient narratives, for, as is well known, these look upon the patriarchs in general as the ancestors of Israel.[2] Jacob is identified with Israel, and his brother Esau is Israel's neighbor Edom; Laban is called the Aramean, and in the legend he concludes a treaty with Jacob, which was understood to apply to the two peoples, Israel and Aram. And it is plain that the deception of Esau by Jacob is meant to represent the retrogression of Edom before the younger people of Israel. Further, the twelve sons of Jacob bear the names of the twelve tribes of Israel. And although some of the patriarchs bear names unknown to the documented history of Israel, it still seems legitimate to suppose that these refer to earlier prehistoric peoples and tribes, whose history found an echo in these legends and can still be reconstructed from them with the use of a little skill.

Now it cannot be disputed that there is some justification for this view. These stories contain elements that must be understood in that way. When twelve sons are ascribed to Jacob, that really means only that the people of Israel were made up of twelve tribes, just as the sons of Judah are simply the clans of the tribe of Judah. We shall encounter other examples of the same kind of interpretation. It must, however, have been very natural for the ancient Israelites to conceive peoples and tribes as persons, and to interpret their history and their relations under the form of such events as take place between individuals. Still, the question remains whether the whole patriarchal history can be thus explained, and whether, therefore, Jacob can be explained as the name of a prehistoric tribe. We must also keep in mind the possibility that these legends contain, along with the history of peoples, some material of an entirely different kind, which is to us completely unintelligible. Fundamental questions of this kind could only be answered by experiment; that is, some daring scholar had, at the risk of failure, to endeavor to apply the principle to the whole of the material.

The credit of having made the attempt to explain the entire Jacob story in this ethnological way belongs to Carl Steuernagel.[3] But the results he obtained turned out so fantastical that everyone could see the impossibility of giving this ethnological interpretation to the entire material. Take, for example, Jacob's contest with the demon at Peniel—a narrative that has many parallels in similar stories and that can only be understood in connection with them. Steuernagel takes this to mean the victorious fight of the Jacob tribe with the inhabitants of the Peniel region. Steuernagel interprets Joseph's coat of many colors, which aroused the envy of his brothers, as a reference to the superior dress of rich descendants of Joseph, which embittered the rest of the Israelite tribes against them! This kind of interpretation has its ultimate roots in rationalism and is nowadays obsolete. Edward Meyer rightly utters a warning against such exaggerations of an idea that, within proper limits, is true and fruitful.[4] The result, therefore, is that, although part of the material must be understood ethnologically, only a part can be so understood, and in the following pages we hope to show that this part is not the most original constituent of the story. In any case we have as little proof of the existence of a "Jacob people" as we have for that of a "Laban people"; and we have no strong reason to assume the existence of either.

If figures like that of Jacob are neither historical figures, nor gods of former days, nor prehistoric tribes, then what are they? The way to the answer has been indicated by Hugo Gressmann in an essay that is (or at least in the present writer's opinion should have been) epoch-making in the history of Old Testament research.[5] He has suggested that these figures were originally the heroes of archaic narratives, that is, so-called folktales, heroes who were only subsequently raised in Israel to the dignity of national ancestors. This assumes the accuracy of the opinion, which has recently come to the fore and which has the support of Wilhelm Wundt,[6] that the oldest narratives of humanity were not myths about the gods, but folktales and narratives that in a later and more developed age were combined with historical reminiscences and have thus become sagas.[7] Following up this view, Gressmann suggests that the patriarchal stories likewise contained an abundance of originally mythical material, and that even the ancestral figures themselves are to be understood in this way. This hypothesis will be thoroughly tested in the following pages as it relates to the figure of Jacob.[8]

SOURCE AND TRADITION

We have to traverse a long road in order to achieve clarity in this matter of the origin; and the reason the whole question has been treated so rarely with success is the fact that this road has not been followed with sufficient consistency.

We must analyze the entire literary composition that is attached to the name of Jacob and try to discover its oldest component parts.

Such an analysis must, of course, assume that the criticism of the sources—the narratives have come down to us in the combined recensions of J (Yahwist), E (Elohist), and P (Priestly)—has been to some extent carried out. This is not completely accurate. Whole generations of scholars have been busied with this task. It was Wellhausen who taught us the nature of the latest source (P) and determined its age. This Priestly writer has touched upon the Jacob stories only slightly. In our present text the sources play a very important part; but the older sources, J and E, were very much alike in these stories, and the detailed separation of these two remains doubtful. Nor has the recent question been settled whether there are two threads to be disentangled in the Jacob stories in J.[9]

When we now raise the question how this cycle of stories arose and how it is to be regarded, we enter upon an area of tradition that is earlier than our sources. The individual Jacob stories probably existed in oral tradition many centuries before J and E, until—first in oral form, then in written form—they were combined in the composite form in which we now have them.

This involves exactly the same presupposition as is made for the Gospel narratives, and indeed for all narratives that have come down to us by way of tradition: as a rule, each story existed as a separate entity in oral tradition. Needless to say, in Israel as elsewhere, each narrative circulated separately, entirely unconnected to others, just as is the case still with our folktales and legends.[10] That this is also the case with the Jacob stories is proved by the fact that the figure of the patriarch differs greatly in the different narratives. In his relations with Esau and Laban he is the skillful shepherd; in the Peniel story he is the strong, fearless opponent; in the Joseph story he is the aged father with a special love for his youngest son. All combinations of individual stories into larger composites invariably belong to a relatively later stage.

Accordingly, in our analysis of the Jacob traditions, we must pay attention to the following issues. First, we have to study each individual story by itself and determine its origin. In particular, we have to notice how the historical element in it is interwoven with material of a different kind—probably taken from folktale—and to ask how this affects the figure of Jacob. Further, we have to determine in what order the individual stories came together into the composite whole. This can be learned from the relative nearness or distance from which they stand in relation to the whole. Such an investigation requires, of course, a certain flair or artistic sense; for many scholars show an unconcealed dislike whenever aesthetics intrudes into research. Unfortunately, however, the legends of Genesis are undeniably artistic productions, and however strongly this claim may be resented, they cannot be understood without a feeling for their peculiar beauty. But, for the comfort of those who are suspicious of all aesthetic judgments, we may state at once that this essay will involve only very simple features of this kind that are easily intelligible to everyone.

Neither J nor E undertook to compose a completely new work. This is the reason we are able to understand the manner in which the stories were gradually combined on the basis of the form of the composite narrative. But in spite of all combinations and alterations and omissions and additions, on the whole they left the arrangement of the material in the form their prede-cessors had constructed it. This will be shown by detailed examples. Israel produced no Homer, so we are in a position—and this is true of the Jacob stories—to distinguish the later parts of the narratives from the earlier. The former are very easily recognizable from the looser relation in which they stand to the others.

By interpolating this investigation into the origin of the composite narra-tive between the criticism of the sources and the question as to the meaning of the patriarchal figures, we obtain a firmer foundation for our study of this latter question. We shall not, as has previously been done, capriciously take any narrative as the real Jacob narrative; we shall take that which is shown by the composite narrative itself to be the kernel of the whole.

It will be best to begin with the stories added at a later time, gradually sep-arate these out, and thus reach the original core. To borrow a metaphor from geology, we shall first remove the upper layers in order to expose those beneath. Here we must distinguish four groups of stories, which we may compare to so many layers of soil. In chronological order these are the four groups:

1. Narratives about Jacob and Esau
2. Narratives about Jacob and Laban
3. Narratives of theophanies and holy places
4. Narratives about Jacob's children

The material in the first and second groups has been worked up into one cycle of stories. At the close of the first set, Jacob flees to Laban. And at the end of his adventures there, he returns to Esau, and then a second part of the Esau stories is narrated. The narratives in the third group are connected with defi-nite localities and have been inserted into the already existing cycle at those points in the narrative where Jacob has reached the specified locality. They include the stories about Bethel, Peniel, Mahanaim, and Shechem. And the narratives in the fourth group cover the birth and later fates of Jacob's chil-dren, including Reuben, Simeon, Levi, Judah, and Joseph.

NARRATIVES ABOUT JACOB'S CHILDREN

Following the plan proposed, we begin with the stories in group four. A glance at the style of the composite narrative shows that these were the last to be inserted into the cycle of Jacob stories. But no conclusion may be drawn from this as to their age as separate stories. In them Jacob plays only a subordinate part. He is the father of the actors in these stories. But the names of the chief figures are those of the tribes of Israel. That is to say, these are tribal legends. The name of Jacob has come into these stories merely because he was regarded as the father of the tribal ancestors. As far as the figure of Jacob is concerned, therefore, all we learn from these is that at a certain time he was regarded as the ancestor of the twelve tribes of Israel, just as in J he bears the name "Israel" (Gen 35:10). For our purpose we might omit these tribal legends altogether, and we linger over them only a moment because we intend to use them afterward to throw light upon the Jacob stories proper.

Reuben

We have only a brief hint of a legend concerning Reuben (Gen 35:21-22) that we have to supplement. It records that Reuben, Jacob's firstborn son, has had intercourse with Jacob's concubine, Bilhah, and has thereby drawn down upon himself his father's curse. As has already been said, in order to under-stand how such a narrative originated, we must carefully disentangle the various components out of which it has been formed. First of all, from other sources we are justified in assuming that the tribe of Reuben, which in the ear-liest period held the leading place among the tribes, had at a later time fallen into complete decay. This fall from its high status is explained in ancient style by the declaration that the national ancestor had cursed Reuben, the firstborn among the brothers. Thus far we have historical tradition in an ancient poetic form. Then the narrative was further developed by transferring to Reuben the popular motif of an adult son who seduces his father's concubine and is expelled from the family (see Homer, *Iliad* 9.447–57). The historical element in this, therefore, is the tradition of Reuben's fall, whereas the actual content of the narrative is derived from the storehouse of poetic invention.

Judah and Tamar

The case is similar to the narrative about Judah (Genesis 38). Here the basis of the story also consists of reminiscences from the early history of the tribe. In the earliest period, Judah contained three clans (Er, Onan, and Shela), of whom the first two perished early and two new ones (Perez and Zerah) were formed. This was put into legendary shape by saying that Er and Onan died early, while Perez and Zerah were born after Er and Onan's deaths. We are then told that the two who died early had one wife, Tamar; but in her widowhood she succeeded in acquiring legitimate heirs (Perez and Zerah) by her father-in-law. The detailed narrative about Tamar, the story of her ardent loyalty in her widowhood, is based on the same motif as the novella of Ruth and is fictitious not historical in its origin.

Dinah

The same holds true with the narrative about Dinah, Jacob's daughter (Genesis 34). There must have been an ancient historical tradition telling how the tribes of Simeon and Levi attacked the town of Shechem in central Canaan, and how the town was retained by the Canaanites. The other tribes of Israel rendered no help, and Simeon and Levi were dispersed and destroyed. This assumption is all the more justifiable because it is entirely in agreement with what we learn from other sources regarding the subsequent fates of Simeon and Levi. Now legend has transformed these events in the following manner. It represents all the parties concerned—including Shechem—as young men. Both parties (and here the fictitious element enters) begin to quarrel about a woman, the sister of Simeon and Levi, who has been raped and carried off by Shechem. In order to avenge this dishonor done to their sister, the two brothers took and killed the rapist, thus earning their father's curse.

Joseph

While in these cases the real basis of the legend is historical, and the fictitious element is the addition (that is, the legend has a historical core), it is, of course, possible to conceive the reverse situation so that folktale contributes the important parts and the historical names are a mere external attachment. This is the case in the Joseph novella. This narrative, given in great detail in our text both in J and E, deals in its essential parts with brothers who envy their youngest brother, a finer fellow than any of them, and determine to get him out of the way. At first the wicked plan succeeds. The poor lad becomes a miserable slave and is taken away to a distant land. But then the tables are turned. Owing to his abilities, he gains the high esteem of the king and attains an outstanding position. When, under the pressure of necessity, the wicked brothers go to the same country, they are delivered into the hands of the influential official, whom they do not recognize as their brother. But he does not pay them back in their own way for the evil they had done to him. There is a touching scene of recognition in which he forgives and helps them. The expert will see at first glance that this is a folktale whose leading motifs are found again and again in the tradition of all peoples. In fact, even many of the details—for example, the boy with his predictive dreams that people unsuccessfully attempt to frustrate as well as his brothers throwing him into a well—occur in all versions of the story. This folktale was rendered suitable for use in Israel by receiving the addition that this youngest brother, the clever one, was the ancestor of the tribe of Joseph, and the other brothers were the fathers of the other tribes. In all this the only historical presupposition is that the tribe of Joseph was considered to be the youngest and best among the tribes. When the narrative was further expanded, very few historical elements were added. The essential parts of this narrative are thus derived from folktale.

Finally, something should be said as to how the statement originated that all these tribes and peoples were each derived from an ancestor, whose names were supposed to be contained in the historical national names. The tribe of Joseph, for example, claims to be derived from a man of that name, and therefore calls itself "the sons of Joseph." This fundamental statement rests to some extent, as can be shown by numerous examples (especially from Arabs and Turks), on a certain view of history. There are tribes that have been formed by a large and ever-increasing number of people attaching themselves to the family of an old sheik. The actual memory of this inherited or adopted ancestry, of course, has in most cases faded in time so that nothing but the historical name is left. It is intelligible enough that the nation at a later time occupied itself with the question "Who really was this man whose name is continually on everyone's lips?" And the storyteller gladly seized the opportunity of filling this gap in the tradition. We have, then, to think of such an origin for the ancestral figure when a people calls itself "the sons of so-and-so." That is, for example, the case with Israel and Judah, but not, by the way, with Abraham; for ancient Israel never called itself "sons of Abraham." Nor is it true of Jacob, because the historical narrative never uses the expression "sons of Jacob," but always "sons of Israel." The figure of Jacob, therefore, like that of Abraham, must go back to a different origin.

The narratives already dealt with represent the top layer of the Jacob stories. They are further connected with the rest of the Jacob cycle by the insertion in the Laban stories of a passage dealing with the birth of Jacob's sons (Gen 29:31-35). As the composite narrative shows, therefore, this passage represents a later dovetailing and was invented for this very purpose by the narrators, who intended to tell stories about these sons afterward. The passage, then, is not based on ancient popular tradition, and the vague style of its narrative clearly reveals this. For example, it is very noticeable how large a portion of it consists of ingenious explanations of the names of Jacob's children.

NARRATIVES OF THEOPHANIES AND HOLY PLACES

Another and deeper layer consists of a few local legends dealing with theophanies and holy places. In our present text they are inserted into the Esau and Laban stories. On his way from Esau to Laban, Jacob reaches Bethel; on his return journey he briefly visits Mahanaim, Peniel, Shechem, and—according to E—he comes a second time to Bethel.

Brief Reports

We have only one brief note about Mahanaim (Gen 32:2). There Jacob saw the march of an army of God's angels and therefore called the place "camp of the armies."

Other brief local traditions are mentioned regarding places in the vicinity of Shechem (Gen 33:12-30; 35:4, 8, 14). There Jacob is said to have buried images under a terebinth and to have purchased a sacred enclosure, erected a stone, and called on "El, God of Israel." At the same time we are told that he buried Rebecca's nurse at Bethel under the oak of weeping and set up a stone over her grave.

These are all local traditions that, in view of their form, should be called "reports" rather than legends, and in their original form they resemble the short "reports" that are still in circulation among the people in many parts of Germany. They are only very loosely connected with the composite story of Jacob, both in content and in form. The compilers of the sources have inserted them at suitable places in their narrative. They were able to do this because the framework of the Jacob story that they possessed told of journeys of Jacob in the course of which he could have passed through these places. In so doing they have, as a rule, followed the plan of putting the religious material first and then adding Jacob's secular adventures connected with the place in question. The fact that this artificial expedient was adopted betrays that these materials were only added to the rest when the tradition was committed to writing. There is a further indication that they were inserted at a later time and do not belong to the oldest narrative. This is particularly clear in connection with the notice about the burial of Rebecca's nurse, who is suddenly introduced here without any germane connection with the story. Why should Jacob be carrying his mother's nurse about with him wherever he went?

How then may the idea have arisen of transferring these trifling incidents to the hero of the Esau-Laban stories? The feature common to them all is that they deal with holy or venerable places in Israel. They must have been attributed to Jacob at a period when the latter was looked upon as national ancestor. It was due to the ancestor that he should have founded these places, or at least given them their names. In the same way, Shechem, Bethel, Hebron, and

Beersheba were attributed to Abraham. Beer-lahai-roi, the sacred place of the Ishmael tribe, was attributed to Ishmael's mother, Hagar. And a few places were attributed to Isaac. That this explanation is correct is also evident from the fact that the memorial stone at Shechem bears the name "El, God of Israel." We may perhaps assume that tradition in Israel at one time called the founder of this holy place "Israel." In any case, we get no light here on the figure of Jacob.

The Fight at the Jabbok

The case is the same with the more expanded narratives of the same group. There is, first, the Peniel story (Gen 32:23-32). Alone at night, on the bank of the Jabbok—so we learn apparently both from J and E—the national progenitor was attacked without any cause by an unknown character and fought with him in mortal combat without weapons. Despite severe injury, Jacob bravely maintained his ground. Then the adversary fell to pleading: "Let me go, the morning breaks." At the dawn of a new day the demons of the night had to disappear. The words revealed to Jacob that his foe was a spirit, one of the beings called *elohim,* and with great presence of mind he utilized the opportunity and forced his adversary to "bless" him (that is, pronounce a magic word over him) lest he allow the specter of the night to escape from his iron grasp.

This narrative has hardly anything in common with the other Jacob stories. In particular, the figure of the patriarch contained in it is entirely different. Here he is a brave hero who is not afraid in a dangerous situation and is a victor over men and gods. In the other stories he is a clever deceiver. What a contradiction arises from the joining of these very different legends in one figure! The same man who has just fought so bravely against a more-than-human foe tries in the immediate sequel to escape the anger of his brother by large gifts and smooth words. With great confidence we may here again infer that it was only at a later period that this story came into this connection and that it had originally no reference to Jacob.

What was this narrative originally? It was merely a local tradition about some hero or other, a story circulated at Peniel about a contest with a demon of the night. This explanation is supported by the existence of numerous parallel stories of similar night contests with a demon and which, as has recently been suggested, go back ultimately to the experience of a nightmare.

But why should this story have been connected with Jacob instead of with some other figure? It was done by someone who identified Jacob with Israel. This is clear from etiological features. The fact that the "sons of Israel" do not eat the sciatic nerve of an animal is said to be due to the fact that in the struggle the god struck Jacob on the thigh. That is to say, a food custom peculiar to the Israelites is explained from an experience of their ancestor. Again, the change of name from Jacob to Israel is mentioned in the story. The one formerly called Jacob is, from then on, to be called Israel; that is to say, his name means "struggler with God," for the divine being says he has "struggled with God and men." Here again it is natural to suppose that this story was told with reference to and in explanation of the name "Israel."

The Dream at Bethel

Finally, we address the Bethel story (Gen 28:10-22). In Bethel, Jacob happens to sleep on a certain spot; and Bethel was a particularly venerated sanctuary to historical Israel. There he sees, according to E, a ladder stretching from heaven to earth, sets up as a memorial the stone on which he rested, anoints it, names the place, and vows to offer his tithes there.

Like the preceding story, this one also ascribes to Jacob the foundation of a sacred place. That is, a local tradition is again transferred to him as Israel, father and founder of the holy places of his people.

This narrative, handed down from ancient tradition, was now interwoven by the compilers of the Genesis sources with the Esau-Laban cycle. Jacob passes the place on his way from Esau to Laban and makes a vow to be fulfilled if God will graciously guide him and bring him home. This is the story according to E. According to J, God promises him this of his own accord, and then adds the promise to bestow on his heirs the land on which he was now encamped. Here, therefore, the present connection of the narrative within the composite story has been utilized to fill out the somewhat bare and scanty Bethel tradition with richer detail.

Here again it is clear that compilers are at work, but the attainment of congruity in the character of Jacob is not successful. Jacob had just deceived his father and brother in disgraceful fashion, and now he approaches God with a pious vow and is even abundantly blessed by him. These compilers, morally and artistically great, have tried to knit the whole structure more firmly together, and in so doing were naïve enough to introduce their own pious thoughts. But they were also undiscerning enough not to see how unsuitable a representative of these ideas the rascal Jacob really was. To produce a consistent picture they would have had to suppress or completely recast some of the stories. But they did not have sufficient courage for that. A similar verdict must be passed upon the beautiful prayer of Jacob before his meeting with Esau (Gen 32:10-13), which was probably inserted by a still later hand and which is equally out of keeping with the rest of the picture of Jacob. The later date of these features of the Bethel story is also proved by the fact that J conceives Jacob as the ancestor of Israel. It is to him and to his seed that the land is promised.

Thus far we have examined two of the strata of the Jacob narratives, the tales of the tribes of Israel and the local tales of holy places and theophanies. Both have been ascribed to Jacob under the presupposition that he is identical with Israel, the ancestor of the people and the founder of its holy places. The writer of J shows a delicate perception when, in the later passages of his narrative—from Peniel onwards—he uses "Israel" instead of "Jacob." In neither of these layers have we found the real kernel of the Jacob stories.

THE JACOB-ESAU NARRATIVES

The case is quite different with the two deeper layers that treat Jacob's relationships with Esau and Laban. Together these narratives constitute a beautifully finished cycle of tales. It consists of three parts:

Jacob-Esau stories, part 1: Genesis 25:1—27:46
Jacob-Laban stories: Genesis 29:15—32:1
Jacob-Esau stories, part 2: Genesis 32:4—33:17

That is to say, the narrators have presented the Esau narrative in two portions and inserted the Laban tradition between them. Evidently that was done for the sake of the fine artistic impression produced by such a whole. The conclusion brings us back to the starting point. The connecting link between the two is, as we have seen, Jacob's journeys. As we shall see below, this motif has been taken from the Laban story. Furthermore, the narrators have sought to attain a still closer unity by all kinds of cross-references. Consequently Rebecca, Jacob's mother, must advise her son to flee to Laban, and when he arrives there, Jacob has to tell Laban all that has happened.

The two threads of narrative have been further assimilated by the invention of a relationship between the figures in the two strands. The mother of the deceiver in the Esau story is the sister of the deceived Laban. In spirit also the two strands have been brought into unity. In the earlier form of the narrative the questionable behavior of Jacob is recounted with complacency, but later hands have toned down this original note and have added religious considerations, as far as that was possible—a procedure in which they have been surpassed by Bible expositors, both Jewish and Christian, even to the present day.

Further, a romantic turn has been given to most of the separate stories, but this has not been carried out so fully here as in, say, the Joseph story. The originally separate tales have not, however, been brought into complete agreement, and some ragged edges have been left. That Jacob, in his flight from Laban, is bound to fall into Esau's hands, neither Jacob nor the narrator himself sees; it is only after Laban has left Jacob that this new danger occurs to Jacob and to the narrator.

Our first task is to compare the first and second parts of the Esau narratives. The second part claims to be the continuation of the first. At the outset Esau is highly enraged by Jacob's deceit and is still full of anger against his brother. But Jacob, returning from his sojourn with Laban, has to enter Esau's territory. How will he fare there? The continuation has not maintained complete consistency with the presuppositions of the first part.

As we shall show in detail, the theme of the former narrative is the contest between the shepherd and the hunter. Jacob, the shepherd, wins the blessing from Esau, the hunter. When the brothers meet again later, Jacob is still the shepherd, but Esau is now no longer the solitary hunter. He has become the leader of a band, gaining his livelihood in the desert at the head of four hundred men, and all that is left of the main theme of the earlier story (their contest) is that Jacob once more outwits Esau by his cleverness. So the theme or plot of this second part is: How is this astute shepherd (Jacob) accompanied by a large family and encumbered with numerous flocks of sheep and goats, to escape in spite of all these impediments from this robber chieftain (Esau), who is so angry with him on account of his former trickery? The second part is therefore a later invention, not completely unified with the first. But the reason for the invention of such a sequel is clear. The old tale was so beautiful and so popular that a sequel was necessary. The listeners insisted on hearing more about Jacob and Esau, and the skillful storytellers complied with this demand all the more readily as it gave them an opportunity of supplying a fine frame for the Laban story. Parallels to this kind of invention of a sequel are abundant in literature. In the Old Testament itself we have a similar second part of the Samson-Delilah story (Judges 16), and similar continuation of the story of the Shunammite woman (2 Kgs 4:1-6).[11]

But the content of the story itself is the best proof that this is how it arose. It is well known that "sequels" of this kind rarely reach the level of the first production. Here too the sequel is inferior both in freshness and in power to the first part. Furthermore, consider the localities of the stories. The scene of the first part is somewhere in southern Canaan, with little importance attached to the exact location. The only important thing is that shepherds and hunters live together there. But the second part takes place in an entirely different country, east of Jordan in Mahanaim and Peniel. It is easy to see why this portion of the story must be located there. The scene is set there because Jacob is there at the close of the Laban story, and this proves that the second part of the Esau narrative presupposes the preceding Laban tale. It was meant from the beginning to be the conclusion of the complete composite Esau-Laban narrative. We are told of the clever ruse by which Jacob outwitted his brother there. In

Mahanaim he divided his flocks and servants into two camps. If Esau should attack the one, probably the other will be able to escape. He arranges his family in such a way that those least dear to him are put first, so that at least Rachel and Jacob in the rear might be able to flee. He sends a large flock in front as a present for Esau, subdividing this flock again into five parts in order to make it appear more imposing. In all these "dividings" we have an echo of the name of the place where this is said to have happened, Mahanaim, "two camps," or "several camps." And this also includes a play on words: *maḥane* "camp," and *minḥah* "gift/offering." Thus no small part of the narrative is drawn from the name of the place, while other motifs are borrowed from the name "Peniel" and the word "Ford of Peniel."[12] The result is that the story has been built upon an imaginative interpretation of the names, such as in the story of the birth of Jacob's children. This is further evidence that this is not an independent, ancient story of popular origin, but one that owes its existence to later narrators. This is not the soil out of which the Jacob figure arose.

The Jacob-Laban Narratives (part 1)

What remains is only the Jacob-Esau narratives (part 1) and the Jacob-Laban narratives. These are the real kernel of the whole composite Jacob narrative.[13] Here we have two very ancient folktales, dovetailed into each other at a later time. We must first try as far as we can to get at their most ancient meaning.

The Jacob-Laban narrative is composed of strands from several separate stories. The preface is a brief narrative, relating "How Jacob comes to Laban" (Gen 21:1-14). The first member of that family that he sees is Rachel, afterwards so dear to him. He gains her favor and that of her father by taking her part against the other shepherds and watering her flocks for her. Exactly similar details are narrated about Moses, who in the same way gains the love of Zipporah and a friendly reception from her father. The story is therefore in no way particularly characteristic of Jacob.[14] Tales like these are "fatherless" and are easily transferred from one person to another, just as the clouds on the mountains detach themselves from one peak to gather around another.

All the more significant for our purpose, therefore, are the ensuing stories in Gen 30:25—32:1, which have been blended into a splendid unit. These stories highlight the conflicts between the equally matched Jacob and Laban. The former, who seems to have a very lucky hand in things pertaining to shepherd work—and who is therefore of great value to the rich flock-owner Laban—is tricked by the latter into serving him fourteen years without pay. Jacob has fallen in love with the fair Rachel and willingly serves her father seven years in order to win her. But when the time for the marriage arrives, he is put off with the less attractive Leah and must serve another seven years for

Rachel. Thus far Laban has tricked Jacob very badly. Now, however, Jacob has his revenge. During the ensuing six years Jacob contrives by all manner of strategems to get into his possession a large part of Laban's flocks and is even clever enough to escape from Laban with all his family and all his rich possessions, awkward to handle as these are. No doubt the oldest form of the tale gave all this with broad humor, thoroughly pleased with the way in which the cunning Laban was paid back with compound interest. In a later time, storytellers felt somewhat uncomfortable about these events (although their morality could hardly be impeached), and the story was retold as indulgently as possible for Jacob and to show how justifiable his conduct was. Jacob is Laban's son-in-law. The two have a dispute about their shares—as fathers and sons-in-law may often do. The popular version is decisively on the young man's side. At first, it is true, the older man is more astute; but in the end the young man has learned something and completely outwits the older man. At this stage the narrative is altogether a splendid specimen of the racy, popular tale. That type of story delights in the theme of "diamond cuts diamond" and loves to give the young man the advantage over the elder.[15]

Jacob and Laban are shepherds. Evidently the people among whom the stories were current were themselves shepherds, and what we have here are shepherds' tales. Laban is a Syrian (Aramean). As we have already shown, this proves that Jacob and Laban were not originally related to each other; in fact, they belong to different peoples. This feature also (that is, that men of different ethnic groups are shown disputing or bargaining together) is a frequent subject in popular tales. In the Old Testament we find Joseph opposed to the lewd Egyptian woman. The *Thousand and One Nights* tell of "the faithful" struggling with Jews, Christians, and Africans; and German tales are fond of introducing the Jewish character. And when Laban is specifically called an Aramean the presupposition is that the Aramean shepherds lived fairly close to the Hebrew shepherds and that they were considered to be specially astute and deceitful. The reason for Jacob coming into contact with these foreigners is stated as due to the necessity of his leaving his home country and seeking refuge in another land. The young man away from home gaining a girl's love and cleverly surmounting all the difficulties that her father puts in his way is found again and again in folktales. This, therefore, is the original place for the motif that is used as the connecting link between the Jacob-Esau and Jacob-Laban cycles—that Jacob is on his travels.

The scene of this tale is, according to J, the very large city of Haran in Mesopotamia, but in the narrative itself no mention is made of such a populous place. On the contrary, the narrative presupposes an extensive pastureland on which the flocks may feed, sometimes days' journeys apart from each other. The original form is found in E, which speaks of the "East country."

Eduard Meyer has identified this as the great steppe to the east of Damascus.[16] From this localization we can read the entire history. Aramean sheepbreeders, we shall suppose, once pastured their flocks in the Syrian/North Arabian steppe, till at a later period they made their way into Mesopotamian and made Haran their capital. The Laban tale followed them there. Originally, however, Jacob was a guest among the Arameans of the "East country," the most distant point between them and the Hebrews being Mizpah to the east of the Jordan.

At the close of the tale, according to E, a treaty was made between Laban and Jacob. With great reluctance Laban had to let Jacob go, taking his family and his flocks with him, but he exacted from him the promise not to wrong his daughters by marrying other wives.

In J the story is different. According to this account the treaty made on this occasion was of historical and national importance. Jacob and Laban mutually agreed upon a frontier that was not to be crossed by either with hostile intent. Jacob stands here, then, for the people of Israel and Laban for the people of Aram, and the frontier they fix is what the two peoples shall respect. Now it is noteworthy that the idea that both men are national ancestors appears nowhere except in this one passage in the whole Laban story, and that only in J. Up till now both have been merely individuals; and although Laban is occasionally called "the Aramean," he is never called "the father of Aram." We conclude, therefore, that Jacob in these stories was originally a private individual, but he was subsequently transformed into the ancestor of Israel. By this transformation, legendary and historical elements have been combined, just as in the tribal legends of the sons of Jacob, which we have already discussed. The latter narrative is an instructive parallel, in which historical matter has been added to what was originally a folktale, but in which the ancient material has been kept very clear and the added historical matter is very loosely attached.

The original figure of Jacob in the Laban narrative, therefore, is the figure of a shepherd, a very shrewd man, temporarily a guest among foreigners (Arameans), who marries there and outwits his astute father-in-law—altogether the very epitome of the hero in a folktale.

THE JACOB-ESAU NARRATIVES (PART 2)

We have to compare this Jacob of the Laban stories now with the Jacob of the Esau tales (Gen 25:21—28:22). Here again our first task is to get at the oldest meaning of the narrative, and so get at the original figure of the hero.

In this passage also our sources have put a national interpretation on the events—clearly in J, less clearly in E. In a brief passage prefixed to the whole we are told that the mother of Jacob and Esau, while the children were still unborn, was conscious of unusual disturbances in her womb. In her trouble she consulted the oracle and received the answer:

> Two nations are in your womb,
>   and two peoples, born of you, shall be divided;
> the one shall be stronger than the other,
>   the elder shall serve the younger. (Gen 25:23)

At the end of the tale of Jacob's deception the blessing, which he extorts from his blind father, declares:

> Let the peoples serve you,
>   and nations bow down to you. (Gen 27:29)

The nations indicated here are clear. Jacob is, of course, Israel, and Esau refers to Edom. Esau is to bear the name Edom ("red man") because he exchanged his birthright for stew (Gen 25:34). In the story of the birth there are hints of the same effect: when Esau was born he was red (Gen 25:25) and like a hairy cloak to the touch. This last is a humorous reference to Edom's country Seir (Deut 2:5), the name of which resembles in sound the Hebrew word for hair. This identification of Esau with Edom is also found elsewhere, especially in the genealogical lists given in Genesis 36, where Esau is identified with Edom, or, according to another view, with Edom's father. In the prophetic writings as well, the Edomites are occasionally called "the house of Esau." But Seir is undoubtedly the name of a Horite primitive people that occupied the country before Edom and were afterwards subdued and absorbed by it, so that Edom could also in poetical language be called by that name.

Now the Jacob-Esau stories told how Jacob defrauded his brother of his birthright and of his father's blessing. The word "birthright" is also used elsewhere in similar connections with reference to peoples. The meaning is that the one people surpasses the kindred one in age, power, and wealth. And, similarly, the blessing of which Jacob deprived his brother means the bestowal of the better country and the superior power. According to this view, therefore, the saga is supposed to mean that Edom, although it was the more important people in earlier days, has had to relinquish its power to Israel, which was previously inferior to it, and is, in fact, now under its dominion. We know enough of the history of both peoples to understand the meaning of this—Edom is an older people than Israel. It abandoned nomadic life earlier than Israel and had a king at an earlier period than Israel. Israel subsequently obtained the richer territory.

> May God give you of the dew of heaven,
>   and of the fatness of the earth,
>   and plenty of grain and wine. (Gen 27:28)

So we read in the "blessing of Jacob"; and in the end Israel, under David, subdued Edom.

Thus the most natural supposition would be that the tale arose merely as a poetical representation of this national relationship. Against this, however, there are several weighty objections. First of all, the striking fact that in both cases two names are used for one figure suggests that the process was not an entirely simple one. Jacob and Israel on the one hand, and Esau and Edom on the other, surely cannot be the same, seeing that they bear different names. Besides, the tale speaks not of Israel and Edom but of Jacob and Esau, whereas, conversely, the historical accounts never speak of Jacob and Esau, but always only of Israel and Edom. This leads us to conclude that the figures in the tale arose in some other way and were transferred to the two tribes only in later tradition. Again, in the narratives there is very little mention indeed of these peoples or of national relationships. Apart from the hints and allusions at the end and at the beginning of the narratives, the characters make the impression throughout of actual individuals.

It is noteworthy that, when they are looked at more closely, these stories do not at all fit Israel and Edom. In the folktale, Jacob is, to be sure, astute; but there is little bravery about him. When his brother is angry with him, he flees. He obtains the birthright entirely by means of superior cunning. But in the historical accounts Israel overcame Edom by force of arms (2 Sam 8:13-14); and fierce Joab—David's commander, who subdued Edom—would hardly have felt honored by being compared to wily Jacob. The same is true of the figure of Esau. In the folktale his chief quality is thoughtlessness or guilelessness. He allows himself to be overreached. But in the historical accounts, as various biblical references show, Edom was renowned precisely for its sagacity and wisdom.[17] In the folktale, the two brothers are shepherd and hunter; but there is no proof that these were the chief occupations of the two peoples in the historical periods when they lived side by side.

We have many reasons, therefore, for the supposition that it was later redactors who gave these stories a new interpretation with a reference to national relationships, and that the narratives had originally a quite different meaning. This supposition will seem less difficult when we remember that exactly the same is true of Jacob's adventures with Laban. We must, therefore, try to read the Esau stories without this new turn that has been given to them. What then would be their meaning?

The main root of the narratives consists of two folktales, both of which tell how the precedence passed from Esau. They both deal with what is really one theme, although according to one version, this took place by purchase; and according to the other it was through deception. Both are at one also in the statement that the two are brothers—an interjected introduction calls them twin brothers. They also differ in occupation and in natural gifts. Jacob is a shepherd and Esau is a hunter. In all their main features, the narratives are based on this difference of occupation between the two.

The Birthright

The first legend tells how Esau comes home from the chase starving (Gen 25:29-34). He has caught nothing that day—so it is understood—and is ready to devour whatever he can find. Jacob, however, who had remained comfortably at home, has something to eat even today; he has prepared for himself a tasty stew. The implication is that, although he was a shepherd, he also did some field work. Thus the foolish Esau turns over his birthright for the stew.

This narrative sets in contrast types of two different occupations, which is a frequent subject of folktales. In German folktales we find the juxtaposition of farmer and woodcutter, cobbler and tailor, shepherd boy and king's daughter. It is also a familiar feature of this kind of tale that the representatives of the occupations are brothers. "A certain man had two sons: the one was a cobbler, the other a smith." That is a typical opening of a German folktale. Israelite saga also focuses on two brothers: Abel, a shepherd, and Cain, a farmer. Another tradition, almost entirely lost, told of three brothers: Jabal, a shepherd; Jubal, a musician; and Tubal-cain, a smith (Gen 4:20-22). That the different actors are conceived as brothers is explained by the fact that the relationship of brotherhood is one of the simplest family relationships, just the type that primitive narrative is able to conceive and handle.

The regular motif of such "tales of occupation" is that the one claims to be superior to the other.[18] Such stories would be told where representatives of the occupations lived together and one was keen to increase its importance and its superiority over the other. In the German folktales the point usually is, "Who is to win the bride?" Abel and Cain dispute as to whose sacrifice is to gain God's favor. Here Jacob and Esau dispute about birthright. This, it should be understood, carries with it the whole inheritance left by the father and the dominion over the other. Admittedly it belongs by right to the hunter, but the shepherd has purchased it from him. Such a tale can only have originated in a country where shepherds and hunters lived together, as is still the case, for example, among the Targi in the Sahara, among the Masai, Abyssinians, and others. Those who tell each other stories of this kind are shepherds them-

selves, and they relate with pride and glee how the hunter, although he was
the firstborn and his occupation was considered the superior one, had to take
an inferior place behind the shepherd. That the occupation of the hunter is
considered superior is also found elsewhere. The Targi are divided into the
nobility, who carry on hunting, warring, and raiding; and the shepherd class,
which ranks below these elite warriors. In its naïve way, the tale has given the
historical process by which the hunter gave way before the shepherd; but it
also reveals splendid powers of detailed observation. The hunter's only skill is
that of knowing how to kill the animal that comes into his power. He lives,
therefore, from hand to mouth. If he comes home empty-handed some days,
he must just go hungry. But as long as he has something to eat today, he does
not trouble with tomorrow. "He ate and drank, and rose and went his way.
Thus Esau despised his birthright" (Gen 25:34). On the other hand, the shepherd is a man of a different type. "While the hunter remains an impecunious
man, who needs to find his living day by day, the shepherd is to some extent a
capitalist, living on his interest."[19] He does not kill the animals in his care but
draws daily profit from them. He has food every day and wisely thinks not only
of today but also of tomorrow. Thus Jacob the shepherd proves superior to
Esau the hunter. The whole narrative is thus to be understood as a folktale
dealing with men of different occupations.

The Blessing

In the related narrative of Jacob's deception, the same motif undergoes
another twist (Gen 27:1-45). In this tale, what belongs to Esau and what Jacob
desires is the father's blessing. The blessing occupies the place held by the
birthright in the other story. There is a simple philological explanation of this
interchange. In Hebrew, *bekorah* (birthright) and *berakah* (blessing) have a
phonetic resemblance. Such wordplays were always popular in Israel. The
blessing in question, moreover, implies a precedence of the one over the
other. It implies the better inheritance and dominion over the brother; in
effect, it amounts to the same thing as the birthright. In form, such a blessing
is a magical word. Once pronounced it cannot be recalled. And the old man
cannot utter it until after he has "strengthened his soul" by a good meal. The
dying father is anxious to give this blessing to his firstborn. He loves him, for
(as it is naïvely put) he loves the venison he provides. So he sends him afield to
secure this delicacy for him. The mother, who prefers her quiet son, Jacob, has
overheard the conversation and secures the blessing for her own favorite by
killing two young goats and tying their skins round his neck and arms. To the
touch, he is exactly like his brother; so E tells it. In J, the ruse by which Isaac is
deceived is even subtler. Jacob puts on his brother's best clothes, and these
have their owner's characteristic odor.

This story is also completely on the level of the folktale, where the same plot is frequently encountered: how the clever but weak one outwits the strong but stupid one, and where there is a special fondness for the childish, roguish exchange of clothes. There are tales in which the prince puts a sheep's stomach over his curls and is then taken by everyone for a bald person. In Grimm's tale of "The Seven Young Kids," the wolf has many disguises. As Thimme says, "In the tale there is no feeling of moral indignation at such roguery, because laughter over the success of the trick displaces all moral resentment."[20]

Our tale shows representatives of two occupations in conflict, and the shepherd supplants the hunter. The latter is pictured as belonging to a rough type of humanity—he is as hairy as a goat and his odor is so strong that it is even perceptible in his new clothes. On the other hand, the shepherd is more civilized. His skin is smooth, and he attaches more value to personal cleanliness. The hunter roams about outdoors and is his father's favorite; but the mother loves the quiet Jacob best, who stays around the house. The hunter's venison tastes better than the tame meat provided by the shepherd, but the art of cooking is already able to conceal such differences. The hunter is a violent man; Esau intends to kill his brother. But the shepherd does not deal in violence; he avoids the open crime, but he is clever and achieves his goal through trickery.

In view of all this, one cannot doubt that the Esau stories are really examples of tales of occupations, with a plot of shepherd versus hunter, and that the ethnological color of the narrative was added at a later stage. In all these compositions we see the same principle at work; we are dealing with ancient folktales interwoven with historical reminiscences.

In the Laban stories the plot is similar. They deal with the young astute shepherd and his successful contest of wits against a man who is really his superior. It is easy to understand how the two similar cycles of stories attracted each other and were connected to the same person. But when we compare them in respect to originality, there can be no hesitation. Unlike the Esau stories, the Laban stories do not bear the marks of great antiquity and of distinct individuality. Rather they belong to the "fatherless" tales, which can easily be connected to another person. This finds confirmation in the arrangement of the composite narrative, which places the Esau stories first and the Laban stories second.[21]

CONCLUSION

The Esau stories are the real kernel of the Jacob tradition. Jacob is the archetypal shepherd who ousts the hunter. The name Jacob is simply a proper name of that period, such as the heroes of German folktales also bear. The same is true in Babylonian literature. The name Jacob (*Yaqubum*) is abbreviated from Jacob-el (*Yahqub-il, Yaqub-il*),[22] and it occurs in the time of Hammurabi. The name was also known in the West, which we learn from the list of Thutmosis III (c. 1500 B.C.E.), where it appears as the name of a Canaanite town. Names of similar formation in Canaan are also to be found in the Tel El-Amarna period.[23] Thus it is not surprising to find this same name in an ancient Israelite folktale. The objection—raised more than once in recent years—that Jacob was not a Canaanite name, has little force, for we know practically nothing of the names from that ancient time. And why should folktales be confined to the most common names? Regarding the name Esau we can say nothing at all. Whether it is in any way connected with the Phoenician Usos, the hunter and the enemy of his brother Samemrumos, must be left an open question.

The subsequent history of the Jacob figure was probably as follows: First is the story of Jacob outwitting Esau. Then a second story was connected to it, which also dealt with a young, clever shepherd. In this way the Jacob-Laban story was added. Simultaneously, a continuation was invented for the Esau story—what we have referred to as the Jacob-Esau story, Part 2. The biggest step, however, was taken when Jacob was declared to be the ancestor of Israel. At that period a new meaning was given to the older tales: Esau was identified with Edom and Laban with Aram. At the same time, the name Jacob was inserted into a whole series of other tales that dealt with the tribes and with the sacred places of Israel. The complete figure thus arose through the addition of the Israel tradition to the Jacob tradition.

It is also possible to give some indication of the time when this process took place. The new interpretation introducing Esau dates from the time subsequent to the conquest of Edom by David (after 980 B.C.E.). The addition of the blessing (Gen 27:40) seems to indicate that Edom afterwards threw off the yoke of Israel (840 B.C.E.). The same period is indicated by the Laban stories, because in the boundary treaty with him not a word is said about the Syrian wars (860-770 B.C.E.). The redactor did not dream that the Syrians would one day break out in rage against Israel and dismember it. The introduction of the political reference, therefore, dates from the time of the early kingdom in Israel. But the original Jacob story must be much older, existing since the primitive age of Israel when people were mostly shepherds and hunters. Another consideration supports the same date. After its unification under the first kings, Israel again began to be conscious of its unity, to ask about its ancestors, and to choose as these the most popular figures that its traditions provided.

The compelling motive for this growth and transformation of the Jacob figure is quite clear: the people loved it. In Jacob, ancient Israel joyfully recognized itself, and so selected him as its ancestor. Of course this popularity cannot be seen without some regret. But we must remember that the Germans take pleasure in the character of Baron Münchhausen, and that the Greeks saw in Odysseus a popular hero, if not an ancestor. Above all, we must remember that, alongside of Jacob, Israel chose another and nobler figure for an ancestor: Abraham.

NOTES

[1.] The Pan-Babylonian School refers to those scholars in the late nineteenth and early twentieth centuries that attributed Israelite and other societies' stories to Babylonian sources. See, for example, Hugo Winckler, *Die babylonische Weltschöpfung* (Leipzig: Hinrichs, 1906); and *idem, The History of Babylonia and Assyria,* trans. and ed. J. Alexander (New York: Scribners, 1907). For an analysis, see Jonathan Z. Smith, *Imagining Religion: From Babylon to Jonestown,* CSHJ (Chicago: Univ. of Chicago Press, 1978) 24–29.

2. Julius Wellhausen, *Prolegomena to the History of Ancient Israel,* trans. J. S. Black and A. Menzies (Edinburgh: A. & C. Black, 1885; reprinted with foreword by D. A. Knight, Scholars Press Reprints and Translations Series [Atlanta: Scholars, 1994]; German ed. 1899). 318–42.

3. Carl Steuernagel, *Einwanderung der israelitischen Stämme in Kanaan* (Berlin: Schwetschke, 1901).

4. Eduard Meyer, *Die Israeliten und ihre Nachbarstämme: Alttestamentliche Untersuchungen* (Halle: Niemeyer, 1906) 250.

5. Hugo Gressmann, "Sage und Geschichte in die Patriarchenerzählungen," *ZAW* 30 (1910) 1–34.

6. Wilhelm M. Wundt, *Völkerpsychologie: Eine Untersuchung der Entwicklungs-Gestze von Sprache, Mythus, und Sitte,* 2 vols. (Leipzig: Englemann, 1901–1909) vol. 2, pts. 1–3; *idem, Elements of Folk Psychology: Outlines of a Psychological History of the Development of Mankind,* trans. E. L. Schaub (New York: Macmillan, 1916; German ed. 1912).

7. See Hermann Gunkel, *The Folktale in the Old Testament,* trans. M. D. Rutter, HTIBS (Sheffield: Almond, 1987; German ed. 1917).

8. Other studies preliminary to the present essay are as follows: I have dealt with the building up of the Jacob stories, taking the Esau narratives as the kernel of the whole, in the first edition (1901) of my commentary, *Genesis;* and I have attempted the separation of the historical material from the material of

another kind (following Eduard Meyer) in the 3rd German ed. of the same commentary (1910), trans. M. E. Biddle, MLBS (Macon, Ga.: Mercer Univ. Press, 1997) 285–371. Then I gradually felt the force of Gressmann's hypothesis. Thus the complete idea of the Jacob stories has come to me from several sources. I have discussed it more briefly in the article "Jacob und Esau," in *RGG²*. I have also analyzed the Joseph stories in the same way in "Die Komposition der Joseph-Geschichte," *ZDMG* 76 (1922) 55–71.

9. Otto Eissfeldt distinguishes even a fourth source: the so-called "Lay source"; see his *Hexateuch-Synopse* (Darmstadt: Wissenschaftliche Buchgesellschaft, 1922); and *idem, The Old Testament: An Introduction,* trans. P. R. Ackroyd (New York: Harper & Row, 1965) 194–99. Thus, unfortunately, the analysis of the sources of Genesis resembles, not a well-founded and finely crowned edifice, but—in spite of, or perhaps just because of, all the pains that have been spent upon it—a web of Penelope, on which labor is continually renewed. However disconcerting this may seem, it is not an insuperable obstacle to the study of questions addressed here. For all the sources that scholars have found—or imagined they have found—are in substantial agreement as far as the composition of the Jacob narrative is concerned. In all of them the figure of Jacob is essentially one and the same. (This is scarcely true for Eissfeldt's suggested "Lay source.") The source references provided here (not very important in this connection) are taken from my *Genesis* commentary (3rd ed., 1910; trans. 1997).

10. To my great astonishment, some Old Testament scholars are unwilling to admit this quite self-evident statement and maintain that it is an unjustifiable dismemberment of the sources on my part. I can only attribute such an attitude to a complete lack of acquaintance with the study of folktales and legends.

[Ed.] See now, Susan Niditch, *Folklore and the Hebrew Bible,* GBS (Minneapolis: Fortress Press, 1993); *idem, The Oral and Written Word,* Library of Ancient Israel (Louisville: Westminster John Knox, 1996).

[11.] To Gunkel's examples, one might add the continuation of the Daniel story in the apocryphal books: Bel and the Dragon, Susanna, and The Song of the Three Young Men. The multiple editions of the Book of Esther show this same tendency; see David J. A. Clines, *The Esther Scroll: The Story of the Story,* JSOTSup 30 (Sheffield: JSOT Press, 1984).

12. Gunkel, *Genesis* (1997) 343–45.

13. I am flattered by the support of Hugo Gressmann and Rudolph Kittel in this opinion: *A History of the Hebrews,* trans. J. Taylor et al. (London: Williams & Norgate, 1895) 1.753.

[14.] Note the analysis of the "betrothal type-scene" by Robert Alter, *The Art of Biblical Narrative* (New York: Basic, 1981) 51–62.

15. See my *The Folktale in the Old Testament,* 135–38.

16. Meyer, *Die Israeliten und ihre Nachbarstämme,* 243.

17. For Edom's famous wisdom, see Jer 49:7 and Bar 3:22-23; but also the homes of Job (Uz) and Eliphaz (Teman): Job 1:1 (see Gen 36:28) and Job 2:11 (Gen 36:10-11); and my *Genesis* (1997) 308.

18. See Gunkel, *The Folktale in the Old Testament,* 149–52.

19. Richard Hildebrand, *Recht und Sitte auf den primitiveren wirtschaftlichen Kulturstufen,* 2nd ed. (Jena: Fischer, 1907) 24.

20. Adolf Thimme, *Das Märchen* (Leipzig: Heims, 1909) 56.

21. In this I have the support of Gressmann; see also Kittel, *A History of the Hebrews,* 1.34 n2.

[22.] This is better written *Iaḥkub-ila;* see Martin Noth, "Mari und Israel: Eine Personennamenstudie," in *Geschichte und Altes Testament,* BHTh 16 (Tübingen: Mohr/Siebeck, 1953) 142.

23. Kittel, *A History of the Hebrews,* 417 n2.

A SELECT JACOB BIBLIOGRAPHY

Bledstein, Adrien Janis. "Binder, Trickster, Heel and Hairy-Man: Rereading Genesis 27 as a Trickster Tale Told by a Woman." In *A Feminist Companion to Genesis,* edited by A. Brenner, 282–89. FCB 2. Sheffield: Sheffield Academic, 1993.

Coats, George W. "Strife Without Reconciliation—A Narrative Theme in the Jacob Traditions." In *Werden und Wirken des Alten Testaments: Festschrift für Claus Westermann,* edited by R. Albertz, 82–106. Göttingen: Vandenhoeck & Ruprecht; Neukirchen-Vluyn: Neukirchener, 1980.

Cross, Frank Moore. "Reuben, the Firstborn of Jacob: Sacral Traditions and Early Israelite History." In *From Epic to Canon: History and Literature in Ancient Israel,* 53–70. Cambridge: Harvard Univ. Press, 1998.

Fishbane, Michael. "Composition and Structure in the Jacob Cycle (Gen. 25:19—35:22)." *JJS* 26 (1975) 15–38.

Fretheim, Terence E. "Jacob in Tradition." *Int* 26 (1972) 419–36.

Furman, Nelly. "His Story versus Her Story: Male Genealogy and Female Strategy in the Jacob Cycle." In *Feminist Perspectives on Biblical Scholarship,* edited by A. Y. Collins, 107–16. BSNA 10. Chico, Calif.: Scholars, 1985.

Gottwald, Norman K. "Sociological Method in the Study of Ancient Israel." In *Encounter with the Text: Form and History in the Hebrew Bible,* edited by M. J. Buss, 69–81. SemeiaSup 8. Philadelphia: Fortress Press; Missoula, Mont.: Scholars, 1979.

Hendel, Ronald S. *The Epic of the Patriarch: The Jacob Cycle and the Narrative Traditions of Canaan and Israel.* HSM 42. Atlanta: Scholars, 1987.

McKay, Heather A. "Jacob Makes it Across the Jabbok." *JSOT* 38 (1987) 3–13.

Morrison, Margaret A. "The Jacob and Laban Narrative in Light of Near Eastern Sources." *BA* 46 (1983) 155–64.

Noth, Martin. *A History of Pentateuchal Traditions,* translated by B. W. Anderson. Englewood Cliffs, N.J.: Prentice-Hall, 1972.

Thompson, Thomas L. "Conflict Themes in the Jacob Narratives." *Semeia* 15 (1979) 5–26.

———. *The Historicity of the Patriarchal Narratives: The Quest for the Historical Abraham.* BZAW 133. Berlin: de Gruyter, 1974.

Westermann, Claus. *Genesis 12–36,* translated by J. J. Scullion. CC. Minneapolis: Augsburg, 1985.

4

The Hagar Traditions

Of all the books of the Old Testament, Genesis probably interests both theologians and laypersons most. For certain phases of our general theological and religious attitude it is of the greatest importance how we regard the individual narratives of Genesis—stories that have been dear to us from earliest youth. Old Testament theology, moreover, has devoted a great—indeed an immense—amount of study and intellect to the interpretation of Genesis. In the nineteenth century, Old Testament research was occupied especially with tracing the sources of Genesis (by general consensus). And though the combination of the sources of this book is far too complicated ever to warrant the expectation of a final and complete solution of all the problems involved, the result has been such that we may now point to it with grateful pride in our predecessors in this research. Particular respect and gratitude is due to Julius Wellhausen, the Old Testament scholar who taught us how to judge correctly the relative age and character of the sources.[1]

And yet, if we consider the commentaries on Genesis and ask them what, after all, has been the outcome for the real purpose of all work on Genesis—the living, historical-theological understanding of these narratives—we cannot give a really satisfactory answer, despite the appreciation of what has been thus far accomplished. While dealing with the preliminary questions, the really vital matter has been neglected; the chief emphasis of investigation has been laid upon literary criticism and the combination of the sources. This has been the case not only with Genesis but also to a large extent with the rest of the Old Testament—and frequently with the New Testament. Now all literary criticism is in the nature of preliminary work—an insight that should never be overlooked. Ultimately the important thing is not to know by whom and when a book was written, and what its sources are. The real question for scholarship should always be: How is this book to be understood? And it is very clear that theological exegesis has fallen short in this respect.

Exegesis is considered tedious and often justifiably so. This is because exegesis is occupied too exclusively with preliminary questions, with matters of textual criticism, grammar, archaeology, and lexicography, with introductory discussions, and—especially in the case of the New Testament—with logical connections. All this is well and good provided it remains merely preliminary and keeps within proper limits. The most important issue, however, is to understand the flesh-and-blood writers who speak to us here, to draw near to them in spirit, to put ourselves in the same place when they rejoice and when they grieve, when they pine and sigh, and when they exult in their song of thanksgiving. This living understanding of the book is true exegesis.

It may be said in reply that we should not blame past scholarship too much for spending so much time over preliminary matters and failing so largely to reach the matter of prime importance because these very preliminaries had to be taken care of first. I am quite willing to accept this explanation, and only ask consent to my proposition that it is now time to begin energetically with real exegesis. Now, what appears to be the object of such exegesis in Genesis? This I propose to show by an example in what follows.

HAGAR'S FLIGHT: GENESIS 16

1. *Now Sarai, Abram's wife, bore him no children. She had an Egyptian maid whose name was Hagar.* The narrative makes an entirely new start, assuming only one thing, that there is a man by the name of Abram; everything else is told within the story. We infer from this that the narrative once existed independently. In oral tradition every story is told as complete within itself; the connection in which we find the stories at present was supplied afterward.

The slave, Hagar, is the property of Sarah, not of Abram. According to Israelite custom, parents could give a young woman a slave as dowry. The slave was thus her personal property and not, like the other maidservants, at the disposal of her husband. This slave, Hagar, is a foreigner, an Egyptian, which was probably a very common thing in an Israelite family. These items ought to mean something—just what we shall learn subsequently.

2. *And Sarai said to Abram, "Behold now, Yahweh has prevented me from bearing children; go in to my maid; it may be that I shall obtain children by her."* The great mysteries of generation, conception, and birth are derived in all antiquity from the deity, in polytheistic religions usually from a goddess. In Israel this, along with many other matters, had been transferred to Yahweh, who thus receives many—and sometimes quite varied—epithets.

An old Israelite legal custom is referred to here: the wife, if barren, may offer another woman as substitute and adopt the latter's children. It cost Sarai some struggle to surrender the slave (her personal property) to her husband, of course; but she controls herself in the hope of thus obtaining children. Childlessness is a misfortune and a disgrace, while motherhood brings honor and dominion in the household. The slave is not consulted in this surrender; it is a great honor for her to have intercourse with her master.

4. *And he went in to Hagar, and she conceived; and when she saw that she had conceived, she looked with contempt on her mistress.* The slave woman, shown too much honor, grows arrogant. And the narrator makes plain that he strongly disapproves of such action on the part of the slave, emphasizing the words "she despised her mistress." This must not occur, for the slave must honor the master.

5. *And Sarai said to Abram, "May the wrong done to me be on you! I gave my maid to your embrace, and when she saw that she had conceived, she looked on me with contempt. May Yahweh judge between you and me!"* Sarai is so indignant that she even invokes the righteous judgment of Yahweh against her husband, for she feels that she has deserved reward and not insult from Abram.

6. *But Abram said to Sarai, "Behold, your maid is in your power; do to her as you please." Then Sarai dealt harshly with her, and she fled from her.* Abram, always pliable, renounces his claim to his concubine for the sake of peace in the family. The phrase "she is in your power" indicates a legal act, an assignment of rights; consequently, Hagar is now once more Sarai's slave. Before this, Sarai could not help enduring contempt; now she turns the tables and shows Hagar who is mistress. What she did to her, as well as what Hagar had done before to offend her mistress, the narrator fails to tell; ancient narrative is very sparing of such details. It is not to be supposed that she treated her gently, for an Israelite slave was used to sound beatings.

The few details make the three characters perfectly clear. Abram is pliable and yields to his wife; at her request he takes Hagar as a concubine, and again at her bidding he dismisses her. Sarai is the impulsive woman, proudly conscious of her position as wife, in passion cruel and very subjective. In order to obtain children she gave Hagar away, and yet she regards this very act as deserving of recognition from her husband. And so, in her passionate indignation at the injustice done her, she sets herself up as unselfish before Abram—psychologically quite true to nature. The Israelite husband probably sighs in secret over his irritable wife. Finally, we come to the slave, whose fluctuating fortunes entertain and move the audience. First she is a slave, then her master's concubine and mother of the heir, and as such impudent toward her childless mistress; then she is severely abused and offended in her maternal pride. Thus, husband, wife, and maid, are clearly Israelite archetypes. That they act just as they do seems to the naïve legend quite a matter of course, for this is the way of Israel.

From this point on, Hagar is the leading character. "And she fled from her." In the construction of the narrative this sentence is the climax of all that has preceded it—the object of which is to explain her fleeing—and the introduction for all that is to follow. What are we to regard as the motive of Hagar's flight? The narrator informs us that Hagar was with child, and that she dared to flee into the wilderness, where deprivations, violence, and murder threatened her. It was, then, an act of desperation and of defiance: better all the dangers of the wilderness than the insults in the tent of Sarai! Thus we have a complete picture of Hagar: when it was well with her, she treated her mistress with insolence; when she is humbled she runs away in defiance. At the same time, we are not to lose all sympathy with the unruly Hagar; for afterwards the legend tells us that the deity himself took care of her. The judgment of the god is of course the judgment of the narrator himself, who takes pleasure in the unbending will of the stubborn woman.

7. *The angel of Yahweh found her by a spring of water in the wilderness, the spring on the way to Shur.* In connecting the elements of the story, we have to consider that Hagar has come to the fountain to drink; just as any travelers and Bedouins come to the spring. It seems that Hagar is acquainted with the desert. "The spring" is a definite spring, the location and the name of which are given at the close of the story. The phrase "the spring on the way to Shur" anticipates this description, and it is a proper addition as far as it goes. The spring is on the road from Canaan to Egypt, which suits the circumstances perfectly: the fugitive Hagar is fleeing to her old home in Egypt. The old narratives always fit closely into the surroundings in which they take place; they do not originate in the study and are not learned accounts but popular tales, told in the very places they discuss. There Hagar meets the divine being who bears the name "Yahweh's angel."

Now we are struck by the fact that afterward Hagar believes that she has seen Yahweh himself: "So she called the name of Yahweh who spoke to her, "You are *El Roi* [a God of seeing]" (16:13). This strange confusion of Yahweh with Yahweh's angel is not rare elsewhere in the old narratives and has been the occasion of curious conjectures and still more curious attempts at explanation on the part of modern scholars. In all cases where the given statement of facts seems to be absurd in an otherwise reasonable tradition, the explanation is to be found in the existence of a history in which a peculiar distortion has made apparent nonsense out of what was originally intelligible and simple. Older versions introduced Yahweh himself in such cases; later editors and copyists were offended by the notion of Yahweh's being too intimately involved with the world and preferred to speak of Yahweh's angel in these passages—that is, an inferior divine being. But this modification is not carried out consistently; in some places Yahweh's name remains. And this results in the apparent absurdity that an angel of Yahweh appears, but Hagar declares that she saw Yahweh. This substitution of a divine being for the deity is a process that we find frequently elsewhere in the history of religion.

We can go a step further. Later Ishmael receives his name from the fact that "God hears." But this name is not Shemayah "Yahweh hears," but Ishmael "El hears." From this we conjecture that the oldest version of the story did not contain the name of Yahweh at all, but spoke of an "El," that is a god. The correctness of this inference is shown by Hagar's comment: "she called Yahweh who spoke to her 'El Roi.'"[2]

So El Roi was undoubtedly the original name of the deity in this narrative. Accordingly, we perceive three stages of religious development in the legend. Originally, the deity was El Roi; then Yahweh was introduced, and El Roi became an epithet of Yahweh; finally, Yahweh's angel took the place of Yahweh.

Furthermore, we are able to say something about the nature of this El Roi. This god appears at the spring, he is a spring-deity, and indeed the deity of a certain spring, the spring Lahai-roi. It is not accidental that the name of the deity, El Roi, and that of his spring, Beer-lahai-roi, are found together. This god is the deity of this spring. And so we obtain a glance into an ancient religion that believes in local deities, specifically in deities of springs. What we know of the pre-Israelite religion of Canaan agrees entirely with these inferences. The pre-Israelite religion of Canaan worshiped a great number of such local deities, the baalim; and in Canaan, as well as in other lands, springs were frequently held sacred. In the earliest periods, people saw a reflection of the deity in the living, gushing, life-giving water. When Israel occupied Canaan, it also adopted some of the Canaanite deities, religious rituals, and legends; and, to a certain extent, they identified these deities with their own Yahweh.[3] The god of the spring, El Roi, is thus regarded as equivalent to Yahweh here.

In the same way, the epithet of Yahweh at Bethel is El Bethel (Gen 35:7); at Beer-sheba, El Olam (Gen 21:33); and at Jerusalem, El Elyon (Ps 73:11). All of these names were originally the names of the local deities of these places and were only transferred later to Yahweh by Israel.[4]

But now it is very important to note that the relation between the spring and the deity, which must have once been very close, has become very loose in the present form of the story. The deity is no longer represented as coming forth from the spring or vanishing into it. This feature is common in the legends of Genesis: the deity and the place of worship are always rather loosely connected. Israel identified Yahweh with the local deities to a certain extent but did not think of Yahweh as so closely connected with the locality. So the history of the Hagar stories is a small episode in the larger process of the adoption of Canaanite worship by Israel.

The deity appeared to Hagar at the spring and spoke with her. Such appearances and conversations on the part of the deity are nothing rare in ancient legends. Incidentally, it is very common for the deity to appear unrecognized or in secret. A divinity is too awesome to appear openly; a human would die of terror if the deity's true nature is recognized. Accordingly, legends tell how the god lifts the veil gently and gradually until recognition occurs. But at the moment when this happens, the god vanishes. Thus it occurs here.

8. *And he said, "Hagar, maid of Sarai, where have you come from and where are you going?" She said, "I am fleeing from my mistress Sarai."* It is assumed in this conversation that Hagar did not at first recognize the god. In her eyes he is merely "a man." The man speaks to her, not she to him; she would not dare to do so because he looks so frightful. But his words are wonderful. She does not know him, but he knows her and calls her by name. Hagar cannot fail to wonder whether this is perhaps a man of God. Then he continues, "Where have you come from and where are you going?" There are questions of surprise and also of interest: Why are you, a woman, here in the wilderness? But Hagar answers as though through her closed teeth; no whimpering and complaining, but only the fact that she is fleeing.

11. *And the angel of Yahweh said to her, "Behold, you are with child."* Hagar's pregnancy—such is the assumption of this remark—has thus far been a secret; and the man knows even this most intimate secret! Accordingly, she is inclined to believe him when he continues: *"and you shall bear a son; you shall call his name Ishmael, because Yahweh has given heed to your affliction."* The legends are fond of telling how an oracle is pronounced regarding an unborn child; what the man becomes later in life is prophesied to his mother before his birth. So his later fortunes are not a matter of chance but divine destiny. And even his name is not left to the whim of his parents but is fixed by the command of God. And God imparted also even the significance of the name. The ancient Israelite people devoted much attention to the significance of names; almost every old legend contains such interpretations, which are often ingenious and full of meaning. But the boy is to be called Ishmael because God has heard of "your affliction." The original uses the same expression as before in "she dealt harshly with her." God has heard of this mistreatment, heard even now as he hears Hagar speak. But these words are a new puzzle to Hagar; how does this remarkable man know that God has heard of this mistreatment? And now she even hears a prophecy from his mouth regarding the destiny of her son.

12. *"He shall be a wild ass of a man, his hand against every man and every man's hand against him; and he shall dwell over against all his kinsmen."* These words are intended to comfort Hagar and encourage her to endure all her hardships here, for a reward is in store for her trouble. The legend details the destiny of Ishmael to be become a Bedouin with unmistakable satisfaction. It compares the Bedouin with the animal that shares the desert with him. The wild ass is untamable and fond of freedom; he laughs at cities and the herder; but indeed his food is scanty—a splendid picture of the nomad. And further, Ishmael's life is a constant warfare, and he is every man's foe: a lot enjoyed by men of heroic type, but on the other hand, full of dangers. "And he shall dwell over against all his kinsmen," a situation more beneficial to him than to the kin whose cattle he robs and whose fields he plunders. The vigorous description of the destiny of Ishmael may serve as a warning to the modern teacher not to get too mild a conception of the story's tone. For the legend thinks, rather, that this untamable Ishmael is a worthy son of his bold and defiant mother, who also refused to bend her neck under the yoke, but spurned a life of security because it was also a life of humiliation. And such as she is as she stands at this moment before the god, defiant and at odds with the world, so her son is to become: unruly, freedom-loving, and the foe of all the world. Now comes the conclusion. As is customary in old legends, the place, and in this case the god also, receives a name.

13. *So she called the name of Yahweh who spoke to her, "You are El Roi [a God of seeing]"; for she said, Have I really seen God and remained alive after seeing him?"* The explanation of the name has become unclear in the text; from the sense of the connection we should expect perhaps "the end of my distress." The narrator of the legend reflects upon the meaning of the name El Roi, the original and precise meaning of which is scarcely known to him, and interprets it in his own way. The name of the spring is also explained.

14. *Therefore the well was called Beer-la-hai-roi; it lies between Kadesh and Bered.* The conclusion of the narrative is lacking. We expect to be told further how Hagar remained at the spring; how she bore Ishmael there and gave him the name; how Ishmael grew up and became a tribe that had its seat by this spring and this El for its god. Why this conclusion is lacking will be explained below.

The Original Meaning of the Legend

The name Ishmael appears elsewhere in ancient legends and histories as the name of a Bedouin group. Plainly the Ishmael described in our story is, according to the legend, the ancestor of the group that is said to bear his name. This is made perfectly clear by Gen 21:18, according to which Ishmael the boy became a great people. The same thing is true of many personages in Genesis, especially of Jacob and Esau; Judah; Joseph and Jacob's other sons; Moab and Ammon; Shem, Ham, and Japheth; and many others. All these in history and in reality are peoples and tribes; in legend and poetry they are regarded as individuals, ancestors of the peoples they personify. We need not raise the question here how extensively this view is to be applied to the characters in Genesis. I am showing here only that the legend of Ishmael, if I understand it correctly, requires this interpretation. When this legend describes Ishmael's love of freedom and his quarrelsomeness, it means by this not only that there once lived a man named Ishmael who had this character; but it desires at the same time to characterize the habits of his descendants, the Ishmaelites. When it gives the name of the spring beside which Ishmael's birth was prophesied, this is no fiction. That spring, we must conclude, was the chief seat and sanctuary of the tribe of the Ishmaelites. Likewise when the legend reports the name of the deity who appeared to Ishmael's mother, it means that this deity, El Roi, is the tribal god of Ishmael.

Finally, the name of the mother, Hagar, is no invention. There must have been a primitive tribe named Hagar, from which the tribe of Ishmael was derived. The mother of Ishmael is a slave; this feature also has its significance. Those who tell one another this story, and who derive their origin from Isaac, the legitimate son, insist that they are nobler and more legitimate than their brother Ishmael. Furthermore, Hagar is an Egyptian, and Ishmael is therefore not pure stock, but only a half-breed. Such mixtures of Bedouin tribes and fugitive Egyptians have been proven on historical grounds.[5] Ishmael is the older group, the firstborn; this feature is also confirmed by the facts. When Israel came upon the stage of history, Ishmael was already forgotten. Thus, if we understand how to read these ethnographic legends, we can derive from them much information that is sometimes of great historical value. This information is often the more valuable because these legends reach back into ancient times, times from which we have no historic reports. We have no other historical information about this group of Ishmael with its center at Beer-lahai-roi. Moreover, no argument is needed to prove that these legends themselves become much more vivid when we understand their ancient meaning.

Many of the legends of Genesis aim to answer questions, and we fail to understand them if we do not recognize this purpose. Thus the legend we are considering asks the questions: Where does Ishmael get its name? How does it come to have this location, this reputation, and this god? The need to furnish answers to these questions led to our legend, or at least gave it its character. That is, our legend treats the origin of the tribe of Ishmael. The chief question is this: How does it happen that Ishmael, our elder brother, has become a

Bedouin? He is surely Abraham's son, conceived in Abraham's house, and yet a child of the desert, born beside a spring in the wilderness; how can this be? The legend answers: When his mother had conceived him she became a fugitive, and thus he was born in the wilderness.

The Antiquity of the Legend

Our legend must be very ancient, since it knows so much more of this Ishmael than we can find in any other historical account. The characters, moreover, are quite primitive. We can distinguish in the legends of Genesis two types: an older type, in which people are depicted as they are—from life; and a later type, which describes religious ideals. Very clearly the present legend belongs to the older type. The conception of deity is also primitive: the god sides with the defiant Hagar. A great number of the legends of Genesis are not of Israelite origin; many were simply adopted and amalgamated by Israel. Such may be presumed from the outset as the case with the legend of Ishmael. Just as, for instance, the Kyffhäusser legend has, as a matter of course, its home at Mount Kyffhäusser,[6] so it is natural that the tribal legend of Ishmael should have been originally told in the Ishmael group and have had its home at Beer-lahai-roi. This is borne out by a number of features, especially the vigorous description of the Bedouin life. Of course, the Ishmaelites must have told the story somewhat differently; they would not have made their ancestor the son of a fugitive slave. In our version we have the story as it was told in accordance with Israelite tradition.

The Style and Preservation of the Legend

The legend is a remarkable model of the oldest narrative style. The first portion of the story, especially, is distinguished for the variety and truthfulness of its images. At the same time, the legend is distinguished by its strict connectedness of action and especially by its admirable compression. The narrator achieves wonders in the omission of everything not absolutely essential; the main thread of the action is held with great energy. Such admirable art can only be the product of a long artistic tradition; we cannot but assume that it was cultivated in Israel by a class of professional storytellers. Ancient legends usually show their great antiquity by the omission or veiling of some of their elements that had become offensive to later times. Thus it is here. The legend has forgotten that the god was the local god of the spring, and the spring was really a sanctuary. How and where the god came, where and when the god disappeared, and when Hagar recognized the god—all this the legend leaves out. The result is an interesting intellectual chiaroscuro, which is characteristic of the ancient legends.

THE EXPULSION OF ISHMAEL: GENESIS 21:8-21

8. *And Abraham made a great feast on the day that Isaac was weaned. 9. But Sarah saw the son of Hagar the Egyptian, whom she had borne to Abraham, playing with her son Isaac. 10. So she said to Abraham, "Cast out this slave woman with her son; for the son of this slave woman shall not be heir with my son Isaac."* With clever and natural touches the legend indicates the motives for the expulsion of Ishmael. At the bottom of it was Sarah's jealous love for her son; for maternal love may become most terrible cruelty if anyone tries to harm a beloved child. To give us a vivid picture of this, the legend takes us to the day of the weaning of Isaac. This is the day on which after the dangerous years of infancy—for the weaning occurred in about the third year—the mother rejoices in her darling and regards him with special tenderness. On this day, Sarah happens to notice Ishmael playing with her child. This element of "playing" (*meṣaḥaq*) is derived from the name Isaac (*Yiṣḥaq*), for the legends are fond of such clever plays on the names of persons and places. The thoughts of Sarah as she sees the children playing are not provided, in accordance with the custom of ancient narrative method; we have to guess them from the context. The mother is thinking—what else should she do on a day such as this?—of her child's future and is already planning for him, for mother-love has far-seeing eyes. And so when she sees the two children playing together it occurs to her that they will divide the inheritance when they are men. And so she demands of Abraham that he cast out Hagar and his own son. The master has the right to dismiss his slave and expel his children entirely in accordance with his personal whim. It should be noted that Hagar has in this case a different position in the household from that of the former account (Genesis 16). There she was Sarah's property; but here she belongs to Abraham, and she is at the same time his concubine; in this account she has nothing whatever to do with Sarah.

The older account went on to tell at this point how Abraham, being pliable, obeyed his wife; he does so with heavy heart indeed, though not on account of the slave—for slaves are plentiful—but on account of his son whom he is to cast out among strangers. But we may infer that she pursued him with her remarks and worried him so that his breath grew short as with one dying. The oldest account, intimate with human nature, probably regarded this yielding on Abraham's part as quite intelligible; the later version, which wished to see in Abraham a moral ideal, took offense at his casting out his own child.

Accordingly, a later hand has interpolated here the following: 11. *And the thing was very displeasing to Abraham on account of his son. 12. But God said to Abraham, "Be not displeased because of the lad and because of your slave woman; whatever Sarah says to you, do as she tells you, for through Isaac shall your descendants be named."* That is, the descendants of Ishmael shall forget that they are derived from Abraham, so that he, nevertheless, will become no real son. And the Lord further comforts Abraham as to Ishmael's fate: 13. *"And I will make a nation of the son of the slave woman also, because he is your offspring."* That these words are not a part of the original narrative is evident for many reasons, especially the following: If the ancient legend had known anything of this command, it would have mentioned it at the beginning of the story and have built up the whole story on this alone—as in the story of the sacrifice of Isaac. For the pious, a command from God is an adequate motive and permits no other subordinate motive. On the other hand, when the ancient legend shows such care to depict the jealousy of Sarah, it does so with the intention of explaining the expulsion of Ishmael from this and this alone. If in accordance with this we omit the command, the story gains in beauty and consistency of form and at the same time in antiquity and force of substance.

Thus far the events took place in Abraham's tent. The legend now goes on to narrate the fortunes of Hagar and Ishmael. 14. *So Abraham rose early in the morning, and took bread and a skin of water, and gave it to Hagar, putting it on her shoulder, along with the child, and sent her away.* With deep sympathy the legend now tells of Hagar's expulsion and distress. A skin of water and a loaf is all she receives for the journey; how will she fare when this little supply is exhausted? Will she find her way in the pathless land? *And she departed, and wandered in the wilderness of Beer-sheba.* So Abraham's home is to be assumed to be not far from Beer-sheba. 15. *When the water in the skin was gone, she cast the child under one of the bushes.* 16. *Then she went, and sat down over against him a good way off, about the distance of a bowshot; for she said, "Let me not look upon the death of the child."* Now mother and child get into the most terrible mortal danger: the way is lost, the water is out; all that is left is to die. The story is evidently nearing its crisis, and on this account becomes unusually detailed: the situation is described closely and an exception is even made to the general rule against reporting thoughts directly. In her despair she cast the boy, whom she had been carrying, under a bush. Naturally the boy is exhausted sooner than his mother; he will die first. But the mother's eye cannot endure the sight of his death anguish; she therefore goes away some distance, but not—O loving and inconsistent mother heart!—not too far. Once more the affecting scene is described: *And as she sat over against him, the child lifted up his voice and wept.* The scene is meant to be impressed deeply upon our hearts. Here sits the mother waiting for the death of her son, and there lies the boy panting and crying for water. At this point we are to suppose a pause.

Then follows the third portion of the story, the turn of fortune, the rescue of Ishmael. 17. *And God heard the voice of the lad.* This statement, which puts an end to all the distress, echoes in the hearts of the listeners: God heard, for he is a God of mercy. God hears even the voice of weeping children; no one is too slight, not even a weeping child, for God to show compassion. The saying is repeated in what follows. The angel exclaims to Hagar: God heard the voice of the lad. The narrator emphasizes the statement this way because in it he has reached the point. He proposes to take up this phrase later in order to explain the name of Ishmael. It must be admitted that the narrator has worked up to this point, which he had in view all the time, in a remarkable manner. This is the supreme art of storytelling.

And the angel of God called to Hagar from heaven, and said to her. . . . The Elohist, to whom we owe this beautiful account, speaks here of the angel of God, as in the other account the Yahwist speaks of the angel of Yahweh. Here too it is to be supposed that the original form of the story spoke of God himself, and that the later time substituted "the angel of God" out of religious respect. The same religious consideration explains also why the angel calls "out of heaven." In the older legends the deity himself comes to earth and appears like a human among humans, as in the first version of the Hagar story. But later times took offense at such an anthropomorphic conception of God and preferred to say that God remained in heaven and talked with the patriarchs from there. In the present case, the two views are combined: it is only an angel who speaks, and even he remains in heaven.

But the angel calls to Hagar, *"What troubles you, Hagar? Fear not; for God has heard the voice of the lad where he is."* The place where the boy lies is a definite place, a place where God hears, that is, a sacred place. This is a particularly fine touch, which we must not miss: in her supreme distress, when in her despair Hagar threw the lad down, she hit upon a place where God is near and listens; when her need was greatest, God's help was nearest. 18. *"Arise, lift up the lad, and hold him fast with your hand"*; do not give him up, for he is destined to do great things; *"for I will make him"*—an overexuberant prophecy, especially to an ancient audience—*"a great nation."* Thus the angel gives Hagar new courage. 19. *Then God opened her eyes, and she saw a well of water. She sees all at once what she had not noticed before, a well*. This touch, too, is true to life. As a deep hole in the ground, such a well may be hidden from the eye by the slightest elevation of the surface and is often not easily recognizable from a distance. Whether the well was already there, or whether it was called forth at the moment of God's word, we do not learn; the delicate tale draws a discreet veil over this point. In the original form of the story this well was without doubt a sacred well, a well at which God appears, God hears.

And she went, and filled the skin with water, and gave the lad a drink. Here is a touching trait: we are not told that Hagar herself drank; that is mother-love. The story is now finished; the only other things the reader expects are the provision of of names, customary at the conclusion, and some notes as to Ishmael's future fortunes. Later editors have omitted the giving of names, because the same names were already explained in other stories. But originally the name of Ishmael must have appeared here; it is evident that the original narrator must have provided this from the fact that the name of Ishmael has been avoided in the story up to this point, and has only employed the expression "the lad." Next, according to the context, the name of this well was Beer-sheba: Hagar wandered in the wilderness of Beer-sheba. We may presume that the narrator interpreted this name as the well of "the one crying for help" (*be'er šew'a*): this is why he recounted that the lad "cried for help." The fortunes of Ishmael continue. 20. *And God was with the lad, and he grew up.* The growth of the lad in the midst of the dangers and hardships of the wilderness can only be explained as a miracle of God. And—when he became a man—*he lived in the wilderness of Paran* (between Canaan and Egypt, or *Mṣr*). 21. *And his mother took a wife for him from the land of Egypt.* This was originally a variant of the note that his mother was an Egyptian or a Musrith.

COMPARISON OF THE TWO ACCOUNTS

The two accounts agree in situation and details. The actors are the same: the jealous Sarah; the pliable Abraham; and the slave Hagar, who bears a child by Abraham before her mistress has a child. The principal action is also the same in both: first they describe a scene in Abraham's tent in which Sarah, jealous and cruel, urges Abraham and Abraham yields, and at the close, Hagar's leaving Abraham's tent and going into the wilderness. Consequently, Hagar gets into dire straits. Then the deity intervenes. He reveals himself at the well and is moved by the misery of the fugitive. Thus Ishmael receives his name, "God hears," and the well too is named. Ishmael grows up in the wilderness and becomes a nation. The two accounts answer the same question: how did the people of Ishmael originate? And how did they come to be in the wilderness? How do they come by the sacred well where it dwelled, and come to be called by the name of Ishmael? The two accounts also agree in many details. For example, the deity who speaks begins speaking with a question to Hagar.

The conclusion from all this is that the two accounts are variants of one and the same story. The existence of such variants is not surprising but rather the rule. These stories existed originally in oral tradition, and though we may have good reason for supposing our tradition to be very persistent and faithful, it is a matter of course that it cannot remain absolutely unchanged. Each one tells the story a little differently. When religion, ethical views, and aesthetic taste change, legend slowly follows them. Thus there arise variants and new versions. Such variants are found in the Book of Genesis in great numbers. The two accounts of Hagar are one of the most interesting examples of this.

The later collectors and editors, who put together all the material known to them, could not avoid the task of combing the variants into some sort of rational arrangement. It is particularly instructive in the story of Hagar to watch the editor at work. We have the first account from the hand of the Yahwist, the second from the hand of the Elohist. The editor who made them both a part of his work is therefore the editor of both the Yahwist and Elohist, the so-called Jehovist. He could not leave the stories exactly as they were: Ishmael cannot be born, named, and brought up in the wilderness twice. Accordingly, in the first version the editor left out Ishmael's growth, and in the second his birth and name. But this was not sufficient. If Hagar flees in the first version and is cast out in the second, then she must have returned to Abraham in the meantime; the editor was consequently obliged to state this expressly and give some rationale for it. To this end he interpolated a command of the angel in the first account: "Return to your mistress, and submit to her" (16:9). And so poor Hagar has to go back home, only to be cast out later. The editor seems to have felt how difficult this made Hagar's lot, and in order to soften the matter a little he added a promise: "The angel of Yahweh also said to her, 'I will so greatly multiply your descendants that they cannot be numbered for multitude," (16:10). That these words are an interpolation is evident from many indications, not only from the heavy style of "the angel of Yahweh said to her" three times, but especially from the fact that this command is not in accord with the whole course of the story.

In the original story, Yahweh intends to comfort Hagar for her humiliation, but he is also sending her back into slavery. In the original form of the story, Hagar has not yet recognized the deity, while the addition ignores this fact. Moreover, the promise that Hagar's descendants shall become a whole nation is too early here, for the story does not tell until later in the sequence that Hagar was to bear a son; the reverse would be the natural order. And so although the additions are not entirely consistent with the original legend, but actually spoil it, yet we must admit that the editor has performed this difficult and thankless task skillfully and with fidelity to the tradition.

But these are observations of minor importance. It is far more important and interesting to compare the two versions. We have noted that such variations are often not accidental but are small reflections of great changes in the spiritual life of the people. Accordingly, when we examine these variations we are no longer concerned with the works of individual authors or editors, but in fact with the great currents of Israel's life.

The two versions differ greatly in many details and especially in their overall tone. In the first version, the tone is hearty and vigorous, while the second version is tender and emotional. This very important difference is especially evident in the way the character of Hagar is drawn. The first narrator enjoys the unbending force of the spirited woman; but the second story weeps over Hagar as a poor outcast slave. Accordingly, Hagar's fortunes differ greatly in the two versions: in the first case she flees in defiance; in the second she is driven away against her will. In the first case her distress consists in the mistreatment her maternal pride cannot endure, and the mistreatment affects herself alone; in the second case the distress consists in the expulsion itself—in the wilderness both mother and child incur the danger of death. For this reason the narrator of the second version lays all his stress upon the description of the misery of mother and child; the first version does not include a single syllable for this misery. In the first version Sarah is jealous of the arrogant slave who is elevated to the rank of concubine; in the second, her jealousy is aimed at the slave child whom Sarah is not willing to have share the inheritance with her own child. In the first version, Hagar is acquainted with the wilderness: she goes, as her situation suggests, to the spring in the wilderness. But in the second version she loses her way in the wilderness: not until God opens her eyes does she find a well. In the first story, God hears of the mistreatment of Hagar; in the second, he hears the weeping of the child.

All these differences result from the one central difference: In the first story Hagar is painted in strong colors and vigorous shading; she is the genuine, defiant, untamable ancestress of the Bedouin. In the second story the local colors are faded and Hagar has become the purely human figure of an outcast mother with her perishing child. From this point of view there can be no doubt that the first version is far older than the second. Later eras had quite forgotten who Hagar really was: they no longer knew the tribe of Hagar. And the wilderness had grown more remote to the people of later time, who were themselves peasants or townsfolk; it seems to them only a land full of dangers, without paths or water. But at the same time—and this is the chief point—the times had become gentler and took more delight in tearful tales than in vigorous ones. We can find evidence elsewhere in Genesis of the increase of more tender moods in later times.

This later origin of the second version is plainly seen in the fact that in the first version Ishmael receives his name, as is fitting, at his birth; but in the second he is not named until he is half-grown, which is clearly unnatural. The religious conceptions of the second version are also later than those of the first. In the first, the deity appears on earth in person; in the second, Hagar merely hears a voice from heaven. In the first, the deity is pleased with the strong and vigorous woman—which draws a comparison to the intense story of Samson; in the second, the religion too has become much gentler: the thought of God hearing the child's weeping goes straight to the heart. The fact that the spring was a place of worship is not prominent in either version; yet the first has preserved the primitive name of the god of that locale. In any case, the second version is not slavishly dependent upon the first, but the changed form has been produced by a genuinely poetic soul and is at least the equal of the original: each in its way is a gem of legendary narrative.

CONCLUSION

I have tried first to render the old legends alive again to the reader and to introduce the moods and conceptions of antiquity—especially the religious and ethical life as displayed in these old stories. At the same time, I have tried to show the peculiar beauty of these remarkable narratives and to interpret their style. But everywhere in the course of the investigation we have been led back to a history. For this is characteristic of the human mind, that it has a history; and it is impossible to interpret even the slightest spiritual human product unless at the same time one gives its history. In these old legends, in which ancient Israel expresses itself without reserve, the history of Israel's spirit is preserved. I have tried in the present study to give a few, humble illustrations of this. I chose this particular legend because I believe that I could best exemplify the manner of investigation in a theme that does not involve dogmatic theories—as might be true in the case of the Paradise story. When all the stories have been investigated in this way, then we shall be prepared to draw pictures of ancient Israel that shall be true to life, along with a history of its religious and ethical life in earliest times.

NOTES

1. Julius Wellhausen, *Prolegomena to the History of Ancient Israel*, trans. J. S. Black and A. Menzies (Edinburgh: A. & C. Black, 1885; reprinted with foreword by D. A. Knight, Scholars Press Reprints and Translations Series [Atlanta: Scholars, 1994]; German ed. 1899).

[2.] Since Gunkel wrote before the discovery of the texts from Ugarit, he was unaware that El was the name of the high god in Ugaritic mythology, the one who created the other gods. See Marvin H. Pope, *El in the Ugaritic Texts*, VTSup 2 (Leiden: Brill, 1955); Frank Moore Cross, *Canaanite Myth and Hebrew Epic: Essays in the History of the Religion of Israel* (Cambridge: Harvard Univ. Press, 1973) 13–75; *idem*, "El," in TDOT 1.242–61; and Wolfgang Hermann, "El," in *Dictionary of Deities and Demons in the Bible*, ed. K. van der Toorn, 2nd ed. (Leiden: Brill, 1999) 274–80.

[3.] On Canaanite religion, see: Patrick D. Miller Jr., "Aspects of the Religion of Ugarit," in *Ancient Israelite Religion: Essays in Honor of Frank Moore Cross*, ed. P. D. Miller et al. (Philadelphia: Fortress Press, 1987) 53–66; Michael David

Coogan, "Canaanite Origins and Lineage: Reflections on the Religion of Ancient Israel," in *Ancient Israelite Religion*, 115–24; Othmar Keel and Christoph Uehlinger, *Gods, Goddesses, and Images of God in Ancient Israel*, trans. T. H. Trapp (Minneapolis: Fortress Press, 1998); and Patrick D. Miller, *The Religion of Ancient Israel*, Library of Ancient Israel (Louisville: Westminster John Knox, 2000).

[4.] On the divine epithets, besides the works mentioned in note 2 above, see Martin Rose, "Names of God in the Old Testament," in *ABD* 4.1001–11; Albert de Pury, "El-Olam," in *Dictionary of Deities and Demons in the Bible*, 288–91; and Eric E. Elnes and Patrick D. Miller, "Elyon," in ibid., 293–99.

5. Professor Hugo Winckler at Berlin says that the word *miṣrith* (Gen 16:1) is not related to *miṣraim* (Egypt), but to *Mṣr*, a name of a Bedouin tribe in the south of Palestine, a hypothesis which I consider quite probable. According to the old account, Hagar is at home in the wilderness.

6. According to a familiar German legend, Emperor Frederick Barbarossa sits at a marble table within the Kyffhäusser, a mountain in the Thuringia region of Germany.

A SELECT BIBLIOGRAPHY ON HAGAR AND ISHMAEL

Eph'al, Israel. *The Ancient Arabs: Nomads on the Borders of the Fertile Crescent, 9th–5th Centuries B.C.* Jerusalem: Magnes, 1982.

Hackett, Jo Ann. "Rehabilitating Hagar: Fragments of an Epic Pattern." In *Gender and Difference in Ancient Israel*, edited by P. L. Day, 12–27. Minneapolis: Fortress Press, 1989.

Irvin, Dorothy. *Mytharion: The Comparison of Tales from the Old Testament and the Ancient Near East.* AOAT 32. Neukirchen-Vluyn: Neukirchener, 1978.

Jeansonne, Sharon Pace. *The Women of Genesis: From Sarah to Potiphar's Wife.* Minneapolis: Fortress Press, 1990.

Knauf, Ernst Axel. "Ishmaelites." In *ABD* 3.513–20.

McEvenue, Sean. "A Comparison of Narrative Styles in the Hagar Stories." *Semeia* 3 (1975) 64–80.

Teubal, Savina J. *Hagar the Egyptian: The Lost Tradition of the Matriarchs.* San Francisco: Harper & Row, 1990.

Trible, Phyllis. "Hagar: The Desolation of Rejection." In *Texts of Terror: Literary-Feminist Readings of Biblical Narratives*, 9–35. OBT. Philadelphia: Fortress Press, 1984.

Weems, Renita J. "A Mistress, a Maid, and No Mercy." In *Just a Sister Away: A Womanist Vision of Women's Relationships in the Bible*, 1–21. San Diego: LauraMedia, 1988.

5

The Prophets: Oral and Written

ATTENTION TO GENRE

The first question that must be asked when examining an ancient writing in a literary, historical way concerns the genre of the writing. Perhaps the modern reader will be surprised that we place this task at the beginning. Therefore we need to explain why this problem is the initial and basic one, and why recognizing this causes difficulties for contemporary interpretation. In treating modern literature one deals predominantly with outstanding individual poets and writers. A discussion of writers seems so important that literary history, at its height, takes the form of biography. Thus literary history of the German classical period is basically concerned with studying the great classical authors, principally Goethe. That those authors themselves made use of certain genres that had developed before they came along is so obvious that it is scarcely considered. Literary history is not written for someone who is so unlearned as to be unable to distinguish between drama and narrative or between historical narrative and a novel.

In addition, the genres that once existed have been so obscured in the poetry of modern peoples that in many cases it is senseless to distinguish them. But the matter is quite different with ancient writings like those of Israel. Here there are many genres that, initially, were completely unknown to modern readers—genres to which modern readers can become accustomed only with a great deal of difficulty. This is especially true of the prophets, who have scarcely any parallel in contemporary literature and whose style of speaking is thus at first completely foreign to us. Moreover, we must further recognize that genres played a far greater role in the literatures of ancient peoples than they do today, and that in antiquity the individual author-personalities, which appear to dominate modern literature, recede into the background in a manner that initially is strange to us.

This phenomenon has its foundation in the characteristics of the intellectual life of ancient culture. At that time individuals were more bound by custom and much less distinguishable from one another than they are today. Ancient customs that guided the life of the individual in prescribed paths also controlled the poet and the writer. Writers chose and spoke about their material using the styles and genres that had been implanted in them from their youth and that appeared to them to be the natural expression of their thought and sensitivity. They were more bound to the style than to the thought. Even when they were able to think and utter something new, they were still bound to the traditional forms of expressing it. Out of this situation comes what is for us the strange monotony dominating such genres. As a result, the prophetic writings have surprising similarities to one another. For example, we could insert passages from Isaiah into Amos or Micah, and no one but the specialist will notice. Moreover, the sorts of speeches that spring from lesser intellects are often related so closely that frequently no individual peculiarity is apparent at all.

Now, to be sure, ancient Israel also had great writers with personal—indeed the most personal—characteristics. That it did produce such authors makes it famous among the peoples of the ancient Near East. And among them the most original were surely some of the prophets. Here in Israel something characteristic took place that was unknown elsewhere in the Near East: the individual came to the fore. Powerful personalities arose, grasped by the storms of the age, trembling with passion, who, touched by the deity in secret hours, attained the sublime courage to proclaim thoughts that they—they completely alone—perceived within themselves. And the form in which the prophets wrote must naturally also bear witness to this originality. But great as the originality of the prophets as authors may be, these writers cannot be recognized apart from the genres that preceded them: they began with the traditional genres, and these they used and modified. Until we know that *Faust* is a drama and *Werthers Leiden* is in the form of a diary, anything that we say about Goethe's literary activity is uninformed. Anyone investigating an author without knowing the genre he or she uses is building a house beginning with the roof. Thus we conclude that the first task in examining the literary history of the prophets is to describe the prophetic genres and their style. Not until this is done can we begin to recognize the special quality an individual prophet has as a writer.

ORALITY AND SOCIAL SETTING

The prophets were not originally writers but speakers. Anyone who thinks of ink and paper while reading their writings is in error from the outset. "Hear!" is the way they begin their works, not "Read!" Above all, however, if contemporary readers wish to understand the prophets, they must entirely forget that the writings were collected in a sacred book centuries after the prophets' work. The contemporary reader must not read their words as portions of the Bible but must attempt to place them in the context of the life of the people of Israel in which they were first spoken.

Here the prophet stands in the forecourt of the temple; around him are the men of Judah who have come to Jerusalem for a festival worship service (Jeremiah 26). Or the king and his court have gone out into the open in order to supervise the work on the city's water conduit. The curious people crowd around; then the prophet steps into their midst (Isa 7:3). A delegation from afar comes to Jerusalem to offer an alliance to Judah; Isaiah speaks to them on the street as the procession of foreign figures approaches the royal court (Isaiah 18). Another time he meets the girls and women of Jerusalem at the Feast of Tabernacles, perhaps while they are performing their dances (Isa 32:9-13), or he speaks to priests and prophets who delight in imbibing wine at the sacrifices (Isa 28:7-8). Amos may have slipped his frightful funeral oration over Israel's fall into the jubilee festival at Bethel (Amos 5:2-4). Such situations of prophetic activity are still reported about Zechariah (Zech 6:10-15; 7:1-14) and Haggai (Hag 2:10-14).

Not infrequently the people themselves sought out a prophet: thus, after the death of Gedaliah the leaders of the army and the people asked Jeremiah for advice, and King Zedekiah secretly summoned the prophet in order to ascertain from him his personal fate (Jer 38:14-23). The elders of the people who were carried off to Babylon came to Ezekiel's house (Ezek 8:1; 14:1), and crowds of ordinary people also marveled at this strange figure (Ezek 33:31). Wherever possible, one should picture in the mind's eye a similar situation for every prophetic word, even when one is not expressly stated.

Wherever it is impossible to conceive of the prophet himself delivering a prophetic word to an audience, such a word certainly belongs to a later time of prophecy. For example, when Deutero-Isaiah addresses the heathen (Isa 49:1), this is no longer an actual but a contrived speech. In addition, the precise description of the temple and the land at the close of the Book of Ezekiel (chaps. 40–48) was certainly never delivered to the people but was a written composition. Previously it was thought that among the major prophets, public activity was least visible in Deutero-Isaiah; but even here some things indicate it: descriptions such as Isa 49:2-4 and 50:4-6 are inconceivable without personal experiences. To be sure, in the Babylonian exile, public activity was to a great extent no longer possible.

ECSTASY AND DELIVERY

Now we turn our attention from the audience to the prophets themselves and visualize the manner in which they spoke. Here too it is difficult to perceive the matter correctly. We hear the texts of the prophets read formally in a liturgical framework in our worship services and we may easily be led into thinking that they were speaking like our preachers, with whom we are apt to compare them. Those Israelite prophets, however, spoke much differently. There an ecstatic man shouted his wild threats among the people; there his speech often was a strange stammering, a marvelous gibberish.

And we see how he conducted himself! He collapsed in bitter pain, weeping and wailing about the coming disaster (Ezek 21:6 [MT 21:11]; he beat his breast and clapped his hands; he wobbled like a drunk; he stood there naked or with a yoke around his neck or madly swinging a sword in his hand (Ezek 5:1-17; 21:8-17 [MT 21:13-22]! We must especially keep the "signs" of these men before our eyes when we read their words. Men who did such exceptional things could not have spoken calmly and prudently. When we constantly find things in their speeches that are foreign, powerful, and baroque, we then may hope that we understand them correctly.

The normal beginning of their speeches "Thus Yahweh spoke to me" certainly shows us that they typically spoke not during their ecstasy but later when they had become calmer. But one should not make a law of this, as was done in the struggle against the Montanists! For we also have texts that, at least in form, were spoken immediately during the prophetic experience (Jer 4:19; Isa 21:1-4; 63:1-6; and the Balaam oracles). In the passages before us, there is a continuum from a passionate way of speaking to a very quiet and thoughtful style, such as we find, for example, in the concluding passages of Ezekiel.

WRITING

The history of the prophets' development from speakers to writers is a long one. The first ecstatic *nebi'im*, whom we meet with Saul, wrote nothing and had nothing to write, for nothing is written in such wild conditions. Even men like Elijah and Elisha were not writers: they acted through their own person and did not contemplate an impact in the future. In addition, the people they addressed read little. To be sure, we learn from the later literary prophets that the prophetic style was already clearly developed at this time; but that does not mean much was written at this time: the style can take definite form in oral speech. Nonetheless, we do have individual writings from this period; there are the blessings of Jacob (Genesis 49), Moses (Deuteronomy 33), and Balaam (Numbers 23–24), whose style combines the emulation of the prophetic artistic form with the form of the praising and blessing of an ancient ancestor or a man of God. We may regard it as typical that these extant fragments appeared under other names and that no writings have been preserved from the renowned prophets of ancient time. We may assume that the recording of prophetic utterances began in this manner, under a name from ancient times or perhaps without any name at all.

Men like Amos and Isaiah were not originally writers. But the real reason that these men increasingly resorted to writing is that times had changed. More was being written in other fields than it had been in previous days. Isaiah complained as if it were something new that treaties were being written at that time (Isa 10:1). Specific reasons for such literary activity of the prophets are also transmitted to us. Jeremiah began dictating to Baruch, his loyal friend, when he was prevented from speaking personally to the people (Jeremiah 36). Amos became a writer when he was expelled from the Northern Kingdom by royal decree. In other places we hear that it was their contemporaries' unbelief that provoked the prophets to write: Isaiah relates an oracle before witnesses in order to be able to prove even to the unbelievers that he prophesied a certain event (Isa 8:16; 30:8). Or he publicly exhibits a tablet with an inscription (Isa 8:1). Or the prophets, when living far away from those to whom their prophecies pertain, send them a letter: such prophetic letters must have passed back and forth between the Judeans in Babylon and Jerusalem in the final years before Judah's fall (Jeremiah 29). On another occasion, Jeremiah had an oracle about Babylon written down and given to a man who was going there so that he might read it aloud there and cast it into the Euphrates (Jer 51:59-64).

We can trace how this literary activity began in a small way and finally eventuated in large books. It began with brief words such as Isaiah wrote or sealed, or with a few extensive proverbs or poems. A paper such as this, comparable perhaps to our political ditties, then circulated through the land as a tract, was read, discussed, and copied everywhere; and if it was relevant, could surely have had a powerful effect. An example of this sort of prophetic word is Isaiah's irate poem against the steward Shebna whom he addresses without respect and threatens with banishment to Babylon (Isa 22:15-19). One might well suppose that for months such a poem was the talk of Jerusalem, where it echoed on every street corner, to the bitter consternation of the high and mighty. Oracles of this sort often bore on their brow the name of the prophet who witnessed in his person to their truth. But very frequently they were nameless: the same sort of anonymous oracles were later given the names of known prophets and incorporated into their books.

The prophets themselves treated these pages, which are so precious to us, quite casually: they thought only of momentary results and not at all of later generations. They were convinced that their prophecies were not related to a far distant future but that they would soon be fulfilled. And also when, in order to sharpen their effect, primitive collections were made by the prophet himself or by the reverential hand of a student, there was scarcely any thought of arranging things logically or chronologically. It is a weakness of Israelite literature that the collected works it produced generally give very little evidence of organization, or none at all. Those collecting such a "book" hardly felt that they were creating a carefully organized work of art, but rather that they were writing down whatever was at hand. This explains why, for example, the "genuine" portions of the prophet Isaiah are currently in complete disorder. Thus a poem's refrain is divided into two parts,[1] while in contrast we find in chap. 22 two passages whose contents have nothing to do with each other placed together only because they both begin with similar words (vv. 1 and 16); or in chap. 28 an oracle against Samaria, contrary to all chronology, comes directly before much later ones against Judah and Jerusalem.

Also, the prophets themselves were not concerned about writing down the passages in their original form, but they subtracted from and added to them entirely as they saw fit. A clear example of such subsequent expansion by the prophet himself is the oracle about the steward Shebna mentioned above: when Isaiah republished this passage, perhaps in a collection, he added to the threat against this hated man a brief appendix (certainly genuine, by the way) in which he, in Yahweh's name, appointed Eliakim, Yahweh's faithful one, as Shebna's successor (Isa 22:20-23). This oracle must have been fulfilled later, but the new minister practiced such nepotism that the prophet felt constrained to add a second appendix in which the successor too was to be deposed (Isa 22:24-25).

No doubt people were fairly casual in dealing with anonymous fragments. These must have appeared throughout the years, and people must have waited continually for their fulfillment. Again and again the fragments must have been copied, but with each copying they were almost certainly altered and new elements were added to them. Thus, for example, in Isa 19:1-14 we have an old poem about Egypt's defeat to which a fifth-century Egyptian Judean added a continuation (vv. 15-25) that corresponds to it in form and content. In the first passage, there are wrath and fury over the foreign land, in the latter, a worldwide universalism. In the first passage, there is a clearly metrical organization,[2] in the latter, an "exalted prose." The prophetic word of uncertain provenience in Isa 2:2-4 is handed down in Mic 4:1-3 as well, but the final lines do not agree in both versions and obviously are additions (Isa 2:5; Mic 4:4-5). So too, other words from later prophets are taken over; Jeremiah scorns the way the "lying prophets" have "stolen" from one another (Jer 23:30). This is how words from more ancient and from more recent times can happen to stand right next to one another in the later prophetic books. Thus Zech 9:10 says that the chariot and war horse have been driven out of Ephraim and Jerusalem—an oracle that can be understood only as coming from the time when Israel's own kingdoms were independent—but it is immediately followed by mention of a future war for Judah's independence from Greece (Zech 9:13).

Accordingly, it is understandable that our present "books" of the prophets, which originated earlier or later—sometimes by many centuries—after their appearance or death, and which passed through the hands of many "redactors," depict a variegated world. Sometimes they contain many things that do not come from the old prophets, so that, for example, the Book of Isaiah can more accurately be termed an overview of Hebrew prophecy than a "book of Isaiah." Not until Ezekiel are things different: this man, accustomed as priest and jurist to scrupulous order, and convinced that his prophecies about Israel would be fulfilled only after centuries, wrote what was the first book of prophecy.

From Individual Units to Books

The history of the growth of the prophetic books belongs together with the history of the gradual development of the individual units of which they are composed. It is one of the inherent laws of a genre that its units have definite limits that are traditionally prescribed. Moreover, one of the fundamental preconditions for aesthetically evaluating as well as for factually understanding a genre is that one keep in mind the whole that the writer intended. The tradition that we have received in fragmentary form, however, leaves us almost completely at a loss. The prophetic words and speeches have come to us virtually without any formal dividers. The superscriptions, which come from ancient time and are found here and there, and the chapter divisions, which come from much later, sometimes give us a correct starting point; but in general the fragments that are separated from one another by chapter divisions are much too large.

In order to comprehend the deplorable condition in which our prophetic books are found we should imagine something like Goethe's poems written one after another without any indication of where one poem ends and another begins, with only larger chapter breaks indicated, and then with the verses chopped up into individual sayings. In such a situation the scholar's first task must be to lift out the individual, original, independent portions—a task that in no way has yet been accomplished with the prophetic writings.

Contemporary scholars especially, following the modern German feeling for style, continue to identify far too many units; and they otherwise show a great deal of uncertainty in identifying the fragments.

This is not the place to explore with the reader that vast enterprise. It must suffice to mention that one must pay special attention to certain beginnings and endings that are repeated frequently. Examples of such beginnings include the well-known words "Thus says Yahweh" and "Hear!"; examples of endings include "says Yahweh," "Thus spoke the mouth of Yahweh," "I, Yahweh, have spoken it," and "And they shall know that I am Yahweh."

The oldest units of prophetic style are also the briefest; they are the puzzling words and collections of words that echo the odd cries of the ancient *nebi'im*. The prophets of a higher sort adopted such a way of speaking in order to give their thoughts a sharp and impressive expression. Such words are then publicly displayed by these men on something like a sign or are given as names to their children (Hosea 1; Isa 7:3; 8:3).

The next stage following this is for the prophets to express themselves with great clarity in brief statements, made up of two, three, or a few more long lines. Examples of this are Isa 1:2-3; 3:12-15; 14:24-27; 17:12-14; 40:1-2, 3-5, 6-8, 9-11; Amos 1:2; 3:1-2; 5:1-3; 9:7; Jer 2:1-3, 4-9, 10-13, 14-19.

Later the prophets learned to compose longer "speeches," about a chapter in length. These, too, are rarely organized as a unit in a way that corresponds to our feeling for style as it has been informed by the Greeks, but they consist rather of statements that are more or less loosely piled up one after another. The prophet turns from one thing to another, according to whatever his eye lights upon, and he stops when he thinks he has exhausted the subject. Thus it is often very difficult to recognize whether, according to the prophet, a new "speech" is beginning, or whether it is only a part of one, that is, a "word." Such a "piecemeal" style also naturally opens the door for later additions that outwardly can hardly be distinguished from the original text.[3] Yet the outstanding stylists among the prophetic writers possessed the art of assembling the smaller, relatively independent fragments into a larger whole that may be compared to a cyclopean wall. An example of such a style is Isaiah 13, a chapter that comes from the time of the exile; it is composed of many more or less strongly differentiated fragments. Yet when taken as a whole it forms a unit: in the beginning is the summons; in the middle, the battle; in the end, the destruction. At the beginning, there is apparent confusion and darkness; at the conclusion, clarity.

Such organization stands out very impressively from the whole when it is couched in the artistic form of a refrain that comes from lyric poetry; poems with refrains are in Amos 1:3—2:16; 4:6-12; 7:1-9; 8:1-3; Isa 2:6-21; 5:24-30; 9:7—10:4. The seven woes in Isa 5:8-23 were probably first compiled by a collector.

The most artistic are those prophetic units in which fragments of different genres are brought together in the form of a "liturgy."

Finally, entire books were produced. But even in them a logical organization is less evident than a chronological one: a day, month, and year of composition is presupposed for every oracle, so that the entire book takes the form of a collection of documents. A painfully exact organization is obviously foreign to the prophetic way of thinking; it is clear that the spirit of priestly legal scholarship is at work here. And the first who really chose this sort of organization for the whole was Ezekiel, a man of priestly ancestry. The later prophets then copied Ezekiel: Zechariah 1–8 and the Book of Haggai are arranged in the same way. In contrast, Deutero-Isaiah was written without any organization: his work can be compared to a diary in which he wrote the words that came to him every day without any further organization.

From all of this we conclude that in interpreting as well as in criticizing the prophetic books one must use the criterion of "context" only with great caution; and also that in attempting to indicate the structure of prophetic books such as Amos or Deutero-Isaiah one must first investigate whether such a thing exists at all.

The complete picture of the history we have just outlined shows us that the number of units gradually increased. This is a manifestation that also has many counterparts in other Israelite genres, and the explanation for it lies in the development of culture and the increasing artistic ability evident in it.

FROM POETRY TO PROSE

Another line of development in the prophetic passages leads from poetry to prose. By its nature, enthusiasm speaks in prophetic form; rational reflection, in prose. Prophetic "speech," therefore, was originally in the form of poetry. Those who, like the prophets, received their thoughts in hours of great inspiration and who now, filled with overflowing emotions, proclaim them are capable of speaking only in poetic rhythms. Thus the clearer the prophetic element is in the content, the more pronounced is the poetic form. To be sure, once again here our traditional Greek feeling for style is different from the Hebraic, in which speech and poetry are not mutually exclusive. It was not odd in ancient Israel for the prophetic oracle to speak in verse; after all, the style of oracles was otherwise poetic in form. In the sanctuary, Yahweh's reply was given in verse (for example, Gen 25:23) no differently than were the words of the Delphic Apollo.

Two genres can be distinguished in the metric form of poetic prophecy: the strict style, in which the same verse dominates the entire poem, and the freer style, which is expressed in different verses according to the ebb and flow of the sentiment. The first style appears to belong more to sung poetry, while the second more to spoken poetry. Examples of the former genre are Isa 1:10-17; 2:2-4; 3:12-15; 28:1-4; Jer 2:1-3. Examples of the latter genre are Isa 1:2-3 and 29:1-7. Future scholars will have a great deal more work to do in establishing the metrical organization of the prophetic poems; thus the six-colon poem (2 + 2 + 2), discovered long ago by Edward Sievers, is still far too little known. Yet one has to guard against wanting to alter the texts in order to create an overall regularity. Perhaps someday it will be concluded that the freer style appears more frequently in the prophets than the stricter one, and that in general the formation of regular "stanzas," that is, conjunctions of long lines, appears rather infrequently.[4]

Judged according to aesthetic standards, many of the prophetic speeches are beyond comparison, and they are among the most powerful passages of the Old Testament, which is so rich in powerful words. Hardly anywhere in the entire world is there religious poetry that is comparable in force and power to these prophetic writings.

From the beginning, some individual elements in the prophetic passages were prose. The narratives are almost always so, regardless of whether the prophet is speaking about himself or others are speaking about him. But prose has also crept into prophetic speech itself. The speeches in Zechariah 1–8 and those in Haggai are in prose, but in the books of Jeremiah and Ezekiel prose and poetry stand alongside each other. We may assume that this transition from poetry to prose can be explained by the fact that at this time the prophets were starting to be transformed from ecstatics into preachers and religious thinkers. Accordingly, the manner in which they spoke gradually became calmer: the rhythm of their words became freer and freer until it finally became prose. When Jeremiah proclaims the law of divine activity (Jer 18:1-12), or when Ezekiel describes the temple buildings in the minutest detail (Ezekiel 40–48), that cannot have been done in any but a tone of clear, precise description, that is, in prose. Contributing to this was the fact that the later prophets—in the torah or when recording history—used genres that were by nature prose. This does not mean, of course, that the later prophets did not also continue using the old poetic genres.

DIVERSITY OF GENRES

As we now attempt to delineate the material of the prophetic books and to arrange it according to genres, we face a difficulty that apparently is almost insurmountable. For what we find is an infinite diversity that appears to defy any sort of organization. Here we find narratives of the prophets' deeds and fates reported by contemporary students or by later ones, and alongside them are passages that come from the prophets themselves; among these are compositions written for themselves and for their God, as well as others they intended for their people.

We shall examine the latter first, for they form the real foundation of the prophetic writings. These prophetic oracles are divided into two groups, according to the manner in which the revelation came: visions and auditions, that is, what was seen and what was heard. These images and "words" are characteristically introduced with "Thus Yahweh showed me" and "Thus Yahweh said to me."

Considered as a whole, the words by far outnumber the visions. Thereby they reveal the uniqueness of our prophets. In the final analysis what is significant about them is that they present God's thoughts. It is much easier and more convenient, however, for a thought to take the form of an audible word than that of a visible image. It is noteworthy that visions came so strongly to the fore in later times when the old ecstatic forms of prophecy experienced a revival: so it was with Ezekiel and Zechariah. But it is strange that at the same time visions played a minor role in Jeremiah, and none at all in Deutero-Isaiah.

VISIONS

The visions of the prophets are of the most varied sort. Sometimes they are brief and simple, as when Amos sees a fruit basket (Amos 8:1) or Jeremiah the branch of an almond tree (Jer 1:11); and sometimes they are longer and more detailed, as in Zechariah and Ezekiel. And their contents are very different. There are, for example, faraway things the prophet cannot see by his own powers: before the eyes of the "lookout" appears the Persian army, approaching two by two, as it traverses the pass (Isa 21:6-10); Ezekiel, while in Babylon, sees a vision of things that are happening in the Jerusalem temple (Ezekiel 11). He claims to have experienced there the death of a prominent man, whom he names specifically (Ezek 11:13). Then a figure appears to him that looks like a man but is made up entirely of fire and brightness; it stretches out its hand, grasps him by a lock of hair, and transports him from Babylon to Jerusalem (Ezekiel 8).

Commonly the prophet sees beings from an invisible world. Thus Isaiah saw Yahweh on his heavenly throne with the frightening seraphim hovering before him (Isa 6:1-7). Zechariah saw the mounted messengers Yahweh sends throughout the world and who then return before him to bring him reports of how things are on earth (Zech 1:7-11), the chariots which go forth from him to visit his wrath on the earth (Zech 6:1-8), the form of "wickedness" enclosed in an ephah borne by two women with wings like those of storks (Zech 5:5-11), and among all these fantastic figures also the pathetic Satan who wants to accuse the high priest before the divine tribunal (Zech 3:1). Ezekiel sees the miraculous throne borne by cherubim on which God travels (Ezekiel 1), the seven spirits who carry out Yahweh's commands, and in the midst a figure clothed in linen with a writing case in his hand (Ezek 9:2).

The way the details of such a vision are depicted is naturally dependent on the beliefs of the time: the prophet sees the heavenly things the way he himself and his people believe that they are. Here mythological elements too may intrude to the extent that the faith of Israel had adopted individual mythological elements: the seven spirits of Yahweh are originally the seven Babylonian gods of the planets and the one in the center is Nabû, the god of the art of writing; the messengers of God riding on horses of four different colors and the heavenly chariots drawn by similar horses are really the four winds (Zech 6:4-8), and the four colors signify the regions of heaven.[5] But our explanation is frequently in error when we interpret such visions—the stuff of which is not created anew by the prophets but rather transformed by them—as if they simply went back to the writer's experience or fantasy.

The style of the visions is almost always a narrative one—the prophet reports what he saw in the hour of revelation—but narrative in the Old Testament is almost always given in prose form.[6] More rarely there are poetic visionary accounts that come directly out of experience (Jer 4:23-26; Isa 21:1-10; 63:1-9; compare also the Balaam oracles).

Characteristic of such presentations of visions is a certain secretive tone that we see most beautifully in Balaam's discourses describing by David in Num 24:17. David's name is not mentioned; it is only from afar that we have in changing images the description of a great conqueror who will crush Moab. Thus the poet hides what he saw behind a secretive veil. All prophetic visions, however, must be read in this way. An example is the glorious vision of Isaiah 6. Human eyes had glimpsed the Lord; but the human mouth falls dumb when it attempts to express the unspeakable. The prophet describes God's throne and his long train; his gaze lights on the beings who stand before God, and his ear listens to the hymn that they sing with loud voices. But how the Lord himself appears he does not say. And only for a moment does he see the heavenly vision; then smoke ascends and obscures it from his view.

Much less delicate is Ezekiel's vision of the wheels, in which the writer attempts to depict God's "glory" in detail; but here too the writer is concerned about not saying too much. He is aware that he dare not describe the divine reality, attempting to approach it only by making comparisons: "And above the firmament over their heads there was the likeness of a throne, in appearance like sapphire; and seated above the likeness of a throne was a likeness as it were of a human form" (Ezek 1:26). The fact that this chaste reticence is lacking in Ezekiel's vision of the temple (Ezekiel 40–48) proves that it was not a vision that was actually experienced. This veil of secrecy through which the bright colors of Near Eastern mythology glimmer is what gives genuine visions their unique aesthetic charm.

Such visions are ordinarily connected with verbal revelations. The prophet sees Yahweh sitting on his high and elevated throne, and then he hears the spirits surrounding him who themselves speak (Isa 6:1-8). He sees Yahweh's messengers riding and receives the tidings they bring him (Zech 1:8-11). Ezekiel sees Yahweh's marvelous chariot-throne and then he hears a "voice"—that is, Yahweh's voice—speaking to him (Ezekiel 1). It is significant that the chief emphasis on such a connection between what is seen and what is heard almost always, especially in older times, lies on the words: the chief thing for the prophet is not Yahweh's appearance, but rather what he says, not the description of the messengers' appearance but rather their message. Thus it frequently happens with the prophets that their visions end with more or less lengthy speeches set either in the mouths of the divine persons who appear in the vision or in the mouth of the prophet (for example Isaiah 6; Zechariah 1). This matter of the visions' receding behind the auditions largely corresponds to the fact, which we have already established, that in general there are far fewer visions than auditions, and moreover, that for those words that appear most frequently the text provides no specific indication of how they might have been received. From this we recognize that the prophets put all emphasis on the thoughts that they contained, not on the miraculous way in which they arrived.

A noteworthy connection exists between vision and verbal revelation when the prophet sees something in front of him and simultaneously hears a voice asking him what it is. Thus he sees something indefinite and at the same time has a strong desire to penetrate the mystery surrounding it. Then, however, he recognizes what is presenting itself to him. It is an object of ordinary life, a fruit basket or the branch of an almond tree or a cooking pot. At once, however, he hears again the voice proclaiming to him the meaning of the revelation; what he sees and its significance are connected by a play on words: the almond branch (*šaqēd* is supposed to mean that Yahweh is watching [*šōqēd*]; Jer 1:11-12, 13-14; Amos 8:1-3). Perhaps one may assume that the thought "He watches" was already unconsciously present in the prophet until it finally presented itself perceptually as the almond branch.

In other places where supernatural forms appear to the prophet in a vision, their nature is revealed to him by the "angel who talks with him"; but the interpretation is occasionally still mysterious and unclear (Zech 1:9-12; 2:2, 4, 6; 4:4-6a; the interpretation of Zech 4:14 remains unclear). It would be unseemly to speak more definitely about divine things. This is usually the case in the later "apocalypses" as well.

But do these visions refer to real occurrences, or are they only embodi-ments of thoughts in one's fantasy? This is a question that cannot be answered definitely for each case. On one hand, it is certain that the whole genre origi-nates in actual events, for its existence is inconceivable without them. On the other hand, such experiences are so difficult to put into words that the prophet, as soon as he states them, becomes a poet and an interpreter. Thus, at any rate, these descriptions are not to be taken in the sense of juridical proof of factual events. Moreover, imitation surely plays a significant role—more than it does in verbal revelations. It is certainly no coincidence that the call vision of Jeremiah agrees so precisely, even in wording, with some visions in Amos. This does not need to be conscious imitation, of course. There is also an unconscious dependency that lies deeper and that causes people of the same age and circle—who not only say the same things but also experience, think, feel, and desire the same things—to have an internal dependency. This is the real reason that we can speak so much about a people's intellectual his-tory. Finally, however, we also have to reckon with an artificial embodiment of something in the form of a vision, a case that is revealed especially clearly in Ezekiel's vision of the temple (Ezekiel 40–48). In the very nature of things such precise measurement of a building would not be revealed in the vision, and Ezekiel, who surely knew these things from the earliest days of his childhood as a priest's son in temple, would have needed no revelation to teach him what he already knew well. Thus he adopted here the style of a poem and filled it with content of a completely different sort. In the visions, accordingly, we catch a glimpse of a history that begins with real experiences but that is also presented and interpreted poetically and then replicated by others so that finally an artistic style arises that can also be used by conscious imitators. Where in the entire process each individual vision belongs, however, is some-thing that will be very difficult to determine.

The Yahweh Word

Much more important than the visions are the words the prophet proclaims. But in our prophetic books these are almost all originally spoken by Yahweh himself: what the prophet hears from Yahweh in his solitary room he declares as his "message" to the people. The "I" speaking from him and through him is not he himself, but rather God, just as the royal messenger literally carrying out his commission says, "I [the king]" (2 Sam 3:14; 19:12), or as the demoniac of the New Testament period might answer a question about his name by say-ing, "My name is legion" (Mark 5:9). But sometimes the prophet has such a strong sense of such words being given by God that in his own speech, for example, he is capable of ascribing other words to God so that what results is a two-way conversation between God and the prophet: we might think of the intercessory prayers of Amos (7:2, 4), Habakkuk (1:12-17), and Jeremiah. In this way it is possible for God to answer just the opposite of what one wishes and hopes (Jer 11:14; 12:5; 14:10; 15:1; 19). In the Jewish apocalypse, 2 Esdras, the entire first part is filled with such conversations between a human and the revealing angel.

There is a fluid transition between this form, in which the deity reveals himself through the mouth of the prophet as an "I," and another, in which the prophet speaks about Yahweh's thoughts and plans and therefore calls Yahweh "he." But even in such cases the prophet is convinced that the inner assurance filling him is of divine origin. Alongside these is a third form of prophetic speech that we see especially in Deutero-Isaiah, where the man of God adds his own observations, speeches, and poems to God's words.

Adaptation of Genres

Though classifying these forms has so far presented no particular difficulties, when we examine the content of the words more closely we are confronted with an almost incomprehensible diversity: here we find promises and threats, descriptions of sins, exhortations, priestly sayings, historical reminiscences, disputes, songs of all sorts, religious poems and parodies of profane poems, complaints, and songs of joy, short poetical passages and entire liturgies, parables, allegories, and so on. But it is the task of the interpreter to put the individual passages in order according to genre, for only when we explain their original context may we hope to understand the individual scattered elements. But literary history, if it is to be worthy of its name, must have as its goal the examination of the history that has caused such a diversity.

The fundamental understanding for this history, however, is the recognition that most of the genres mentioned were not originally prophetic: from the outset the prophets were not composers of songs, tellers of stories, or proclaimers of the torah. Only in retrospect did they become such. This means that prophecy adopted foreign genres in the course of its development. The motivating cause of this history is also clear: it is the burning desire of the prophets to gain power over their people's soul. Just as the recognition by contemporary Christianity that traditional forms of preaching and religious instruction no longer go far enough, which has led to the adoption of genres that originally were not specifically religious (for example, Christian calendars, lectures, periodicals, newspapers, and novels; in fact, even "Christian bookstores"); so did prophecy, when its original manner of speaking was no longer sufficient, adopt other genres through which it hoped to reach the people. The fact that the prophets used so many of them is a sign of the zeal with which they contended for their people's hearts.

But then the question arises concerning the actual prophetic genre from which all others must have come. It must be that genre in which what is really prophetic in content and form is most clearly evident. Now, originally, as we have seen, the chief task of the prophets was to announce the future. Therefore we should expect to find the oldest prophetic style in those passages that depict the future and that we call promises or threats, depending on whether they foretell good or disaster. Notably enough, particularly clear examples of this style are the oracles about foreign peoples, such as those in Isaiah 13–21; Jeremiah 46–51; and Ezekiel 25–32. Since the prophets always feel themselves sent in the first instance to Israel, the new forms they use appear principally in the passages addressed to Israel, and the speeches against the foreign peoples resemble a now-dry riverbed that shows us where water previously flowed. If this is correct, then in this really prophetic depiction of the future we should see most clearly the characteristically prophetic, ecstatic form of revelation. That this is largely the case is what we shall see as we now attempt to delineate the style of these prophecies.

SECRECY AND REVELATION

Revelations are received in secret hours: only in darkness and shadow do they appear in the prophet's soul. This style of foreseeing the future is faithfully mirrored in the literature. Thus we have the virtually demonic tone that is characteristic of prophecies as well as of history. As much as possible, names are avoided; even the very well known are unnamed. Thus the threatening enemy is not mentioned by name in the oracles about Edom in Obadiah, about Moab in Isaiah 15–16 and Jeremiah 48, about Egypt in Isaiah 19, about Philistia in Isa 14:29-32 and Jeremiah 47, about Tyre in Isaiah 23, and about Nineveh in Nah 1:15—3:19. Not even in Habakkuk 3 are those who are to be overcome named. Jeremiah prophesied for decades about an enemy from the north without himself knowing who it was going to be, until finally the Chaldeans appeared and he became certain that it was they Yahweh had meant. Amos and Isaiah (in his early period) both avoided using the name Assyria. Even the later imitations of prophetic oracles, in their common spuriousness, name no names whenever they speak like a prophet.[7] And it is completely unprophetic and thus probably to be explained as an addition when a legend prophesies about a God-man: one day a son will be born to David, Josiah by name (1 Kgs 13:2).

Rarely do the prophets give exact numbers, but instead they give very general ones: in three (Isa 16:14), forty (Ezek 29:11), or seventy years (Jer 25:11-12);

when a child that now is conceived is born (Isa 7:14); when the boy can say father and mother (Isa 8:4). For this reason it is impossible to put the word of Isa 7:8, "Within sixty-five years Ephraim will be broken to pieces," in Isaiah's mouth; instead it must read, "In six or five years . . ."

The prophet avoids definite expressions even in ordinary prose and instead employs an indefinite form of words. Assyria, he says, is sent "against a godless country" (he means against Israel; Isa 10:6). Hosea is commanded to love again "a woman who is an adulteress" (it is his own unfaithful wife he is to remarry; Hos 3:1). Yahweh will throw Shebna, according to Isaiah's prophecy, "into a wide land" (the prophet is probably thinking of Babylonia, but he does not say so; Isa 22:18). Isaiah describes the frightful land where people carry their treasures on the humps of camels; but he disdains to utter the name aloud, although at that time he knows it well (Isa 30:6-7).

Likewise, the prophet prefers to use images that reveal something but at the same time conceal it. He says "harvest" when he means judgment, "yoke" when he means slavery. "His yoke shall depart from them" means that they will be free from his domination (Isa 14:25). "Your silver has become dross" means "Your noble customs have degenerated" (Isa 1:22). Thus, ultimately an entire prophetic imagery developed. Joel 4:13 is an example. The uninitiated person will think that the prophet is speaking of the coming harvest; the initiate, however, knows that he is describing judgment upon the foreign kingdoms. One speaking in a mystical manner loves to put together images taken from several different areas in order to indicate through them that the words contain a secret:

> A star shall come forth out of Jacob,
>   and a scepter shall rise out of Israel. (Num 24:17)[8]

Much more, however, do the prophets enjoy embellishing an individual image so that it approaches the "allegorical" manner of speaking. Ezekiel prophesies Egypt's fall under Nebuchadnezzar in the words:

> Son of man, set your face toward the south and preach at noon and prophesy against the woods in the land of the south. Say to the woods in the land of the south, Hear the word of the Lord! Thus Yahweh the Lord has spoken: I will set a fire in you. It shall burn every green tree in you and destroy every dry tree. The blaze will not go out. And all the faces from the land of the south to the north will be singed by it (Ezek 21:1-3).

Understandably enough, the contemporaries of these words did not comprehend them and jeered at the prophet's "riddles" (Ezek 21:5).

Another way of keeping the secret was by using certain words that were clear only to initiates. Thus later apocalyptic speaks of the "man" and the "abomination of desolation"; but prophecy also speaks about the "northerner" (Joel 2:20), the "valley of Jehoshaphat" (Joel 4:12), the "servant of Yahweh," and "Ariel."[9] It compresses entire schemes of thought into short, obscure names such as Shear-jashub "a remnant shall return" (Isa 7:3), or Rahab-hammash-bath "the restrained chaos" (Isa 30:7). Sometimes such words are employed indiscriminately in a mystical, interpretive way: Shear-jashub includes a threat, but at the same time it is a promise (Isa 10:20-23). Jezreel is the name of the place of the blood guiltiness of the house of Jehu and the divine judgment upon it (Hos 1:4-5)—therefore Israel will be destroyed in Jezreel—but at the same time Jezreel is the place where Israel's new kingdom will one day arise (Hos 2:2); and because it literally means "God sows," it is the name of the future Israel planted anew by Yahweh (Hos 2:24-25).

Such obscurity commonly appears at the beginning of the oracle and then it becomes clearer toward its conclusion: so, for example, Isaiah 13 starts in a completely mysterious fashion and not until vv. 17 and 19 do the words "Medes" and "Babylon" occur. In Isa 17:12-14, three successive scenes are depicted without any names: first, the approach of a powerful, frightened crowd of people; then, the sudden appearance of one who rebukes; finally, a headlong flight throughout the land. And only a brief concluding word indicates that all of this will take place in a single night, and shows, although still semi-obscured, those whom this will affect:

> This is the portion of those who despoil us,
>   and the lot of those who plunder us. (Isa 17:14)

In Isa 21:1-10 all the anguish of uncertainty that torments the prophet is depicted, until the redeeming revelation comes at the conclusion: "Fallen, fallen is Babylon."

This secretive tone seems especially appropriate when the appearance of the divine in history is portrayed. Suddenly a voice sounds; the prophet thinks that it is Yahweh's voice, but he is too modest to say so (Isa 17:13; 13:3). Isaiah uses especially bright colors to depict Assyria's coming campaign against Jerusalem (Isa 10:28-34); he names place after place through which the invasion is coming. Then, however, comes the great moment when the miracle enters the world. Then the curtain falls. An image must suffice:

> Behold, the Lord, Yahweh Sabaoth
>   will lop the boughs with terrifying power;
> the great in height will be hewn down,
>   and the lofty will be brought low.
> He will cut down the thickets of the forest with an ax,
>   and Lebanon with its majestic trees will fall. (Isa 10:33-34)

Anyone able to penetrate the obscurity of this image will know what Yahweh will do then.

Again, Isa 40:3-5 speaks about a way leading over mountain and valley, through the midst of the desert, that is to be leveled for Yahweh. Will God come through the desert? Whoever understands it, understand it; and whoever does not recognize it, will someday recognize it when their eyes behold it!

Precisely when the prophets, as they so often do, adopt the most ancient material of mythological origin, themselves trembling inwardly at what is to come, the only thing allowed is a hint from afar. Thus the prophet speaks in deepest secrecy of the child that is to be born for us (Isa 9:5). But can a child bear the great name of "Wonderful Counselor, Mighty God, Everlasting Father, Prince of Peace"? Can a boy help us in the storms of this time? Yes, that is the great, divine mystery!

The marvelous passage about the future ruler who comes from Bethlehem, "whose origin is from old, from ancient days," leads even deeper into the world of mystery (Mic 5:1-4). But here too there are a multitude of questions: How can the one who comes from ancient days return? How can the dead become alive? Who are those who are given up until "she who is in travail" gives birth? Who gives them up and to whom? And who is "she who is in travail" herself? And when what follows mentions the "rest of his brethren," who one day shall return, who is "he" of whom it speaks? Only one thing is certain: the prophet is not thinking about answering such questions. In similarly obscure passages in the New Testament one finds, "Let the reader understand" (Mark 13:14); the prophet does not make it any easier.

And now the miraculous "servant of Yahweh" is even to lead Israel out of captivity and to preach to the heathen—the one whose mouth proclaims the word of God and yet accomplishes nothing, the one who is abused and dishonored but who does not despair, indeed the one who ultimately is given up to rejection and loathing, to death and burial, but who still attains his glorious goal! We might guess that the prophet is doing something more than describing himself in terms of human sensitivity; but nowhere does he clearly explain the secret of this image. No wonder that in every age those who read this text have pondered that question, especially when even the prophet's contemporaries could not have been entirely clear.

No doubt it was with all deliberateness that the prophets hid even that which was completely clear to themselves: Isaiah thinks that Assyria will plunder Damascus and Samaria, but he says so quite indirectly: "The spoil speeds, the prey hastes" (Isa 8:1-3). He explains this word only to the extent of saying "The wealth of Damascus and spoil of Samaria will be carried away" (8:4).[10] He does not name the plunderer himself, whom he knows full well. He is content to speak about the roar of kingdoms when he means the masses of people who are approaching Jerusalem in the Assyrian armies (Isa 17:12). The modern interpreter, when knowing the time and circumstances of an oracle, is in a position to replace the unknown elements with known ones, but when the tradition is lacking, we often fumble in complete uncertainty for an explanation.[11] In such cases may we be preserved from cheap guesses that do not improve after they become fashionable. May we also not proceed to accept additions and glosses too soon, before we really understand the text. We should generally read such passages with an attitude completely different from that with which they have usually been read: we should recognize that we are hardly in a position to penetrate all these secrets without further ado, and we should guard against prematurely destroying by our interpretation the impression that the prophet wanted to achieve.

DISJOINTED STYLE

Another feature of prophetic predictions is their peculiarly disconnected style. Prophetic recognition is not something that is coherent and complete but is rather a sudden, lightninglike illumination. This observation is also important for reproducing the prophets' thoughts, which the modern scholar, using his own thought patterns, too often tries to comprehend and reproduce in some sort of systematic arrangement. Thus even a man like Isaiah is aware that he has proclaimed different things at different times (Isa 28:23-29). And this abrupt, sudden manner is echoed in the style of the prophetic oracle.

The prophet, therefore, loves to begin a speech with a powerful opening: he jumps into the middle of a subject with both feet, often without introduction, without any concern for whether the hearers understand a thought that may perhaps be quite alien to them: let them open ears and eyes (Isa 6:9) and regard it as madness!

> Go not forth into the field,
>   nor walk on the road;
> for the enemy has a sword,
>   terror is on every side! (Jer 6:25)

Thus Jeremiah once began. How one would have looked at these words with amazement: Where is the enemy from whom we should flee, now that we are at peace?

Similar beginnings are "Blow the horn in Gibeah!" (Hos 5:8); "On a bare hill raise a signal!" (Isa 13:2); "Get you up to a high mountain, O Zion, herald of good tidings!" (Isa 40:9). These are all interjections that at first are totally unintelligible. It is equally powerful when the passage begins with a question that is a question for no one but the prophet. "Now why do you cry aloud?" the prophet begins (Mic 4:9), but none of the bystanders hear any cry. Likewise, "Who is this that comes from Edom?" (Isa 63:1); and "Who is this, rising like the Nile?" (Jer 46:7).

And the way the prophets continue is often just as disjointed as their beginning. Purely individual features, taken out of context, are piled up one on another. Block is piled upon block, mere fragments, which, however, when one looks at the whole, present the impression of a skillfully created picture. It is thus that we read such a magnificent passage as Nah 3:1-3. First, as with Nineveh, so now:

> Woe to the bloody city,
>   all full of lies and booty—
>   no end to all the plunder!

Then the attack of the enemy:

> The crack of whip, and rumble of wheel,
>   galloping horse and bounding chariot!
> Horsemen charging,
>   flashing sword and glittering spear!

And then, in conclusion, the result:

> Hosts of slain,
>   heaps of corpses,
> dead bodies without end—
>   they stumble over the bodies!

In Jeremiah 46, we observe a magnificent poem portraying things without any transitions: Egypt's expedition, its defeat on the Euphrates, its absolute destruction.

This defeat is emphasized when the prophet's speech turns from proclaiming doom to proclaiming deliverance, thereby giving the impression that Yahweh is creating something new. Examples of this are Isa 29:5 and especially the brilliant conclusion of Isaiah's call vision, where the final threatening word that only a stump will remain of Israel's oak is powerfully and cleverly turned around: "The holy seed is its stump"; someday a new, holy shoot will spring from this stump (Isa 6:2). But let no one conclude from such alleged "lack of context" that things are spurious, as certainly is often done!

CONCRETE IMAGERY

A further conclusion to be drawn from the style of the prophets' revelation, as well as from the nature of Israelite thought in general, is that their prophecies are extraordinarily concrete, abounding with the most specific and extremely vivid elements. The prophet does not say, "The desolate Babylon will be inhabited by swamp animals," but he uses the word "hedgehogs" (Isa 14:23). He depicts the manner in which the discarded idols will someday be thrown "to the moles and to the bats" (Isa 2:20). He calls the high trees the "cedars of Lebanon" and the "oaks of Bashan" (Isa 2:13); the large ships, the "ships of Tarshish" (Isa 2:16). He makes it clear that the princes of the royal house are following strange customs by saying that they wear foreign attire (Zeph 1:8). If the matter itself is not graphic, a clear picture is introduced: years whose time is limited are "the years of a hireling" (Isa 16:14); Israel's faithfulness to Yahweh at the beginning of its history is its honeymoon (Jer 2:2); someday Israel will be as few as ears remaining in the valley of Rephaim, as fruit remaining after the olive harvest: "two or three berries in the top of the highest bough, four or five on the branches of a fruit tree" (Isa 17:4-6). That is speaking concretely!

The prophet does not depict the entire context, but he knows how to lift a small scene out of the whole and paint it in such a lively way that it reveals everything else. We may think of mood pictures like Isa 3:6-8, where the total collapse of a state is depicted in a gruesome manner: one who still has a mantle must become king, something against which he protests with all his might. Or consider Isa 4:1, which depicts the lack of men after the destruction: seven women will take hold of one man. Or Zech 8:23, where it is made clear how the heathen will long for Yahweh in the last times: ten men of the heathen shall take hold of a Judean's robe, saying "We want to go with you!"

It is especially in accord with the prophets' bold spirit, which always penetrates to ultimates, for them to depict with particular vividness the final state of the place or person about which they are prophesying:

- Babylon is pools of water (Isa 14:23);
- Mount Zion is a joy of wild asses (Isa 32:14);
- a deathly stillness dominates the land (Isaiah 6–12);
- a piece of ground that now is planted with valuable vines is briers and thorns (Isa 7:23);
- where once was cultivated land there is nothing being raised but cattle: then a man will have a cow and two sheep, and because they give so much milk he will be able to eat curds (Isa 7:21);
- one will haul bodies out of the houses in silence in order not to provoke Yahweh's anger once more (Amos 6:9-10);

- Zion will be a plowed field, a terror or a reproach to the people; and even the dead are stirred up when the one who has been overcome enters Sheol (Isa 14:9-11).

Thus the prophets understand how to let a whole series of events reveal what is to occur from the perspective of the final outcome.

PROPHETIC PASSION

But there is no characteristic in them that comes to the fore more clearly than the enormous force of their passion. It is their religious passion, as we have seen, that motivates them; and such passion streams out in torrents from their words to anyone who reads them. But the prophets are completely different from us northern Europeans in terms of reserve! They are all impressed that the coming one they proclaim is colossal, shocking, frightening, or conversely, gloriously inspiring, thrilling, wonderful. The intent of much in their oracles is to kindle this ardor in their hearer's heart. The prophet of doom wants to trouble a proud, self-satisfied people; the prophet of deliverance wants to encourage the despondent. This tension with the recalcitrant populace causes the prophets to become agitated, and their sharpest expressions appear still insufficient. To the prophets of doom no picture is too horrible or too cruel for them not to use it and revel in it. Those who are murdered lie around like dung (Jer 8:2); one stumbles over bodies (Nah 3:3); children are dashed to pieces (Hos 14:1), women are ravished (Isa 13:16), pregnant women are ripped open (Hos 14:1); terrible fear grasps the army, no one can flee (Amos 2:14-16); even the body of the dead king is abused (Ezek 32:4-8), buried like an ass (Jer 22:19); his name is forgotten (Isa 14:20), his sons are slaughtered (Isa 14:21); the field is laid waste (Isa 6:11), the vineyard is a thorn hedge (Isa 7:23); "and though a tenth remain in it, it will be burned again, like a terebinth or an oak, whose stump remains standing when it is felled" (Isa 6:13).

These men also rage against the sanctuaries of their people: no sympathy, no mercy, no patience, nothing but furious wrath! The people are abruptly scolded for abandoning the national Yahweh-religion for the worship of Baal. The prophets describe with joy how the golden idols will be thrown to the moles (Isa 2:20); "dung" will be said to them (Isa 30:22).

They close their eyes to the necessities of national life: for them alliances are nothing but idolatry (Isa 7:1-9), and they explain that juvenile craving is the reason for importing horses from Egypt (Isa 30:16). We have to conclude that today's historians must be cautious about using the prophets' words to describe the circumstances of their time, and especially about using the prophets' judgments.

Just as exaggerated on the other side are the promises of the prophecies of deliverance, the moon will shine like the sun, and the sun sevenfold (Isa 30:26); all the heathen will come to worship Yahweh (Isa 2:2-4) and to serve Israel (Isa 14:1-2). No word is too glorious, no image too exaggerated to express how glorious everything will be! Even the wild animals will lose their evil nature: the lion will lie down with the lamb (Isa 11:6-9). Indeed, a new heaven and a new earth will appear (Isa 65:17).

This passion of the prophets erupts in a multitude of plays on words, analogies, allusions, ironic and sarcastic expressions. Their inner emotion is revealed in a constant to and fro, in a flickering unrest (in Hosea and occasionally in Jeremiah); but sometimes their sentences also roll majestically with pathos like the mighty waves of the sea (Isaiah).

The prophets especially love depicting in sharp colors the difference between the present and the future: the gluttons and spendthrifts of Jerusalem, the whole boisterous throng, will be swallowed by the gaping mouth of the underworld (Isa 5:14); the women, now proudly going around in their stylish finery, will then be brought low (Isa 3:24). The proud ones, who have borne seven sons, have lost everything and now must mourn (Jer 15:9). The joyful noise of the winepress is stilled, and the din of the battle cry grows loud (Isa 16:9-10). The cities of the land are in ruins (Isa 17:9); the palace is desolate, and the noise of the city is stilled (Isa 32:14).

Or, in contrast: the desert becomes a gorgeous garden (Isa 41:18-19), mountains and hills will be made low, and every valley exalted (Isa 40:4); the thirsty will drink water (Isa 41:17-18); the imprisoned will be set free (Isa 42:7); the lame will leap like a hart (Isa 35:6); the worm Jacob will become a sharp threshing sledge and thresh the mountains (Isa 41:14-16). In such contrasting activities the Israelite sensitivity, as we see, reconciles the strongest and most baroque elements.

And the prophets often add the impression that the one who is coming will do this at the very outset. Thus they describe the onset of the future:

> Therefore all hands will be feeble,
>> and every man's heart will melt,
>> and they will be dismayed.
> Pangs and agony will seize them;
>> they will be in anguish like a woman in travail.
> They will look aghast at one another;
>> and their faces will be aflame. (Isa 13:7-8)

Or the rejoicing:

> You have multiplied the nation,
>   you have increased its joy;
> they rejoice before you
>   as with joy at the harvest,
>   as men rejoice when they divide the spoil. (Isa 9:3)

Some prophetic passages are quite full of such images of the mood of the future, for example, extensively described woes (Isaiah 15–16). A special favorite is to begin with "Cry," "Rejoice," or the like (Isa 23:1; Zeph 1:11; Joel 1:5-12; Jer 22:20; 25:34; Zeph 3:14; Zech 2:14; 9:9). Here is one of the places where prophecy can make a transition to lyric poetry. In this way, the prophets attempt to draw their people who are living in the present into the mood of the future.

And everywhere at the culmination of their speaking we find the wondrously powerful mythological images that terrify the human heart, or that captivate and thrill it. Fire destroys the universe (Mic 1:4; Zeph 1:18; 3:8; Deut 32:22); a storm breaks out over the earth (Isaiah 2); the earth is broken asunder (Isa 24:19-20); the heavens roll up like a scroll (Isa 34:4a); the stars fall from heaven (Isa 34:4b); the sun loses its radiance and the moon its shine (Isa 13:10). And in the proclamations of deliverance: Zion will become the highest mountain on earth, the seat of the highest God (Isa 2:2) and the site of paradise (Isa 51:3); Jerusalem a fairyland city, its pinnacles of agate, its gates of carbuncles (Isa 54:11-15)! Such mythological images appear more frequently in the later prophets and the "apocalypticists," where the myth of the conquest of Leviathan appears especially often (Isa 27:1; Daniel 7; Rev 13:17; and other passages) but are also not unknown in the earlier ones.

Prophetic Grammar

We conclude this discussion of the authentically prophetic manner of speaking with something about their "style" of syntax. It is one of the peculiarities of certain genres that they favor particular sentence structures. Characteristic of Hebrew narrative, for example, is the constantly repeated "and then," "and then." Naturally the prophets prophesy in the future tense (imperfect or *waw*-consecutive + perfect). In addition, however, they especially like to use a curious perfect tense, ordinarily used to express acts completed in the past. When they use this tense to introduce the future it expresses their total confidence that the prophecy is true; the prophets thus do not see the expected event in front of them, like ordinary people, but behind them: in their eyes it has already occurred.[12]

Moreover, it is noteworthy that they couch their address in the second person. Thus their speeches ordinarily begin with the exhortation "Hear!" This way of speaking is explained by the vocation the prophet has received from Yahweh: as his "messenger," the prophet is to deliver the words he has received from Yahweh to those to whom they apply. He must meet face to face with anyone to whom Yahweh sends him, whether king or prime minister! But when the person is far away, a letter (Jeremiah 29) or a message (Isaiah 18) may suffice. Or when the prophet prophesies against foreign peoples, he turns his face in the direction they live (Ezek 25:1; see 6:2; and Jer 3:12) and he is convinced that they will hear his words, for, after all, these proceed from Yahweh's mouth. That explains the prophetic practice of summoning and speaking to all people, places, and kingdoms, near and far, even Bethlehem Ephrathah (Mic 5:1), the mountains and hills (Mic 6:2), Nineveh (Nah 3:5), the Chaldeans (Hab 2:7-8), indeed all the peoples (Mic 1:2), and finally heaven and earth (Isa 1:2). Clearly such language gives the prophet's way of speaking great animation; the prophet places the fate he proclaims squarely before the eyes of the third party, the listener, in the most vivid manner.

In this way, he often speaks in the form of a command; indeed, there are prophetic speeches or passages that consist entirely or predominantly of one imperative piled upon another (see esp. Jer 46:3-4). They are commands of God or of divine beings whom the prophet has heard in his ecstatic state. As an example, one may cite a passage such as:

> On a bare hill raise a signal,
>   cry aloud to them;
> wave the hand for them to enter
>   the gates of the nobles. (Isa 13:2)

Or the prophet himself may speak such commands as Yahweh's agent, convinced that in doing so his words will not disappear into thin air. Thus in God's name, Ezekiel in a vision calls upon breath to enter the dry bones and make them alive: "Come from the four winds, O breath, and breathe upon these slain!" And the breath obeys his command (Ezek 37:9-10). Thus sometimes the prophet, we might say, speaks like a divine stage manager constructing the scenes of world history (Isa 21:13-14). Or he speaks like a watchman on the battlement who sees what is coming and spreads the warning (Jer 4:5-6; 6:1, 25; 8:14; 48:6; Hos 5:8; Zech 2:10-11). Frequently there are exhortations to "weep" or to "rejoice." The prophets especially favor imperatives at the beginning of speeches—a powerful introduction (Joel 4:9; Zeph 2:1).

Another stylistic device that, like the imperative, can be explained as some-thing characteristic of the prophets is the frequent use of questions. Ques-tions play a major role in relating visions (Zech 1:9, 19, 21; 4:4), whether it is the prophet asking the angel standing beside him for information ("What are these?"), or whether he himself speaks to the apparition he sees before him ("Who are you? What do you want?"), or whether he hears a divine voice directed to him ("What do you see?"; Amos 7:8; 8:2; Jer 1:11, 13; Zech 4:2; 5:2). The poetic accounts of visions are also laced with questions: the prophet is amazed at what he sees and hears: What is this? How can this be? The prophet sees a sudden rout before his eyes and cries out in surprise.

> Why have I seen it?
> They are dismayed
> > and have turned backward.
> Their warriors are beaten down,
> > and have fled in haste;
> they look not back—
> > terror on every side! (Jer 46:5)

Or in the twilight he sees a mighty flood and asks:

> Who is this, rising like the Nile,
> > like rivers whose waters surge? (Jer 46:7)

The best example is the fantastic bloody image in Isa 63:1-6, with its powerful opening:

> Who is this that comes from Edom,
> > in crimsoned garments from Bozrah,
> he that is glorious in his apparel,
> > marching in the greatness of his strength? (Isa 63:1a)

Such questions occasionally also begin or interrupt the prophetic words (Mic 4:9; Zeph 2:15; Jer 49:1; other examples include Isa 19:11; 66:8; Jer 2:10-11, 14; 22:28; 30:6).

All of these characteristics we have mentioned show us how much of the prophets' revelations of the future demonstrate an original style that is authentically prophetic.

THE PROPHETS AS POETS

This ancient prophetic style never disappeared entirely but rather continued to be nurtured into the later period and into the final age. But, under the hand of the great writers, a great many other genres took their places alongside it. Usually these genres were already in existence, and the writers filled them with their special prophetic content.

In this we may distinguish two different lines of development: the prophets as poets, and the prophets as thinkers.

First, let us take the prophets as poets. Long before the prophets and those contemporaneous with them, there must have been in Israel a richly developed literature with secular and spiritual content. Israel was a people that knew how to sing and enjoyed singing. Songs embellished all festivities. The singer's voice resounded at victory celebrations; at the royal court the oracles echoed in praise of the ruler and proclaimed victory. Having a feast without singing songs was inconceivable. Even at night the watchman sang high up in the tower, and young men returning home perhaps struck up a satirical song about faded beauty. Burials too were accompanied by songs. But singing had its special place in worship. On festal days, hymns to Yahweh echoed in the sanctuary; there when the people were beset by any kind of need they joined in their songs of complaint. There were also songs by individuals in Hebrew worship. Even in ancient times it must have been customary to combine different kinds of lyric passages in an impressive "liturgy."

The prophets adopted all of these and some other lyric genres and used them for their purposes: there was no better way for them to bring the voices of the future to the people who were so fond of poetry than to express the future in poems. If they want to depict the anticipated destruction of an enemy before the souls of their contemporaries in an impressive fashion, they sing a victory song flavored with mockery (Isa 37:22-29; 47). If they want to depict the greatest joy, they recall the "voice of the bridegroom and the voice of the bride," that is, wedding songs (Jer 33:11). If they want to depict the attitude of blasphemers who have forgotten God, they put a frivolous drinking song in their mouths (Isa 22:13; 56:12). Another time the prophet uses a deeply sensitive watchman's song, "Watchman, what of the night?" to show the human longing for new light (Isa 21:11). Indeed, the prophet does not scruple to cite a frivolous song ridiculing a harlot: an unusual contrast, such a serious man and such a tune (Isa 23:16)! Deutero-Isaiah, who prophesies Cyrus's triumphal procession, imitates royal oracles for that purpose, something also done in Babylonia, so that these Israelite prophecies correspond quite remarkably with the inscription that the Babylonian priests wrote down for Cyrus somewhat later.

But most frequently it is funeral songs that are found in the prophets.[13] Such songs, originally sung at the bier or at the grave and known by heart, already took on political content in pre-prophetic poetry: the poet, for instance, sings of a fallen city whose citizens have been deported, as of children robbed of their mother (Lamentations 1). The prophets make use of this type of poetry in order to indicate the inevitability of the destruction they foresee: how powerful and impressive it must have been when they lamented those as already fallen who now were enjoying the best of fortunes! The most famous example of such prophetic funeral songs is the word in Amos 5:2 that pictures Israel as a virgin toppled to the ground (Isa 14:4-20; Jer 9:16-18; Ezekiel 19; 26:17-18; 27; 28:11-19; 32). It is customary in funeral songs to sing the praises of the departed, but the prophets insert scorn for their people's fallen opponents. Thus we have bizarre poems in which praise, scorn, lament, and prophecy echo in a confusing mixture (Isaiah 14). It is especially effective when the prophet, following the custom of the funeral song, ascribes words to the mourners: the poet of Isaiah 14 even summons the cedars of Lebanon, indeed, the underworld and the kings who sit there on their thrones, to mourn at the fall of the world rulers. And here, too, mythological images are employed at the height of the mood: the dejected king is compared to the morning star (*hêlēl*), which enthusiastically rose so high and fell so far (Isa 14:12-15), or with the dragon of the Nile that is caught by the deity in spite of its vehemence (Ezek 29:32). Aesthetically, such "eschatological funeral songs" are perhaps the most glorious poems in the prophetic books.

Adapting Religious Genres

Thanksgiving and Pilgrimage Songs

More common than these secular genres, of course, are the spiritual ones that are found in the prophets. When the prophet wants to make it clear that one day a tremendous joy will echo in the now decaying and silent cities of Judah, he uses the most beautiful tones on earth, the "voice of the bridegroom and the voice of the bride." But at the same time there is the "rejoicing of those who bring thankofferings into Yahweh's house," and he introduces their song: it is the well-known thankoffering of the Psalms (Pss 106; 107; 118; 136).

> Give thanks to Yahweh of hosts,
>   for Yahweh is good,
>   for his steadfast love endures for ever! (Jer 33:11)

He clothes the great concept that someday the heathen will turn to Yahweh, in the image of their making a pilgrimage to his sanctuary, and he composes in advance the song they will sing on such a pilgrimage:

> Come let us go up to the mountain of Yahweh,
>> to the house of the God of Jacob. (Isa 2:3)

We shall have to understand these words as an imitation of pilgrimage songs (Ps 100:2b). Likewise, the prophet uses a pilgrimage song to depict the rejoicing of the day when the world empire will collapse before Jerusalem; the joy will be like that of a pilgrim accompanied on a flute:

> To go to the mountain of Yahweh,
>> to the Rock of Israel. (Isa 30:29b)

The wording of the verse above may imitate a pilgrimage song. And how could one better depict the unending joy of the Jerusalem that will one day be free than to give in advance the song that the redeemed will sing when they enter the sanctuary, rejoicing:

> Open the gates,
>> that the righteous nation which keeps faith
>> may enter in. (Isa 26:2)

Hymns

As the funeral songs are significant for the prophets of disaster, so are the hymns for the prophets of deliverance; this genre appears frequently in Deutero-Isaiah. When the soul of the man of God is full of all the glorious things that Yahweh has promised to do, he breaks out in a hymn of joy:

> Sing, O heavens, for Yahweh has done it;
>> shout, O depths of the earth;
> break forth into singing, O mountains,
>> O forest, and every tree in it!
> For Yahweh has redeemed Jacob,
>> and will be glorified in Israel. (Isa 44:23)

The forms of these prophetic hymns are well known to us, especially from the Psalms:[14] there the song begins with a summons to rejoice and gives the reason for such rejoicing by adding a "for"; this is the outline of the hymn in the example above.[15] Or God's mighty deeds are recounted in one participial clause after another:

> Who makes a way in the sea,
> a path in the mighty waters,

> who brings forth chariot and horse,
>> army and warrior,
> they lie down, they cannot rise,
>> they are extinguished, quenched like a wick. (Isa 43:16-17)[16]

Here the prophet so loves to combine this hymnic style with the prophetic style that he prefaces the passage with the prophetic phrase "Thus says Yahweh" and then continues with the hymnic participles.[17] In Isa 63:17 there is the introduction of a hymn solo: "I will sing of your steadfast love, O Yahweh" (see Ps 89:1). A hymn without such an introduction is the one Isaiah hears the seraphim singing before Yahweh's throne (Isa 6:3). The song in Isa 40:12-14 is replete with rhetorical questions that are characteristic of hymns (see Exod 15:11). Such songs of rejoicing are sung by the people in Yahweh's festivals; the prophet reminds them of hymns at the announcement of "the feast," probably the Passover festival (Isa 30:29).

Communal Complaint Songs

In addition, there are the songs of communal complaint, which in various situations of need are performed before the community assembled at the sacred places (for example, Pss 44; 74; 79). While the prophet ordinarily appears before his people on the side of Yahweh, as is appropriate for Yahweh's representative, in these prayers he stands over against Yahweh as the one who prays and intercedes for Israel. Making intercession had long been the prophet's highest right. Even the most terrifying prophets of disaster occasionally break out into short intercessory sighs in the midst of their oracles of disaster.[18] Such prayers are now occasionally converted into entire poems in which the prophet voices a song of complaint for his poor tormented people (Jer 14:7-9; also 14:1-6, 13, 19-22; 15:5-9; Isa 63:7-9). Rather different is the Book of Joel, where the prophet summons the people to a general day of repentance during a great plague of locusts and calls upon everyone to lament and wail.

Another variation on the same genre occurs when the prophet sings the future song of repentance. These men who have to fight so bitterly with their stiff-necked people think with deep emotion of the hour when hard hearts will soften and finally the people will turn to their God. Thus they compose the future song of repentance with longing in their eyes:

> A voice on the bare heights is heard,
>> the weeping and pleading of Israel's sons, . . .
> "Behold, we come to you;
>> for you, Yahweh, are our God . . .

> Let us lie down in our shame,
>> and let our dishonor cover us;
>> for we have sinned against Yahweh our God." (Jer 3:21-25)[19]

Repentance, along with funeral dirges, marks the mood of the future festival described in Zech 12:10-14.

Sometimes the prophet attaches Yahweh's answer to such songs of complaint, whether it is that God inclines his ear to the complaint of his people or that he turns away in anger. Thus the people pray:

> Assyria shall not save us,
>> we will not ride upon horses;
>> and we will say no more, "Our God,"
>> to the work of our hands. (Hos 14:3)

And then the prophet answers in God's name:

> I will heal their faithlessness;
>> I will love them freely,
>> for my anger has turned from them.
> I will be as the dew to Israel;
>> he shall blossom as the lily. (Hos 14:4-5)

Or as the frightening answer comes:

> Though Moses and Samuel stood before me,
>> yet my heart would not turn toward this people.
> Send them out of my sight, and let them go! (Jer 15:1)[20]

What results is a unique mixture of poetic and prophetic styles.[21] Elsewhere in the prophets, especially the later ones, we frequently find passages in which alternating voices speak. In an older epoch, in order to animate their prophecies, they had already introduced the use of speeches, for example, the boasting speeches of the Israelites (Isa 9:8), the Assyrians (Isa 10:8-11, 13-14; 37:24-25), and the wise men of Egypt (Isa 19:11); the expression of despair of the "inhabitants of this coastland" (Isa 20:6), and of Moab (Isa 16:3-6); and also antiphonal speeches in which sudden changes in speakers are sometimes found (Isa 16:3-6).

Liturgies

From that it was a short step to constructing an artful form of liturgy that was used in the worship service and that was obviously of very special impressive force. We know such a liturgy from Psalms 15 and 24:3-6: the lay choir appears at the gates of the sanctuary and asks how one must go about gaining entrance; the priests answer by enumerating the conditions of entrance, and they close with a benediction. This liturgical genre is used in Isa 33:14-16 in order to represent the conversion of sinners in Zion, which will itself one day be saved. Frightened at the terrifying fall of the power of the heathen that they have just witnessed, they approach the sanctuary and ask, "Who among us can dwell with the devouring fire?" (v. 14). In place of the priest, the prophet gives the answer, "He who walks righteously and speaks uprightly" (v. 15); and at the conclusion he promises that those who walk thus will enjoy divine protection in this difficult time (v. 16).

Similar, but without the benediction, is Mic 6:6-8. The contrite sinner recounts in the form of a question all sorts of accomplishments with which he wishes to placate the vengeful God; but the prophet's answer explains the true divine demand to him. The prophets filled such liturgies for worship services with their spirit and enriched them with their manner of speaking. Thus at the conclusion of this development appear extraordinarily rich creations that cannot help but have their effect on us, insofar as we understand them.

One of the most glorious liturgical productions is the passage in Mic 6:2-8, whose second part we have just discussed. First comes a "judgment speech" that the prophet addresses to Israel in the name of his God, a speech with a majestic beginning (v. 2) and—in real contrast to that—poignant reproaches (vv. 3-5). Then the second part follows: the man broken by this accusation enumerates the sacrifices he is prepared to offer to placate God, each one greater than the last, until he comes to the most powerful and gruesome one—the offer of his own firstborn son (vv. 6-7).[22] But now it is as if the sun is rising: God proclaims with sublime words that all of this is nothing! No sacrifice, but rather justice, mercy, and humility (v. 8)!

Even richer is the liturgy in Isaiah 33. Extended poems of this sort are offered primarily by Trito-Isaiah (Isaiah 59; 61; 63:7—65:25) and the apocryphal Book of Baruch (Bar 4:5—5:9).[23] The appreciation of these liturgies has often been missed previously because the voice that is speaking tends to change without specific notice. To be sure, we must proceed with special caution if we are to identify such "liturgies." Not all those passages in which the same subject is discussed back and forth are to be considered a related totality; but rather we must reckon with the possibility that sometimes ordinary individual passages with similar content are juxtaposed without any further connection.[24] It will be the task of further investigation to determine which special connections generally appear in the prophetic "liturgies."

PROPHETIC PERSONALITY

With most of the prophets, their own personalities recede entirely—or almost entirely—behind their oracles. Even Hosea would not have told about his marriage if it had not been an image of a more significant issue for him. Not until Isaiah and Jeremiah, who speak much more frequently about themselves than the earlier prophets do, does this change, and consequently we are much better informed about their personal lives. The fact that accounts about Jeremiah, probably from Baruch's hand, are also of a distinctly historical sort and are much more extensive than anything we have about the earlier literary prophets shows us that there must have been general interest in a prophet's personality. People of this time had developed an interest in observing individuals. In the narratives of Genesis we may also observe the same change toward a way of looking at things that is capable of picking out individual details about a certain person.

Thus Jeremiah is following the trend of his times as the one prophet who more than any other inserts personal comments among the oracles intended for Israel (Jer 4:10, 19-21; 5:4-5; 6:10-11; 7:16-17, 27-29; 8:6, 18, 21, 23; 9:1; 11:14, 21-23; 13:17; 14:17-18; 15:10; 16:1-13). Here we become acquainted with his inner self: a man of tender nature, much too soft for his frightful vocation, suffering bitterly in having to do battle with his people, indeed, even with members of his own family. He was continually vacillating between painful sympathy and raging anger, between merciful intercession and the certainty that here no longer will any prayer be heard, struggling and quarrelling with his God and yet always being overcome by him. So it does not seem strange that he, the most personal of all the prophets, has made a new form his very own; he found it by adopting a genre not previously used by the prophets. We may conclude that such a breakthrough in compulsory use of genres is this man's contribution. The new genre is the individual complaint song.[25]

Such songs were sung at that time in the sacred places, doubtless originally to accompany various purification and penance rituals by those who were sick or suffering. The prophet adopted this genre because it expressed the complaint of and comfort for an individual soul. The heart of the singer of complaints is full of anguish and sorrow, as indeed is the prophet's own! The singers complain, above all, about their physical suffering: the prophet's sore spot is that Yahweh's word has still not been fulfilled (Jer 17:15; 15:18). The singers are surrounded by enemies who doubt their righteousness; how many foes the prophet has because of his prophesying! The singers rise at the end to the certainty that God will hear them and will triumph, sending a terrible fate upon their opponents. To the prophet, God himself announces that he will preserve him and topple his slanderers! It is therefore understandable that Jeremiah formulated his pains and comfort in complaint poems.

Anyone who knows the permanence of such genres, however, will not be surprised to see how faithfully Jeremiah follows the linguistic form of these songs. Earlier scholars, to be sure, assumed just the opposite and regarded Jeremiah as the creator of the entire type of poetry, even calling him the "first psalmist": they did not realize that such genres were not invented by an individual poet but rather developed in a long history. They also overlooked the fact that "complaint poems" flourished even in Babylonia and Egypt long before Israel existed.[26] It is just as erroneous to declare, as Gustav Hölscher has recently done, that these songs of Jeremiah, which so characteristically resemble the Psalms, are not genuine. Instead, as Walter Baumgartner has recently shown, their genuineness is guaranteed by the authentically prophetic element that appears in them along with the common elements of complaint songs. Above all, what the complaint is missing is a Yahweh oracle that has come to the poet personally,[27] something that does not occur in the individual complaint songs in the Psalter and that is conceivable only with a prophet who hears God's word.[28]

Deutero-Isaiah announced the experiences of his life as a prophet in tune with Jeremiah's poems: he speaks about the high goals and the disappointments of his work, and Yahweh announces comforting words to him, entirely in the way that Jeremiah spoke with his God.

All in all, therefore, there is an extraordinarily well-developed prophetic poetry, equally sublime both religiously and aesthetically, which makes it one of the greatest treasures of the Old Testament.

PROPHETS AS PREACHERS AND TEACHERS

As rich as all this is, the prophetic abundance is far from exhausted. A second line of development exists by which the prophets became preachers and teachers. The greatest among them were not satisfied with being only prophets. Although their primary concern was always to proclaim what was coming, they were imbued with the certainty that the future they were foretelling was a divine necessity: they demanded it in the name of religion and morality. They knew Yahweh's reasons for his plans. So the prophets of disaster—for it is precisely they from whom this development proceeded—began speaking about Israel's sins that draw down Yahweh's wrathful judgment or about the sacrilege of the people whom Yahweh will annihilate.

In the style of the speeches that have been passed down, we can still trace how this process slowly took place. In passages of the older style a brief word about the reason for the prophecy is sometimes added to the depiction of the future. Why must Tyre fall? "Yahweh Sabaoth has planned it, to defile the pride of all glory" (Isa 23:9). Why do the Persians overthrow the Chaldean empire? In order to punish the world for its evil (Isa 13:11). Such reasons are often given at the end of the prophecy itself:

> All this is for the transgression of Jacob
> > and for the sins of the house of Israel. (Mic 1:5)

> And for all the countless harlotries of the harlot,
> > graceful and of deadly charms,
> who betrays nations with her harlotries,
> > and peoples with her charms. (Nah 3:4)

> This shall be their lot in return for their pride,
> > because they scoffed and boasted
> > against the people of Yahweh Sabaoth.
> > (Zeph 2:10; see Jer 13:22; 16:10-13)

As the moral idea comes to the fore among the prophets, the references to the sins that have been committed becomes stronger. Thus "invective" appears alongside threat. Both usually stand so closely together in the same passage that first the disaster is announced and then, after a "because," the sins are listed (Amos 1:3, 6, 9, 11), or the invective is followed by a "therefore" and the threat.[29] If the invective comes first, it is introduced with something like "Ah, you who . . ."[30] or "Hear, you who . . ." (Amos 4:8; 8:4). Often it also happens that the prophets in their disregard of exact details switch back and forth, from threat to invective and then again to threat.[31]

This listing of sins by the great prophets of disaster has now become a major point of their entire activity. They feel they are called to be "testers" (Jer 6:27) and "watchmen" of their people (Ezek 3:17); with great elation they distinguish from their own literary activity the pitiful style of the ordinary prophets who speak to people with their mouths (Mic 3:8). Thus a new, really prophetic genre, the independently occurring "invective," comes into existence. Such invectives might begin with the words:

> Cry aloud, spare not,
> > lift up your voice like a trumpet;
> declare to my people their transgression,
> > to the house of Jacob their sins. (Isa 58:1)[32]

It was natural for the prophets to clothe such invective in the form of a "judg-ment speech" of Yahweh, that is, a concrete image congenial to the thinking of ancient Israel and beloved by the prophetic way of speaking:

> Yahweh has taken his place to contend,
>> he stands to judge his people.
> Yahweh enters into judgment
>> with the elders and princes of his people. (Isa 3:13-14a)

And the speech thunders forth:

> It is you who have devoured the vineyard,
>> the spoil of the poor is in your houses.
> What do you mean by crushing my people,
>> By grinding the face of the poor? (Isa 3:14b-15)[33]

Frequently in such a judgment speech there is an indignant question that makes sense by reference to the specific image of an interrogation, "What do you mean?" (v. 15):

> O my people, what have I to do with you?
>> In what have I wearied you? Answer me! (Mic 6:3)

> What wrong did your fathers find in me
>> that they went far from me? (Jer 2:5)

A later prophet depicts Yahweh's judgment at the last day as an occasion for assembling all the heathen and then demanding an answer from them for all the injustice they have done to him and to Israel (Joel 3:1-8):

> What are you to me, O Tyre and Sidon,
>> and all the regions of Philistia? (v. 4)

The same genre of eschatological judgment address, but without such ques-tions, is found in the later apocalypses (the best example is 2 Esdr 7:37-44), and even in Jesus' amazing and captivating discourses about the last judgment (Matt 5:31-48).

FROM THREAT TO WARNING

The movement from threat to warning essentially describes the style of a man like Amos—but not completely, even for him! For the most austere and fright-ening person can also have his fill of invective and threat. He would have been no man at all if a "perhaps" did not creep into his soul: perhaps his activity may bring about a conversion and perhaps then Yahweh will show mercy once again (Amos 5:15; Zeph 2:3; Jer 26:3).Driven by this "perhaps," his prophesying slowly turned from threats and invective to warnings. To be sure, threats and invective were always the first word for the prophets of disaster, but alongside this they gradually began to use warning speeches, penitential sermons. Using this form, they had an opportunity to develop their positive religious and moral demands.

Among the earlier prophets there is little trace of this development. Instead, they were convinced that for such a hardened people as Israel no warning will do any good, and no repentance is possible any longer: if the spirit of harlotry once takes hold, it never again releases its grasp (Hos 4:12)! No, the prophet's own preaching will avail nothing, but it will rather rob the people of the tiny amount of understanding that they still possess and topple them into the abyss (Isa 6:9-10; 29:9-10)! From this mood then come the frightfully ironic warnings—warnings to do evil!

> Come to Bethel, and transgress;
>> to Gilgal, and multiply transgression. (Amos 4:4)

> Add your burnt offerings to your sacrifices,
>> and eat the flesh. (Jer 7:21)

But sometimes the warning does break through, even with the early prophets:

> "Seek me and live." (Amos 5:4-6)

> Hate evil, and love good,
>> and establish justice in the gate;
> it may be that Yahweh Sabaoth
>> will be gracious to the remnant of Joseph.
>> (Amos 5:15; see Hos 2:4; 4:15)

In such words we see how minimally the promise itself appears.

The warning appears more clearly in Isaiah who, despite his certainty that his people are marked for destruction, cannot refrain from speaking about well-being (Isa 1:10-14) and from placing a promise—in case they now obey—alongside the threat (Isa 1:19-20; 7:9; 28:16; 29:5-8; 30:15). During his lifetime, after all, Isaiah never tires of giving political advice (Isa 7:3; 28:12; 30:15).

Even more positive is Jeremiah, who—despite continually reinforcing the same fundamental conviction (Jer 6:10, 27-30; 7:28; 13:23)—cannot refrain from warning and exhorting. In his activity, exhortation plays such a major role (Jer 3:13, 14-15; 4:1, 3-4, 14; 5:20-29; 6:8; 7:1-7; 11:1-5; 13:15-17; 18:11; 21:11-14; 22:3-5; 23:16; 26:13; 27:12) that it may be considered the real content of his message (Jer 25:5-7), indeed, as it is the content of all prophecy (Jer 7:23-26; see Zech 1:4). But this change in his own style of speaking is connected with a thorough transformation in his conception of the prophetic vocation. He is convinced that he is proclaiming not an immutable decree of Yahweh, but rather a plan that allows God to "repent" if the people repent. Not only does the narrow gate of the "perhaps" stand open for the repentant sinner, but the whole gate of divine mercy! Therefore the prophet feels obligated to raise his voice: "Turn back, everyone from his evil way!" (Jer 18:11). A true prophet has the ultimate goal of "converting" the people from their evil activity (Jer 23:22). But in the same way that Jeremiah spoke to the people, Ezekiel spoke to individuals when everything was in ruins: "Cast away from you all the transgressions which you have committed against me . . . Why will you die?" (Ezek 18:31). And even among the later prophets—that is, the prophets of deliverance—the activity of exhorting their hearers to do good is a main focus (Isa 55:6-7; 56:1-2; Zech 1:3-6; 8:9, 16-17; Hag 1:8).

Such words of exhortation, according to the prophets' orientation or the various concrete situations, are connected with promises (Jer 3:13, 14-16, 22; 44:1-2) or threats (Jer 4:3-4; 7:1-15; 13:15-17; 21:11-12), or with both at the same time (esp. Jeremiah 18; Ezekiel 18; Amos 5:4-6). Then the grammatical connection between the two is something like this: "Listen to my voice, and . . . so shall you be my people" (Jer 11:4), or "Circumcise yourselves to Yahweh . . . lest my wrath go forth like fire (Jer 4:4). In some places it is clear that the prophet regards the oracle that he is proclaiming as Yahweh's revelation, but he regards the warning that he attaches to it as his own good counsel (Jer 26:13; 17:13). The style of these warnings is in part poetry but also prose—especially in Jeremiah (the best example is Jer 7:1-34).

As novel as this manner of speaking may be on the whole, it still depends on what is already available. The predecessors of the literary prophets were accustomed to answering questions, a practice that continued into the later period. This practice also had an effect on their style: questions and answers, for example, are sometimes juxtaposed in prophetic speeches (Isa 21:11-12; 14:32). Frequently people address specific questions to the prophets about what they should do in a certain situation, and to this they receive an answer in the form of a suggestion (Jeremiah 42). At the same time, however, the priestly torah (that is, "instruction") had an effect on the prophets.

PRIESTLY TORAH

This priestly torah originated in Israel in the form of oral tradition. It was the chief task of the priests to teach the laity the ordinances of the worship services and also the precepts of law and morality. The torah was usually spoken in prose form—we may think of the Ten Commandments—but also to some extent in the poetic form of torah liturgies that were employed in the worship services. Torah thus emphatically impressed the demands of God upon the laity (see the liturgies mentioned above and Pss 15 and 24:3-5). The liturgical and moral torah was usually in the form of "You shall" or "You shall not" (as in the Ten Commandments) or of the conditional statement found especially in the legal codes, "If . . . thus shall . . . ,"[34] or of an announcement of what is an "abomination" to Yahweh (Deut 7:25; 17:1; 18:12; 21:4).

The prophets also appropriated and made use of this genre. They were sharply opposed to one part of the priestly torah insofar as it demanded sacrifices and all sorts of ceremonies (Jer 8:8), but they thoroughly approved another part, namely, that of the important religious and moral demands (Hos 4:6; Jer 11:1-5; 34:12-16; Isa 2:3; Mal 2:6). It was natural for them to make use of passages from the law for their purposes (Jer 3:1; Hag 2:12-14), or even for them to proclaim the torah themselves, but of course a torah that rejected sacrifices and ceremonies in strident tones (Amos 5:21-24; other examples include Isa 1:10-17; Hos 6:6; Jer 6:20; 7:21-26; Isa 58:6-8; 66:3; Zech 7:4-7). This prophetic torah thus concludes with the third form mentioned above under the priestly torah forms. The prophets also adopted the liturgical torah with questions and answers (Isa 33:14-16; Mic 6:6-8).

A new tone, introduced into the priestly way of speaking by the "Deuteronomist" and in its revisions and supplements, was a peculiarly heartfelt, emotional admonition directed toward the people. This style, in its zeal for speaking to the people's heart, became widespread. This is the same style of speaking that we find in Jeremiah's prose speeches. In its readily understood prolixity it is sharply different from the concise poetic style the same man mastered (Jeremiah 11; 18; 34). Some of this agreement, of course, may result from a subsequent reworking of both texts. Nevertheless, we should not forget that nothing compels us to assume that Jeremiah could have spoken in only one style: for example, the style of Goethe's lyrical poetry in his youthful years and Goethe's mature style in his later narratives are extraordinarily different. We should also not forget that Ezekiel occasionally spoke in the same long-winded torah style (Ezekiel 18). But at whatever time this transition may have occurred, the appropriation of this prolix, quietly flowing torah style is one of the most memorable events in the entire history of the prophetic style.

In these forms of the priestly torah the prophets now either proclaimed

God's will or uttered warnings to those who were good. At the same time they found here a form to express their thoughts about the divine rule over kingdoms and people. The basic teaching of Jeremiah about divine retribution, like Ezekiel's, is in the form of legal statutes: if a kingdom or person whom God threatens turns from its evil, he will repent of his evil (Jeremiah 13; Ezekiel 18; 14:12-20). Developed on the basis of the torah, the most sublime formulation of prophetic abstract thinking (or "religious philosophy") was totally justified retribution.

No matter how foreign the prophetic and the priestly spirits might be to each other, they did borrow from and mutually enrich each other, something that can be seen in the way the prophets speak. In Ezekiel a priestly style is incorporated in the content of the prophecy. We may especially compare the temple vision at the conclusion of his book (Ezekiel 40–48)—in content, a description of the instruments used in worship—with the way the priests later described the tabernacle (Exodus 35–40).

HISTORICAL NARRATIVE

In order to communicate incisively their abstract thinking, the prophets make use of still another genre, the historical narrative. This too happened by itself. Is there anything more natural for a politician—and to a certain extent that is what the prophets were—than to remind people of the past, namely the most recent past, in order to create from it a doctrine for the present (Amos 4:6-11; Hos 5:13; 6:7-10; 7:7, 11; 8:4, 9; 10:9; Isa 7:17; 10:9-11; 22:5-11; Nah 3:8-10; Jer 2:16; Zech 1:6)? Again and again the prophets mention the Exodus from Egypt and the entrance into Canaan, for this period is considered the classical age of their religion, and they themselves rightly feel they are related to the figure of Moses in some way (Amos 2:9-11; 5:25; 9:7; Hos 9:10; 11:1; 12:14; Jer 2:1-3; 7:22). The earliest of them, whose ultimate interest is solely in the present, make very little use of retrospective observations of things long ago. Not until toward the end of the history of Judah, and especially in the period of the Exile, does this change. Likewise, just as German historiography had the task in 1870 of examining how the unification of Germany came about, and as historians of the future will have to explain the collapse of the German empire and the national revolution in 1918, so did the people of Judah have an innate impulse to interpret Judah's fall, as a necessary part of its history writing.

During that time, this task lay upon the prophet Ezekiel's soul; he tried to solve it through a series of glimpses into Israel's history (Ezekiel 16; 20; 23; and earlier Jer 3:6-13). Thus the prophets were attracted to historical philosophy: the powerful idea that history is a unity, a great divine-human activity, is an unforgettable achievement of its spirit. On the other side, to be sure, we should not misunderstand the one-sidedness of this way of looking at history, for its purpose was to give evidence of Israel's sins, which remained significant in all periods. Considering the forcefulness of the prophetic nature and the frightfulness of everything the prophets experienced, this perspective certainly comes as no surprise. That this same consideration was incorporated in the actual writing of history at the same time (Isa 43:27-28; 47:6; 48:3-5) shows us clearly that it was a necessary effect of the events on the thinking of that time.

What is characteristic is that such historical observations were given by Ezekiel in the form of allegory. This preference for allegory (Hosea 1–3) is perhaps explained by the custom of the prophets of interpreting dreams and visions in an allegorical way.[35]

DISPUTATION

Although we have previously seen how the prophetic style was constantly enriched by adopting nonprophetic genres, we now must look at a drama that shredded this style from within. That process occurs by means of the opposition in which even the greatest of the prophets always stood over against their people. How often did these men who lived in the future set themselves against the natural sensitivity of their contemporaries! In times when their contemporaries rejoiced, they lamented, and they exulted when their contemporaries sorrowed! Thus strife and discord were the watchwords of their lives. In fact, even within the prophetic movement itself parties sometimes formed that fought each other with extreme bitterness.

The strife with their people or with their prophetic opponents had a powerful significance for the prophets and was expressed in their way of speaking. Thus the prophetic disputation came into being.

In order to understand such prophetic "disputations," we may imagine concrete situations in which the prophet meets his opponents. There Amos stands before the priest Amaziah (Amos 7:10-17), Isaiah before King Hezekiah (Isaiah 37), Jeremiah before the prophet Hananiah (Jeremiah 28), just as in the older histories Elijah stood before King Ahab (1 Kgs 18:17-18) and the two prophets Micaiah ben Imlah and Zedekiah (1 Kgs 22:24-28). The reader should always imagine such disputes when reading the disputations of the prophets.

The necessity of hearing arguments and answering them explains the prophetic practice of citing the words of the people or the opponent and then refuting them, often in a powerful and brilliant way.[36] So the Book of Malachi is almost entirely couched in speeches and replies; much in Haggai is similar.

To be sure, quoted words are often presented in a very subjective manner by the prophets—not in the way they were spoken but rather how they must have sounded to the prophets' ears. "We are hidden in the temple," Jeremiah has the people say, "in order to go on doing all these abominations" (Jer 7:10); "We have made lies our refuge," the sly politicians say to Isaiah (Isa 28:15; Jer 2:20, 25; Isa 30:16); it is the prophet's conviction that what his contemporaries are doing is an abomination and that their trust rests on lies, but the people themselves would never have admitted such a thing. After all, the prophets straightforwardly called their opponents "lying prophets," a word that today's scholar certainly should not repeat with them.

A great many of the prophets' ideas are to be understood on the basis of these struggles with their opponents, even those that are not expressly indicated as such. Yahweh will protect us for the sake of the covenant, so the people think. No, precisely because of it he will punish you, for precisely because of it can be demanded something from you, replies Amos (3:2). He has brought up us alone, people say; the Syrians and Philistines, too, the prophet adds bitterly (Amos 9:7). When he is called upon to explain why he is prophesying, he makes it clear in an image that he can do nothing else: he has to speak (Amos 3:8). They say, Yahweh's arm is too short to save us. No, he replies, it is your sins; they separate you from him (Isa 59:1-3)! Even some of the unusual baroque phrases can be explained as products of these vocal or silent confrontations with contemporaries' thought. They praise Canaan as a land that is flowing with milk and honey; so it shall be—says the prophet—namely, when all cultivation of fields ceases and only cattle raising is left (Isa 7:21-22). To them Israel is Yahweh's glorious grapevine. That it is, the prophet cries, but he adds grimly: And do you not know that grape branches are good for nothing but burning? And that is what will be come of you (Ezekiel 15)! "Hear," is the way the popular speaker begins everywhere in the world, thereby hoping that his auditors will be able to hear and understand him. "Hear, as much as you will, you will understand nothing," says the formidable Isaiah (Isa 6:9). The songs of joy begin: "Rejoice, O Israel!" But the prophet begins, "Rejoice not, O Israel!" (Hos 9:1). And the same man named his daughter Not Pitied (*Lo-Ruḥamah*, Hos 1:6), whereas other fathers try to give their children beautiful names.

Above all, the style of the prophets changed most strongly in this constant confrontation. For now they felt themselves obligated to blunt the objections leveled against them, to get the obstinate to feel the magnitude of their sins, to show the secure the necessity of judgment; or alternatively, to restore the fallen to confidence with comforting words, to display Yahweh's might to the doubters. These are all tasks far removed from the original prophetic genres. Thus the prophets attempted to work through examples and they yearned for parables (Amos 3:3-8; 5:19; Isa 5:1-7; 28:23-29), or they cited proverbs (Ezek 12:22; 16:44). They clearly expounded the right of a good cause in the form of "judgment speeches" (Isa 41:1-13, 21-29; 43:9-13). In a few prophetic passages this led them away from using the old genres and into developing an excitingly new way of speaking in disputations (examples occur in Jer 2:14-19 and in Deutero-Isaiah).

ADAPTATION

This prophetic writing then had the most powerful effect on later literature: the genres that the prophets appropriated—filled with their spirit—were reused by their students. Thus began a lyricism enriched by the prophets, the writing of Psalms, then a prophetic torah, the "Deuteronomist," and a way of writing of history that we meet particularly in the books of Judges and Kings. Later, these genres, nurtured as they were by the successors of the prophets, had a more profound influence among their people than the prophets themselves had ever had.

LITERARY PERSONALITIES

Not until the work described above has been completed and scholarship is acquainted with the prophetic genres and their history will it be possible to depict with complete certainty the literary personalities of the prophets, some of which are distinctive. Here are a few suggestions about only the most important prophets.

First there is the gloomy Amos, full of wrathful fervor, with his one-sided rusticness. The genres he employs are primarily threat and invective, and he develops those styles fully. Along with threat and invective are a few very simple visions, and here and there replies to the objections of the people. The units that make up the speeches are usually rather short; and as with the earlier prophets, the language is thoroughly poetic, terse and full of images. The book is lacking in organization.

Next there is his contemporary Hosea, who has a richer nature, vacillating between vehement wrath and fervent love. Alongside frightful threats and invectives he places the attractive promise of total divine mercy and individual lyric elements, indeed, things that are already liturgical in form. Above all, however, the conflict with the people comes to the fore and causes his style to disintegrate. Sometimes it seems as if the prophet is addressing his opponents in nervous excitement. Characteristic of him is the lengthy, scintillatingly clever allegory of the first chapter, in the constantly repeated statements of which he may be describing some sleepless nights with groans and tears. The units that make up the speeches are of varying length. Unfortunately the text has been seriously corrupted.

Finally comes the sublime, royal Isaiah, not torn apart inwardly like Hosea, but also not as single-minded as Amos. He combines the messages of disaster and deliverance into a total construct: the "counsel" or "work" of Yahweh. His speech, full of power and vitality, rolls majestically forth. Compared with Amos and Hosea, its units have grown significantly; he also understands how to organize these longer passages as a unit. The disjointed and ecstatic elements, which characterize his predecessors, recede in him. He is frightening in his threats and invectives, which for him are also the starting point of his style. He is powerful too when he turns to the proclamation of salvation; and in other genres as well—in the torah, the parable, the funeral song (in a derived sense, Isa 1:21), the disputation—he is a speaker and poet of the first class. He also has words, along with the "I" discourses of Yahweh, words about Yahweh that express his own prophetic conviction. His masterpiece is the vision of his calling (Isaiah 6), in the recounting of which he organically weaves together a series of genres: the song of the seraphim that he hears bears the form of a hymn; the words the seraph addresses to him when he is empowered are reminiscent of sacramental priestly words accompanying such actions in the worship service; and then there is a cruel inversion of the introduction of prophetic speech (v. 9), as well as a commission of God to the prophet (v. 10), a terrifying threat (vv. 11-13), and at the conclusion a very secretive, indeed distant, promise.

So much for the first generation of prophets in the Assyrian period. The second generation, which experienced the fall of Jerusalem to the Chaldeans, is, from a literary point of view, distinguished from the first by the fact that now the diversity of styles has increased extraordinarily because of the work of the earlier prophets. By this time there are a multitude of prophetic genres enriched by men like Jeremiah and Ezekiel.

The main genres occur in Jeremiah: in his prophetic proclamation of the future, as well as in his threats, the basic element of his style, he displays a strongly ecstatic excitement. In the almost passionate, almost melancholy and sensitive, disputations with his people he is comparable to Hosea. In heartfelt, moving warnings he wants to induce Israel to repent. Characteristic is his adoption of the torah genre, in which he, following the prolix prose style of the contemporary "Deuteronomist," presents his people with an "either/or," at the same time, however, expressing the deepest understanding of prophecy. By including personal elements in his speeches to the deity, he dares to describe his own experiences in detail in order to unburden his woes in prayer to his God, by following the rather precise usage of the genre of individual complaint songs. In short visions he follows Amos's style. There are a few symbolic acts.

His younger contemporary Ezekiel, although similar to him in many respects, is in others far different: Jeremiah is cautious by nature and suffers in the depths of his being, and Ezekiel's basic mood is poured from the same mold. Jeremiah, however, is full of tender sympathy for his miserable people; while Ezekiel is without pity, harsh, somber, even cruel, embittered by the struggle, and severe even in his prophecies of deliverance. Jeremiah represents the apex of prophecy in his opposition to all outward "holy things"; Ezekiel followed priestly ideas. In invective and threats, as well as in his forceful funeral songs and song of derision, in which he adopts older mythological material of many kinds, Ezekiel, full of untamed ferocity, is more baroque than great. In his visions, which in contrast to Jeremiah's are greatly extended, and in his miraculous acts, he shows himself a thoroughly ecstatic personality. In preaching about God's rule over humanity, in the prose style of the torah he follows Jeremiah. He likewise expresses his philosophy of history, demanded by the events of the time, in prose and in great allegorical historical overviews. The priestly spirit appears prominently in his description of the temple, at the book's conclusion. Remarkably, with Ezekiel one finds extreme, frightful, loudly proclaimed passion standing side by side with wide-ranging, matter-of-fact rational exposition. In his case, the units are often very long. He himself has arranged the whole book chronologically.

At the end of the exile is Deutero-Isaiah, the prophet of deliverance. Full of overflowing enthusiasm, he proclaims the liberation of the captives and the radiance of Jerusalem, and he breaks out in ecstatic hymns of jubilation over the greatness of God. With various sorts of observations and proofs, he seeks to lead those who are in despair to the heights of his faith. Invective is completely absent; instead of warning, he proclaims trust and comfort. Filled with pain, he speaks personally about his rejection by his people, with a fervent faith that not even the prospect of his death is able to destroy; this builds on Jeremiah's forms of self-expression. The speeches tend to be long. The units are shorter than in Ezekiel, and the book is without any further divisions.

In the following age, the tones that had sounded continued on, in general without any special originality. This preceding sketch should be taken by the reader not as a "result of scholarship" but as an attempt to master the immense amount of material. The field of a history of prophetic literature is rich indeed; in the future may there be no lack of workers who will understand how to harvest its rich fruit!

NOTES

1. The same is true for the visions of Amos 7:1-9 and 8:1-3, which belong together but have been separated by an account from the life of the prophet in 7:10-17.

2. Three sections, each with four double lines.

3. For such a style, compare the discourses about Babylon placed together in Jeremiah 50–51.

4. It is completely impossible to contemplate such a large composition, one combining seven long lines each. Hebrew poetry lacks the means for connecting such "stanzas" into a whole.

5. Compare Hermann Gunkel, "Mythen und Mythologie in Israel," in *RGG*[2] 4.38–90. [Ed.] See also Bruce J. Malina, *On the Genre and Message of Revelation: Star Visions and Sky Journeys* (Peabody, Mass.: Hendrickson, 1995) 126–28.

6. Exceptions are the visions in Isaiah 6 and Jeremiah 1, for example, which are delivered in free rhythm.

7. Compare 1 Sam 2:27-28; and especially the prophecies of Daniel about the fate of the Seleucids and Ptolemies in Dan 11:5-45.

8. This explains the constantly changing images in the *Odes of Solomon* (*OTP* 2.725–71).

9. The ancient name of Jerusalem (Isa 29:1; 33:7).

10. The phrase "before the king of Assyria" should certainly be explained as an addition.

11. Precisely because of this, we should move especially cautiously whenever a name is mentioned; if we remove it by conjecture, the interpretation will be obscured. This applies to Hab 1:6.

12. On this "prophetic perfect" *(perfectum propheticum)*, see GKC §106n.

13. The credit for being the first to discover this genre within the context of other Israelite genres goes to Karl Budde; recently it has been extensively presented and explicated on the basis of many comparable passages from the most varied peoples by Hedwig Jahnow, *Das hebräische Leichenlied im Rahmen der Völkerdichtung*, BZAW 36 (Giessen: Töpelmann, 1923). [Ed.] See also Aage Bentzen, *Introduction to the Old Testament* (Copenhagen: Gads, 1948) 1.135–38.

14. Compare Gunkel, "Formen der Hymnen" 20 (1917) 265–304.

15. See also Isa 25:1-5; 42:10; 49:13; 52:9; the same structure of a hymn is already in Miriam's song, Exod 15:21.

16. Other examples of the participial style are Isa 40:22-23; 42:5; 44:24-28; 46:10-11; Jer 31:35; 51:15; Amos 4:13; 5:8; 9:5-6; compare also Ps 103:3-5.

17. Isa 43:16-17; also Isa 42:5; 44:24-28; Jer 31:35.

18. Amos 7:2, 5; Jer 4:10; Ezek 9:8; 21:11-12; ironically directed in Hos 9:14; Isa 16:9, 11.

19. Other examples include Hos 6:1-3; 14:3-7.

20. On such rejection of prophetic intercessions, see Jer 7:16-20; 11:14; 14:10-12.

21. Examples of prophetic complaint songs of the people with oracles attached are Jer 3:4-5a, with the answer in v. 5b; 3:22-25 with 4:1-2; 14:1-9 with v.

10; 14:19-22 with 15:1-4; Isa 26:8-14a with vv. 14b-15; 26:16-18 with vv. 19-21; 63:7—
64:11 with 65; Hab 1:12-17 with 2:1-5; Mic 7:7-10 with vv. 11-13; 7:14-17 with vv. 18-
20. See also the oracle in Joel 2:18-27 that follows the summons to repentance
and the complaint song of Joel 2:17.

22. There is also evidence of such great numbers of applications to the deity
among the Babylonians; see Heinrich Zimmern, *Beiträge zur Kenntnis der baby-
lonischen Religion*, Assyriologische Bibliothek 12 (Leipzig: Hinrichs, 1901) 2ff.

23. See also the beautiful liturgies in Isaiah 25–27 and Mic 7:7-10. The Song
of Moses in Deuteronomy 32 also belongs here.

24. See Isaiah 40; Jeremiah 30–31. This against Paul Volz, *Der Prophet Jere-
mia*, KAT 10 (Leipzig: Deichert, 1922) xxxviii.

25. On this genre, see Willy Stärck, *Die Schriften des Alten Testaments in
Auswahl* 3.1 (Göttingen: Vandenhoeck & Ruprecht, 1911) 157ff. Also, Hermann
Gunkel and Joachim Begrich, *An Introduction to the Psalms*, trans. J. D. Nogalski,
MLBS (Macon, Ga.: Mercer Univ. Press, 1998) 121–98. The complaint poems of
Jeremiah are Jer 11:18-20, 21, 23; 12:1-6; 15:10-12, 15-21; 17:12-18; 18:18-23; 20:7-9, 14-18.

26. On Egyptian complaint poems, see Gunkel, "Ägyptische Danklieder," in
Reden und Aufsätze (Göttingen: Vandenhoeck & Ruprecht, 1913) 145–49. On
Babylonian examples, see Willy Stärck, *Die Schriften* 3.1, 34ff. [Ed.] See also
Godfrey R. Driver, "The Psalms in the Light of Babylonian Research," in *The
Psalmists*, 109–75, ed. D. C. Simpson (London: Oxford Univ. Press, 1926); and
Aylward M. Blackman, "The Psalms in the Light of Egyptian Research," in *The
Psalmists*, 177–97.

27. Jeremiah 11:21-23; 12:5-6; 15:19-21; see also 14:11-12; 15:1.

28. In addition, the expressions "as my mouth" (Jer 15:19) and "stand before
Yahweh" (18:20) are genuinely prophetic; likewise the names Anathoth (11:21,
23) and even Jeremiah (15:20-21 and 18:18) agree with 1:18-19.

29. Amos 4:11; 5:11; 6:7; Isa 5:13; 10:16; 29:14; Jer 2:9; 5:6.

30. In Hebrew, *hôy* with the participle or something similar; see Isa 1:4-9;
5:8, 11, 18, 20, 21, 22; 29:15; 30:1; Amos 5:18; 6:1; Jer 22:13-17. [Ed.] On this form,
see K. C. Hanson, "'How Honorable! How Shameful!' A Cultural Analysis of
Matthew's Makarisms and Reproaches," *Semeia* 68 (1994[96]) 81–111.

31. A noteworthy example of such movement back and forth is Amos 2:6-16.

32. Other examples of invective are Isa 1:2-3, 4-9; Jer 2:10-13.

33. This same disguising of invective as judgment address occurs in Isa 1:18-
20; Mic 6:1-5; Jer 2:4-9; Hos 2:4-7. Psalm 82 is a replica.

34. On the cultic torah, see Deut 12:20-31; 13:2-18; Hag 2:12-14.

35. See Gunkel, "Allegorie," in *RGG²* 1.219–20. [Ed.] See also M. Lucetta
Mowry, "Allegory," in *IDB* 1.82–84.

36. Amos 5:14; Isa 22:13; 28:9-10, 14-15; 30:16; Zeph 1:12; Jer 2:20, 25, 27, 35; 3:4-
5; 7:10; Ezek 11:3, 15; 12:22-23; 18:2; 21:5; Isa 40:27; 58:1-3; Hag 1:2; 2:3.

A SELECT BIBLIOGRAPHY ON ISRAELITE PROPHECY

Baltzer, Klaus. *Deutero-Isaiah: A Commentary on Isaiah 40–55*; translated by M. Kohl. Hermeneia. Minneapolis: Fortress Press, 2001.

Blenkinsopp, Joseph. *A History of Prophecy in Israel*. Rev. ed. Louisville: Westminster John Knox, 1996.

Chaney, Marvin L. "Bitter Bounty: The Dynamics of Political Economy Critiqued by the Eighth-Century Prophets." In *Reformed Faith and Economics*, edited by R. L. Stivers, 15–30. Lanham, Md.: University Press of America, 1989.

Dempsey, Carol J. *The Prophets: A Literary-Critical Reading*. Minneapolis: Fortress Press, 2000.

Floyd, Michael H. *Minor Prophets: Part 2*. FOTL 22. Grand Rapids: Eerdmans, 2000.

Gordon, Robert P., editor. *The Place Is Too Small for Us: The Israelite Prophets in Recent Scholarship*. SBTS 5. Winona Lake, Ind.: Eisenbrauns, 1995.

Gottwald, Norman K. "The Biblical Prophetic Critique of Political Economy: Its Ground and Import." In *The Hebrew Bible in Its Social World and in Ours*, 349–64. Semeia Studies. Atlanta: Scholars, 1993.

Grabbe, Lester L. *Priests, Prophets, Diviners, Sages: A Socio-Historical Study of Religious Specialists in Ancient Israel*. Valley Forge, Pa.: Trinity Press International, 1995.

Hutton, Rodney R. *Charisma and Authority in Israelite Society*. Minneapolis: Fortress Press, 1994.

Koch, Klaus. *The Prophets*, translated by M. Kohl. 2 vols. Philadelphia: Fortress Press, 1983–84.

Lang, Bernhard. *Monotheism and the Prophetic Minority: An Essay in Biblical History and Sociology*. SWBA 1. Sheffield: Almond, 1983.

March, W. Eugene. "Prophecy." In *Old Testament Form Criticism*, edited by J. H. Hayes, 141–77. TUMSR2. San Antonio: Trinity Univ. Press, 1974.

Mowinckel, Sigmund. *The Spirit and the Word: Prophecy and Tradition in Ancient Israel*, edited by K. C. Hanson. FCBS. Minneapolis: Fortress Press, forthcoming.

Overholt, Thomas W. *Channels of Prophecy: The Social Dynamics of Prophetic Activity*. Minneapolis: Fortress Press, 1989.

Peterson, David L., editor. *Prophecy in Israel: Search for an Identity*. IRT 10. Philadelphia: Fortress Press, 1987.

Sweeney, Marvin A. *Isaiah 1–39; with an Introduction to Prophetic Literature*. FOTL 16. Grand Rapids: Eerdmans, 1996.

Wilson, Robert R. *Prophecy and Society in Ancient Israel*. Philadelphia: Fortress Press, 1980.

6

The Religion of the Psalms

Discussion about the value of the Old Testament for the Protestant Church has not yet come to an end in Germany. The best interests of our church, however, demand that this discussion should be carried on not with an excess of zeal for or against the Old Testament but with calm impartiality and thorough knowledge of the subject. An Old Testament topic, therefore, is particularly relevant to our business here today.

We shall deal with a theme that lies at the very heart of the Old Testament, or at least constitutes one of its chief interests. In earlier eras, the Psalms were awarded a place almost equal to that occupied by the New Testament. We shall not treat any of the external questions here, although, of course, scholarship cannot evade them: we shall leave unmentioned all critical problems and all questions of date. Now we shall consider exclusively the most characteristic content of the Psalter: the religion that finds expression there.

The material that occupies us now is extremely varied and complicated. It can also be said that until now this subject has been neglected. The task of the present day is to lay a foundation for the understanding of the Psalms. The purpose of this lecture is not to lay that foundation but to offer some results of that preliminary work. A few words about this foundation, however, will make the results more intelligible.

If we are to reach a clear view of these poems, with all their numerous similarities and divergences, the first order of business must be to arrange them in groups according to their genres. This does not mean, however, any capricious classification in accordance with individual taste. Our aim is to restore the arrangement that indicates the origin and source of the Psalms. That is, or should be, the prime interest of all study of the book at the present time and should include a study of the rise and the history of Hebrew psalmody.[1] I shall enumerate a few of the chief results here.

1. If we are to understand the Psalms as living poetry, we must not confine ourselves to the songs contained in the Psalter. The cognate poetry in the narrative books, the Book of Job, the prophetic writings, the Apocrypha, as well as the lyric poetry of other peoples, especially the Babylonians and the Egyptians, should all be included. We are discussing here not only the piety of the Psalter but also that of Hebrew lyric poetry as a whole. Only a brief sketch of the subject can be given here.

2. Our most important task is to understand how this poetry arose. As in the case of all the literature of Israel, we must not think of the Psalms as primarily a written literature. We must put away all thoughts of paper and ink and look on the Psalms as having their source in the life of the people. The Psalms played a part there before they took literary form at all. Most importantly, the singing of psalms was originally a part of worship, both public and private. Eventually, psalm-singing spread beyond the public sanctuary and penetrated into the private worship of pious individuals, who imitated the models and breathed their personal lives into them as well.

3. We are thus able to classify the Psalms by genre.[2] These songs are to be arranged according to the aspect of religious life to which they originally belong:

Hymns: originally sung as choruses or solos at sacred feasts.

Communal thanksgiving songs: related to hymns and used in public thanksgivings.

Communal complaint songs: sung by the choir at times of communal distress or calamity.

Court songs: sung by the court singer in the temple in the presence of the royal court.

Individual complaint songs: originally sung in the sanctuary by individuals in times of personal stress, such as sickness, or in protestation of innocence or in acknowledgment of sin. The songs were then used by such individuals at home to relieve their painful feelings.

Individual thanksgiving songs: originally sung to accompany a thank-offering for deliverance out of great distress.

There are also minor or secondary genres, which bear evidence of having been influenced by the prophetic writings and by the wisdom literature, such as that represented by the Wisdom of Solomon.

Now if we wish to look at the inner life of the psalmists we must start from these genres, especially ones closely related. This examination will offer a clear view of aspects of religious life of Israel that find expression in religious lyric poetry. Such aspects comprise the following:

1. *The religion of the hymns*: in which the fundamental thoughts and feelings find expression.

2. *The religion of the people*: contained in the communal complaints and songs of praise and hymns and in the eschatological poetry in imitation of the prophets.

3. *The religion of the court*: found in the royal psalms.

4. *The religion of the pious individual*: as revealed in complaints and songs of praise and lyric wisdom poetry.

THE RELIGION OF THE HYMNS

The hymns were sung to the accompaniment of instruments by or in the presence of the assembled congregation at a sacred festival.[3] In order to appreciate poems of this kind, we must have a clear picture of such a celebration. From far and near the people gathered together at the sanctuary and are all in a celebrative mood. The grace of Yahweh has blessed the land and there is once more an abundance of bread. Almost all the great regular festivals of ancient Israel were harvest festivals. On these occasions the sanctuary, the priests, and all the worshipers appeared in their finest clothing. It was a time of great rejoicing and of eating and drinking. Most important of all were the varied solemn services in which the individual could take part—including the feasts. The whole assembly also took part joyously in large dance processions.

These festivals were the key days of Israel from the earliest to the latest eras. In the earlier eras they did much to promote the unification of the people, and in later periods they were the actual center around which the Judean community clustered. That community was able to cohere because it had these celebrations in Jerusalem, just as the varied peoples of Islam find their bond of unity today in the celebrations at Mecca. To take part in one of these feasts was the greatest ambition of the Judeans living in the Diaspora. Even if at a later time they had to pine in misery and want, far from the sanctuary, beset by unbelieving enemies, they still remembered with longing those festive times in which they had been able to share:

> how I went with the throng,
>   and led them in procession to the house of God,
> with glad shouts and songs of thanksgiving,
>   a multitude keeping festival. (Ps 42:4b)

The Book of Sirach (Ecclesiasticus) clearly shows the deep impression made on pilgrims by such a celebration, when the high priest came forth from the temple in all the splendor of his official robes and with his own hands laid the sacrifice on the altar, when the attendant priests blew their horns and the singers raised their voices in praise (Sirach 50). At such a moment all present realized their unity as a people—a glorious thought for the Judeans whose lot in life had led them to a distant land. At such times they realized Yahweh's glory and presence. The technical expression for being present in the sanctuary was "to see Yahweh," "to behold the beauty of the Lord," namely to be conscious of his presence.

The spiritual content of such experiences finds expression in the hymns. The leading motifs in these poems are, therefore, zeal, devotion, awe, thanksgiving, and praise. Of course these are the characteristic notes of Israelite religion at all times; but they are especially prominent in the hymns. The same holds true, indeed, in other religions, especially those of Babylon and Egypt; but it is a distinguishing feature of Israelite religion and a token of its outstanding worth that these motifs should be so predominant. "Let my first thought be thanks and praise."

In the Babylonian hymns we frequently find petition added to praise; the deity is first flattered in order that he may be moved to grant the request. Such petition is hardly ever found in the Israelite hymn, and the hymn thus represents the deepest and noblest religious need of humanity: to kneel in the dust and worship that which is higher than oneself. It is no self-seeking piety that finds voice in the hymns.

This explains the splendid objectivity that marks the view of human life in the hymns of Israel. When, for example, the subject of the hymn is Yahweh's omnipotent rule among people, how Yahweh brings low the rich and humiliates the mighty, the poet's heart is filled, not with sadness at the thought of how transitory everything human is but with joy at the thought of God's greatness. The standpoint of the poet is not that of a humanity that rises and falls, but that of God who can bring low or lift up as God wills. Hence, the hymn singer does not shrink from describing the dread side of Yahweh's character, as in that mighty hymn of the thunderstorm, Psalm 29. Even the fact that God is so terrifying is a reason for praise!

This singing of praise to God has, of course, a great effect on the singer. Religious thought gathers strength when it is strongly expressed. The individual worshiper is carried along by the universal enthusiasm. Hence these hymns, in which the whole people can join with loud voice, can be deep experiences for individual worshipers; but this subjective, personal aspect finds little or no expression. The hymn is sung for God alone.

The Israelite hymn has borne the fairest of blossoms. The Babylonian and Egyptian hymns consist mainly of a lifeless enumeration of divine attributes. Even some of the hymns in the Bible are trite enough, but there are many majestic hymns that throb with power and life. "The heavens declare the glory of God" (Ps 19:1a). "Holy, holy, holy is Yahweh of Hosts; the whole earth is full of his glory" (Isa 6:3).

These hymns reveal very impressively the strong enthusiasm of the people for their God. No language could adequately express the feelings of the people as they gathered together for worship. Again and again we come upon the exhortation that not only the rejoicing Judeans should sing praises to the Lord, but that all peoples, all creatures, all realms of nature must add their voices if his name is to be worthily magnified. The hymn of the seraphim in Isa 6:3 was sung with such power that the pillars of the heavenly palace were shaken—that is how Yahweh should be praised! To take part in such worship was the highest duty and privilege of the individual. The heavens are Yahweh's; he has reserved them for himself. But the earth he has given "sons of humanity." The dead cannot praise him; in the silence of Sheol his praise is not heard. But we who live in this world and can sing—let us praise him forever (Ps 115:16). The singing of praise to Yahweh is thus an essential part of religious services and religious life.

Clearly, the objective side of religion is most prominent in the hymn—Yahweh himself, his deeds, and his attributes. That is why we are giving priority of place to this genre. But we must also keep in view the outstanding importance attached to the awe and enthusiasm that are aroused in his presence.

What does the hymn say about Yahweh? Its constant themes are these. God is the incomparable. Among the gods, there is none like him in holiness, power, wisdom, and goodness. His dwelling is in the heavens, and this very fact, that he has his throne in the loftiest part of the world, indicates that he himself is the "highest." The same idea is found in Babylonian and Egyptian hymns, but it is only among the Israelites that his appearance is seen in the terrors of the lightning and in volcanic eruptions (Psalm 29).[4] This is an ancient conception that goes back to the revelation given at Sinai. But the hymns contain various other mythological views of nature. The light is his garment; the clouds are his chariots; the winds and the lightning are his servants. But side by side with this ancient phraseology, there is another, a supernatural manner of speech according to which the phenomena of nature are not only manifestations of God, but the works of his hands. "He commanded and it stood fast" (Ps 33:9). In this connection it is, of course, mainly upon those striking phenomena that the ancients were unable to explain that attention is directed. Well-known examples are found in Job and in the famous hymn of creation: Psalm 104. Here we see also the characteristic optimism of Israelite religion—the world is good, and God is its wise and gracious creator. Such psalms are all the more precious in that they form a supplement to the New Testament, in which comparatively little is said about nature.

The hymns also exalt Yahweh's deeds in the past. In Babylonian and Egyptian hymns dealing with this subject, mythological allusions are frequent, and similar material is not altogether absent from the Israelite hymn.

> You crushed Rahab like a carcass,
>> you scattered your enemies with your mighty arm.
> The heavens are yours, the earth also is yours;
>> the world and all that is in it, you have founded. (Ps 89:10-11)

In the previous verse we read:

> You rule the raging sea;
>> when its waves rise, you still them. (Ps 89:9)

Here Rahab is the sea monster whom Yahweh subdued before creation and from whose power he delivered the world. There is another mythical echo in the majestic Psalm 19, where the glory of the sun is compared to a youthful hero. And there are other similar allusions.

It is no mere chance that the creation myth should find such a prominent place in this hymn genre. The creation of the world by God is one of the chief themes of the hymns even among other peoples, because in that work the omnipotence of God is especially revealed.

This supplies a clue to a part of the history of Israel's religion. The Israelite mind, with its development along its own lines, took up an attitude increasingly antagonistic to myth, and that element became fainter and fainter until it ultimately disappeared. Its place was taken by the sacred legend. We have a whole series of hymns that sing the praise of the God who led Israel in the days of old. These hymns borrow their material for this purpose from the narrative books that were by that time in existence and contained many traditional and legendary elements. Examples are Ps 105:12-15 and Exodus 15. We see here how the great thought—proclaimed with such zest by the prophets—that the history of Israel was a fellowship between Yahweh and his people, edified and helped later generations. This adoption of the legend into the hymn is a phenomenon peculiar to Israelite hymnody. There is nothing like it in the hymns of Babylon or Egypt. The recurrent theme of such legendary hymns is the story of the Passover—a proof of the deep impression made by the feast on the religious mind in Israel.

The hymns also have much to say about Yahweh in the future. He is the God who was, and is, and is to come. The heart of the pious Israelite thrills when he or she thinks of the time that is to come, when Yahweh will reveal himself in his true majesty and ascend the throne of the world. This is another manifest proof of how the preaching of the prophets influenced the hymns. The favorite method of the singer when thinking of this theme was to project himself into these latter days, with the result that to him the coming event was as if it had already happened. This impressive figure, exemplified in Psalms 46 and 149, was borrowed by the hymn singer from the prophets.

There is another way in which we can see how the prophets influenced the hymn singers. Now and again the latter borrowed the finest thoughts of the prophets and embodied them in their hymns. We read in Psalm 103:

> For as the heavens are high above the earth,
>   so great is his steadfast love toward those who fear him . . .
> As a father pities his children,
>   so Yahweh pities those who fear him. (Ps 103:11, 13)

Still another and quite a peculiar result of prophetic influence on the hymns is found in the prophetic invective that is occasionally added to a hymn. While the people assembled in the sanctuary are joyously extolling the greatness of God, they hear in a voice of thunder, which recalls the prophetic style, the exhortation, "Repent" (Psalms 81 and 95). In such hymns we have an impressive presentation of the two aspects of religion—joy in God and the grave demands that he makes.

It was only very rarely and not till a late period that enthusiasm for the Law found voice in the hymns. One example is found in Ps 19:8-11.[5] Sober, earnest study of the Law and the enthusiasm that finds expression in the hymn belong essentially to different worlds.

One step in the evolution of the hymn can also be seen in other genres: it was extended from public worship into personal religion and private devotion. As a rule, the choir sang the hymn; but from the very beginning there was a solo by a skilled singer. Solo hymns of this kind were eventually sung by the individual at times when there was neither feast nor congregation, and a gifted singer could occasionally pour his personal religion into this mold. Psalm 103 presents a fine example of how a singer could pour forth heartfelt gratitude for restoration from sickness in the hymn form: "Bless Yahweh, O my soul" (v. 1); and in Psalm 139 we see how a singer can add to the hymn many profound thoughts regarding the relation between God and his worshiper: "O Yahweh, you have searched me and known me" (v. 1).

In conclusion, through the hymn the pious one kneels in worship and adoration and proclaims with full heart God's glory to all the world.

The Religion of the People

Our first source for the popular religion is the communal complaint song.[6] When harvest had failed, or when pestilence had come, or an enemy was at the gate, the people assembled at the sanctuary, tore their garments, fasted, wept, and prayed. A trumpet was blown in order that the sound might reach to heaven. This was the communal mourning service—an entire people passionately beseeching their God to have mercy upon them.

Part of such a service was the singing of a complaint song. There is the strongest possible contrast between these complaint songs and the hymns. That we should find together in the Psalter the song of praise with its enthusiasm and the complaint song with its note of woe shows the contrasts that exist in the religion of the Psalms. One thing is common to both—they have the same intensity of passion; passionate enthusiasm in the hymn, passionate wailing and praying in the complaint song. This emotional intensity, indeed, is a distinctive quality of Israel, its religion, and its religious lyric poetry.

These complaint songs are so many cries of despair wrung from a tortured people—cries the like of which have perhaps never been heard anywhere else in this world. Let us look first at what they contain. The complaint songs in the Psalter are almost all of a political nature. From the Assyrian period onwards, Israel, which had been hemmed in by enemies throughout its history, was fated to pass from one foreign oppression to another. Even in post-exilic days, the Judean community of Jerusalem was only a small colony, annoyed and oppressed by malevolent neighbors, and as time went on, that community suffered continued disruption, till it was dispersed over the whole Near East. Wherever they went, the Judeans were unpopular, the butt of scorn, and their lives and property were never safe. Besides, their internal conditions were wretched. We hear this repeatedly in the individual complaint songs of the two opposing parties. The rich and the great were on the point of falling away both from their religion and their nationality and showed a disposition to ally themselves with like-minded folks among foreign peoples. They ruthlessly exploited the poor and the lowly.[7] These distressful circumstances, on the surface political and social, were felt by religious minds to be also moral and religious. People of this temper were horrified to see everywhere the same spectacle—lies and disloyalty triumphant, blood poured out like water, captives crying for liberty, the innocent for justice.

Conditions like these were all the more intolerable to people who had been taught by the prophets to love righteousness and justice. But they also constituted a religious problem. God, extolled in the hymns as refuge for the oppressed, seemed to be idly looking on while so much innocent blood was shed. When would God come to strike the oppressor and bring down the proud? God, who had chosen Israel, allowed the heathen to defile his inheritance and merely listened while the foreigner taunted and mocked the puny, miserable country. This scorn from the foreigner was very galling to the proud Judean and is frequently mentioned. Nor was this all. The heathen turned their mockery on Yahweh himself and blasphemed his name, speaking contemptuously of the God whose people they had subjugated. And even Judeans themselves were losing faith and turning away from him, saying, "There is no God" (Ps 14:1). Added to all this was the influence of the polytheism that prevailed in the whole world around them. There were even Judeans who no longer dared to deny that the gods of other countries were real powers, even if they still ranked these deities far beneath Yahweh. Such deities must be vassals of Yahweh, to whom he had entrusted dominion for a time. But they had abused the power he had lent to them and thrown the world into confusion. Lord, Yahweh, take out of their hands the power that is yours, and become yourself the monarch of the world!

These complaint songs are thus the cry of a people that refused at all costs to bow to the fate that providence had laid upon it, and felt anew each day the hurt done to its most sacred feelings. And religion gave the despair an even keener edge. Faith in Yahweh was flatly contradicted by experience. Hence the ever recurring, despairing note "Why?" that characterizes the complaint songs. Why does his wrath burn against the sheep of his pasture? Why have you forgotten the promises of former days? Why did you cause us to err from your ways? There is no attempt and no inclination to mitigate this contrast between faith and experience; it is rather emphasized as strongly as possible in the hope of provoking Yahweh to anger and making him rise up in wrath against the foes. This explains the practice of placing in strong contrast hymns extolling Yahweh's grace and power and poems emphasizing his present wrath and apparent impotence.

As we shall see below, the individual poems exhibit the same passion, and in many cases the same complete despair. Some of the pious, however, were able to renounce all their keen personal desires. The Israelite can attain self-renunciation but has never been able to abandon hope for the people!

Another characteristic feature deserves special mention. The thought of Israel's sin hardly ever appears in the communal complaint songs; indeed, it is frequently disclaimed. Especially in the later period we find a clear consciousness of fidelity to the law.

This reveals one aspect of Israel's communal religion. A second aspect presents a strong contrast to it. The hymns extol God's grace and faithfulness in the present and his wonderful works in past days. Faith found solace in recalling the distant past, because it found there the wonderful works it failed to see in its own day. And in the narratives dealing with these past times the note of penitence was heard, although it was more on account of the sins of the ancestors rather than of their own (see Psalm 106).

Among the Psalms there are also communal songs of praise, originally sung to celebrate great deliverances of the community; but they are few.[8] "They have afflicted me harshly from my youth, yet they have not prevailed against me" (Ps 129:2). "As the mountains are round about Jerusalem, so Yahweh is round about his people" (Ps 125:2). "Blessed be Yahweh, who has not given us as prey to their teeth" (Ps 124:6). Or in the individual songs we hear the pilgrim singing of the splendors of the holy city as he enters Jerusalem (Psalm 122), so that it is not always the note of lamentation and woe that we hear. The religious passion had its moments of relaxation. But even these poems are never without aspirations, although lamentation is occasionally absent; and the dominant note of the Judean mind, when reflecting on the history of the people, is that of grief.

But faith can also shake off despair, and we see it achieving this in the "eschatological psalms."[9] These poems, which treat the blessed latter days, follow both in form and in content the pattern of the prophets and the prophecies of deliverance. The same pattern is also found at the conclusion of the messages of the prophets of woe. In imitation of these writers, the psalmists depict Yahweh's future appearances and repeat his exhortations in the form of a prophetic word of judgment (Psalm 82). Or again, imitating prophetic example, they give in anticipation of the hymn that the delivered people shall one day sing (Psalm 149). Or they sing already of the glory of the holy place where the great deed of Yahweh shall be accomplished (Psalms 46, 48, 76). Or they adopt the style of a royal song, such as was chanted when a king ascended the throne, and transfer it to Yahweh's future reign (Psalm 97). Psalmists can thus dare to assume the predictive mantle of the prophets because they also lay claim to divine inspiration—belief in the inspiration of the minstrel is pervasive in the ancient world. Now and again we find similar eschatological hopes even in the individual complaint songs, especially when certainty of being heard is at its zenith. This shows how deep the hope of Israel's future lay in the individual religious heart. Judaism lives on this expectation, and no pious heart can live without it.

In the substance of their prophecies the psalmists agree on the whole with their prophetic models, but there are also some significant variations. This hope is the deeply felt answer to the lamentations and questionings of the communal complaint song. It is the expression of the immovable courage of faith, of unshaken confidence. That on which your hearts are set, that for which you have longed with floods of tears, shall be when the time has come! And this time is at hand! The words "soon," "at hand" is an integral part of all prophecy of deliverance, and is an indication of the zest with which this future was yearned for.

All woe shall soon be ended! Not forever shall the scepter of the wicked rule the inheritance of the righteous. Not forever shall Jerusalem lie in ruins and Israel be dispersed in exile. The time is coming when Yahweh shall rebuild the city and lead his people home. "May those who sow in tears reap with shouts of joy" (Ps 126:5).

Then Yahweh's dominion will begin. Amid shouts of joy he ascends to heaven and sits on the throne of the world above the cherubim. Heaven and earth now lie at his feet, and the kingdoms greet the new king with exultation.

Then, too, ceases the dominion of the gods. They fall down before Yahweh and all who served them are put to shame. God steps into the midst of their assembly, in which they were inclined to settle the affairs of the world, and addresses them with indignant words: "You are gods, sons of the Most High, all of you; nevertheless, you shall die like men, and fall like any prince" (Ps 82:6-7). In this manner the poet, borrowing a fanciful picture from mythology, describes the victory of the one true God over the many gods of the world.[10]

On that day the dominion of the heathen is also broken. Those who once impudently rose against Yahweh must now learn to fear Yahweh's name. They gather themselves together to serve him and bring him tribute. Then also the truth of religion is demonstrated. People's eyes shall see that Yahweh is the true God and Israel his chosen people. The poor sufferers will rejoice when they see that Yahweh is supreme above all gods, and when the scoffers who formerly mocked God and his people have to admit that "Yahweh has done great things for them" (Ps 126:2). When God is thus glorified, his people share in the glory. When God becomes the monarch of the world, he gives Israel the dominion of the world. They march to the holy war, bathe their feet in the blood of the wicked, and celebrate the wondrous victory with songs of praise on their lips and two-edged swords in their hands (Psalm 149).

This hope comprises all that the Israelite heart desires: deliverance from the power of the heathen, revenge for the violence they have suffered, the dream of world dominion, the deeply felt longing for righteousness on earth and for the revelation of Yahweh, the desire for the triumph of the true God over his heathen rivals. Political, moral, social, and religious elements are all brought into a unity here. But all the gracious gifts sought by the people at that day are summed up in the words "Yahweh will turn the crisis of Israel around"; that is, he will establish Israel as it was before. Both those who announce this message and those who hear it have their hearts filled with religious enthusiasm, delight, and gratitude.

Israelite piety thus oscillates between two extremes: the woe of the present and the ardent hope for the future. Both are felt with equal passion and equal inevitableness. Any account of Israelite religion must exhibit the two side by side. This was felt by psalmists who gave voice to liturgies consisting of heartfelt prayers answered by descriptions of the joy of the last times, or, in a different arrangement, consisting of pictures of the future interrupted by the sighs of the people.

> When Yahweh restored the fortunes of Zion,
> > we were like those who dream.
> Then our mouth was filled with laughter,
> > and our tongue with shouts of joy;
> then they said among the nations,
> > "Yahweh has done great things for them."
> Yahweh has done great things for us;
> > we are glad. (Ps 126:1-3)

Then comes the answer of the congregation. None of the things triumphantly foretold by the prophet have yet come to pass. Yahweh, accomplish it speedily!

> Restore our fortunes, O Yahweh,
> > like the watercourses in the Negeb!
> May those who sow in tears
> > reap with shouts of joy!
> He that goes forth weeping,
> > bearing the seed for sowing,
> shall come home with shouts of joy,
> > bringing his sheaves with him. (Ps 126:4-6)

The beauty of such a poem consists in the success with which the poet has expressed with equal perfection the two aspects of religion—the lament of the people and the hope of the prophets.

In analyzing the Judean hope, two things must be distinguished: first, the demand for justice and righteousness in the world, and for the punishment of the wicked, as well as the longing to see the presence of God, who has kept silent so long—that is a genuine Advent spirit, intelligible also to a Christian. And second, the feverish dream of a tortured people to be permitted one day, in spite of all they have gone through, to play the leading part among the kingdoms—that is, a Judean national desire, which has no appeal for Christians.

In seeking an explanation of the details, it is important to remember that the hopes of the psalmists are tinged with elements that were originally mythological. Of course, that is no part of their religion; it belongs rather to their poetic fancy.[11] It should further be noticed that, in distinction from many of the prophets, the psalmists nowhere make mention of the messiah. The king whose dominion is longed for is Yahweh himself. Here the Psalms follow a definite prophetic direction, with which we are familiar in Deutero-Isaiah (Isaiah 40–55). On the other hand, we hear much about the king in the so-called royal psalms, where we make acquaintance with the religion of the royal court.

THE RELIGION OF THE ROYAL COURT

The royal psalms have preserved a place in the Psalter because post-exilic times interpreted them as referring to the messiah. Later scholars, who did not know what to make of this interpretation, sought to replace it by others equally untenable. It is only in recent times that acquaintance with similar Egyptian and Babylonian poems has made it clear beyond all doubt that the biblical poems of this kind refer to the king who occupied the throne in the poet's day.[12] There is absolutely no reason for interpreting them as referring to any other than the pre-exilic monarchy. Most of the royal psalms might very well belong to the last days of the kingdom of Judah (that is, prior to 587 B.C.E.).

Most of them are clearly connected with the varied royal celebrations that were held at the king's court, especially the royal court at Jerusalem. Every royal court feels the need of festivities to enable it to "bear the tedium of life and the unspeakable monotony of the days."[13] But the festivities presupposed in the Psalms are partly of a religious nature. That holds true not only of Israel. For us, too, the state is one of the highest moral possessions. We too pray God to preserve it; and it seemed a natural thing to every kingdom in antiquity that its king should stand in an especially close relation to the deity. The court itself also cultivated this relation in order that the deity might defend the monarch in his dangerous elevation.[14]

Such religious celebrations were of many kinds. When the young king ascended the throne a great celebration was held (see Psalm 2), and a herald announced to all the world "He has become king" (see 2 Sam 15:10).[15] The anniversaries of his accession or of his birth were also occasions of rejoicing. In Jerusalem there was another festival to commemorate the founding of the dynasty and the building of the sanctuary. The two were one, for David, the ancestor of the dynasty, was also the founder of the holy place. Other occasions for festivity were the king's marriage (Psalm 45), the time when he went forth to war, and when he returned safely, crowned with victory. Although no examples actually occur in the Psalter, we may surely infer that there were days of lamentation when the king fell sick, and services of thanksgiving when he was restored to health (2 Kgs 20:1-11).

On all these occasions songs were sung, and these are the royal psalms. We are to think of them as sung in the presence of the king and his court in the sanctuary by the singers of the royal choir. On the day of the king's accession the choir sang "He reigns"; and at a later time this was sung with reference to Yahweh (Psalm 97). Or the choir announced in the king's name his principles of government in which the whole people should rejoice (Psalm 101). Or at such a celebration the divine oracle spoke (Psalm 110), occasionally from the king's own lips (Psalm 2). Praises and congratulations were expressed on the anniversary of his accession or on his birthday (Psalms 21, 72). When the king went forth to war a singer prayed for and promised Yahweh's help (Psalm 20); when he returned from the campaign a song of thanksgiving was sung (Psalm 18). On the day when the sanctuary was founded a liturgy was performed, giving first a dramatic account of how David brought the ark of the Lord to Zion, and then a prophecy that Yahweh would bless David and his house (Psalm 132).

These royal poems are distinguished by a tone of great extravagance: everlasting life is promised to the king: "He shall reign as long as the sun shall shine" (Ps 72:5). And he shall have world dominion: "May he have dominion from sea to sea, and from the River to the ends of the earth" (Ps 72:8).

In order to understand such words we must know that they are imitations of Egyptian and Babylonian royal songs. In the great rulers of the world empires the petty king of Judah saw exalted types of himself, and much that sounded quite natural on the lips of foreign poets—such as the promise of world dominion—sound somewhat unreal when carried over to the conditions in Judah.

A similar extravagance marks the religious elements in these psalms, but we must again bear in mind the influence of foreign models. We must also remember that the poet is not describing any one actual king, but has in his mind a royal ideal whom he identifies with his own monarch.

The main religious ideas of these songs are as follows. All the glory that surrounds the king comes from God—including all that the king possesses and all the promise that the future holds for him. Yahweh has anointed him with the oil of joy and placed the crown of gold upon his head. It is Yahweh who gives him immortality and deathless glory. Battle scenes are described in which God marches at the king's side and inspires the kingdoms with fear before him. However highly the court poet may praise the monarch, he never forgets that Yahweh is high above the king. The great song of the victory that is promised in Ps 20:6 is not meant to extol the king, but to proclaim the glory of the deity who has helped him.

We hear a great deal about the close relationship between the king and his God. He is under Yahweh's special protection; he is called his consecrated one, his anointed one. Priesthood is also ascribed to him; and, as in the case of the Babylonian and Egyptian rulers, great stress is laid on this. The king occupies the seat of honor at Yahweh's right hand. He is called his son. In one passage, indeed—although the most recent expositors will not admit this—he is called God: "Your throne, O God, is forever and ever" (Ps 45:6).

Here again we must keep in view the foreign model. In the world empires, the rulers were worshiped as gods or as actual sons of the gods. But there is only one passage in our text of the Psalms where we find this monarch called a god. On all other occasions this extreme is avoided. When the king of Judah is called Yahweh's "son," the poet means an adopted son, not a begotten son: "You are my son, today I have begotten you" (Ps 2:7). These words were without any doubt the regular formula of adoption, and "today" here means "the day of your accession."

It is also a part of the glorification of the king that his trust in God and his justice are extolled. The dominion of the world is his, because he regards the poor; and victory, because he is on the side of the right; his deliverance from all enemies is due to his justice. Here again it should be kept in view that the poet is describing his ideal. The true king is good and just; that is the poet's deep conviction, and he immediately adds "You are he." Sometimes we can even read between the lines a word of exhortation or admonition that the poet dares not expressly state. For instance, when he prays for the king, "Give the king your justice, O God, and your righteousness to the royal son. May he judge your people with righteousness, and your poor with justice" (Ps 72:1-2). Or when he puts into the king's mouth a promise to surround himself only with righteous and worthy men, and to banish from his court all slanderers and evildoers (Psalm 101). This is again an ideal of royalty and an attempt to tame the unruly lion brood of the house of Judah.

On the whole, judged by our standards, the religion of the court is largely "Byzantine"; but when compared with the court songs of all the other ancient kingdoms of the ancient Near East, it is much more moderate and sane.

THE RELIGION OF THE INDIVIDUAL

Our chief sources for this aspect of Israelite religion are the individual complaint songs and songs of praise and the proverbial poetry in the Psalter and elsewhere.[16] Properly speaking, the Psalms that present this aspect of religion are the main part of the Psalter. In the first place, they constitute the majority of the Psalms, and secondly, they even found their way into the worship at the royal temple. They include a few that deal with individual religion and to which has been added a prayer of intercession of the king. Examples are Psalms 61 and 84. Such poems of personal religion were so popular and contained such an appeal to every sensitive heart that they were felt to deserve a place even in the worship at the royal temple. Thirdly, in some psalms certain aspects of personal religion have been carried over and applied to Israel. For example, Ps 129:1: "'Sorely have they afflicted me from my youth,' let Israel say." Poems dealing with personal matters really touch the heart quite differently than do those that treat Israel's sufferings and hopes. As a result, poems of personal religion were far better developed than those dealing with communal religion, and communal religion readily borrowed much from the other. The gravest error made by students of the Psalms is that they have completely misunderstood this personal poetry and have taken the living "I," meaning the poet himself, as a mere figure of speech meaning the people.[17]

Let us again look at the origin of these poems and the situation in which they arose, beginning with the complaint songs.

When persons were afflicted with sickness they went to the sanctuary in order to receive the desired healing. They performed ceremonies, such as washings and sacrifices.[18] The hope was to obtain a divine oracle for future healing.[19] The presupposition underlying such ceremonies was that sickness, especially life-threatening sickness, comes from higher powers. To understand this belief we must remember that antiquity was utterly unable to recognize any natural cause of illness and that this made it all the more terrible. In Israel also, in the earliest period, illness was sometimes ascribed to curses that wicked enemies had pronounced.[20] Usually, however, and at a later time always, it was conceived as coming from Yahweh himself, who in wrath thus afflicted a person because of his or her sins. The clearest instance in the Old Testament of a person thus afflicted by God is of course Job. But whatever might have been the cause and origin of an illness, it was to Yahweh alone that a person looked for healing.

It was an essential part of the religious ceremony performed by the sick persons at the sanctuary that they should utter their prayers for healing in song. That this is the origin of the complaint songs in the Psalter is clear from various allusions still preserved for us, such as Pss 5:1-3 and 51:7-12, and it is corroborated by the numerous similar Babylonian complaint songs with which we are acquainted.

The counterpart of the complaint song by the sick person is found in the song of thanksgiving sung by the sick person after being healed.[21] When persons had been delivered from serious illness or from grave danger, they came to the holy place and offered the sacrifices that they promised. A small or large feast (if their means permitted it) was held in which friends and acquaintances joyfully took part. At such a festivity a psalm was sung, which is how the songs of thanksgiving emerged.

In these two genres—complaint song and thanksgiving song—we find the two main currents of personal religious poetry. Of the two, the former is by far the more important and the more developed, which is not surprising. It is human nature that misery is far more deeply felt than the duty of gratitude.

The two genres have passed through almost the same history. Originally sung by the sick person or by the person who had received healing, at a later time they were sung or composed in connection with other misfortunes or deliverances. Their original occasion is still apparent in the metaphors of illness and healing that continued to be used. In the complaint songs scattered throughout the Book of Jeremiah, the prophet's "illness" is the fact that his prophecies remain unfulfilled; and in many of the Psalms, it is difficult to say whether the "sickness" mentioned is literal or metaphorical.

Another important part of the history of both genres is that they passed from use in the sanctuary into the Israelite home. This took place more completely with the complaint songs than with the thanksgiving songs. In the case of the former, the original atmosphere of public worship is hardly ever perceptible in pronounced form—it has to be supplied by the reader. In the thanksgiving songs, the atmosphere of public worship is present even in our text, but here also are songs that deliberately omit all mention of the thankoffering and merely show us the grateful worshiper in the sanctuary singing a song of praise. This stage of development of the genres exhibits a very important change in the nature of religion. In a earlier era, sacrifices and ceremonies were indispensable to give expression to the spiritual life; in a later era, religion has freed itself from this need and become, to some extent at least, independent of these external aids. The religious mind begins to hold the external acts in less esteem. The sufferers are convinced that they receive healing without any intervention of the priest, through God's word alone, and the person who has experienced deliverance knows something that is far better than animal sacrifice. The song of a grateful heart, giving the glory to God, is far more pleasing to him.

It is the prophetic spirit that finds expression in this change in religious thought. The prophets had waged war against sacrifices and rituals, demanding true religion and moral uprightness, and it is therefore to their influence that we owe the new teaching in these psalms. This change was of epoch-making importance. The Psalms would never have become models of our own prayers if, like the Babylonian psalms, they had continued to be bound up with all kinds of ritual acts. The pious heart found courage to express its innermost joys and sorrows directly to God. This emergence of a completely personal religion is one of the greatest things to which the Old Testament bears witness.

These personal songs are more precious to us than the songs of public worship. We have to excise and omit a great deal from the songs of public worship before we can use them for our own needs. Many of these personal songs—though not all—we can make our own as they stand. They are "the Psalter within the Psalter."

Characteristically, it is in songs of suffering that the spiritual life finds strongest expression. This is true of all higher life, especially religious life. Human need leads people to God. When the afflicted see that none other can help them, then from the depths of their misery they lift their hands to God on high. That is why most of the personal songs are songs of troubled hearts.

But why were there so many sufferers in those days? The answer can be read in the way in which the psalmists described themselves. They call themselves the poor, the afflicted, the downtrodden, the humble, the people of the land. They complain of oppression at the hands of the rich, the powerful, the proud, and the insolent. The implication is that the poor are good and that the rich and the mighty have no regard for God. The poor and the rich are contrasted as constituting two different religious parties. Such conditions are familiar to us from the Gospels and from Judean life in the Greek period, when the powerful and the wealthy sided with the ruling kingdoms and adopted their civilization, while the humble people clung to the religion of their ancestors. In all probability, the same was the case in the Persian period, for Ezra and Nehemiah opposed the mixed marriages and disloyalty of the upper classes, including the high priestly families. But similar conditions must have prevailed in earlier periods. Jeremiah calls himself one of "the poor" (Jer 20:13). Wickedness and indifference to the ancestral religion came in along with foreign civilization. The wealthy classes were in constant danger of deserting to the dominant empire. But at that very time there arose among the poor and the oppressed a more heartfelt religion. In every Judean village there were bitter, passionate feuds between these two parties, and it was among the poor and the despised that the complaint psalms originated.[22]

This division of the Judean people into two parties—those who believed in Yahweh and those who had apostatized—was of great importance for the history of religion. Such an inward cleavage always takes place when a national religion, to which all members of the nation belong, is replaced by a deeper religion that lays less emphasis on the mere fact of membership in the nation and attaches more importance to faith and character. Parseeism provides another example of the same phenomenon.

We shall now describe briefly the religious content of these poems, taking first the complaint songs.

Like the communal complaint songs, these personal cries invariably begin with an appeal to the divine name. That is the appropriate beginning of all prayers, and the practice goes back to the oldest prehistoric period. In view of the general belief that there were many gods and many lords, it was necessary to mention expressly the name of the deity one meant to address. Thus the opening words of all prayers contained the name of the deity invoked. But the complaint songs pronounce the name of Yahweh in a special tone. It is with loud cries of anguish, no, with a "roar like that of a roaring lion," that they call upon God for aid.

The primary elements in the complaint songs are complaint and petition. The complaint proper describes the great misery of the poet, with the intention of calling down Yahweh's pity and touching his heart. The sufferer thus eases his own pain—pouring out his heart before God. These outpourings are therefore extremely passionate and are full of vehement exaggeration. The calamity is emphasized—usually, however, in very general terms. A very frequent subject of complaint is the danger of death: unless God hastens to intervene, the petitioner will die. We constantly meet the metaphor of going down to Sheol. The complainer cries that he is already in the depths and makes a lavish use of metaphors that are intelligible only when they are taken together and seen to contain the same fundamental thought. He has already gone down to the pit, the waters have already gone over his head, Sheol has already locked its doors behind him. This metaphor, which has hitherto not been always understood, is a very ancient one. Concerning an unconscious person it was said the soul had left the body and gone down to the realm of the dead, "to the pit" underneath the earth, into the realm of the dark waters of the deep.[23]

A frequent complaint of the psalmist is that concerning his enemies, and here again most of the expressions used are very vague.[24] It is remarkable that these adversaries do not assail the psalmist by open, evil treacherous acts of persecution. Originally they must have been wicked sorcerers who attacked a person with dreadful curses and evil machinations. This idea is common in Babylonian poems. But there is little trace of this dread of magic and evil charm in the biblical Psalms—another great achievement of Israelite religion. The complaint about magical charms has been replaced by one concerning slanders and deceptions. Numerous passages make it clear that the enemies referred to are the rich and powerful among the psalmist's own people. In a few passages they are heathens, among whom the psalmist is forced to dwell. To what extent personal enmities play a part it is difficult to say. In any case, it is enmity for the sake of religion that is most prominent.

We must therefore recall here what has just been said about the strife between the two parties in the country. The Judaism of the time was divided into two bitterly opposed camps—a condition that finds a parallel in the rivalries of the Jesuits and the Freemasons in Roman Catholic countries. The point in dispute was the question: How are happiness and earthly success to be attained. This was the desire of both parties. Even the religiously minded sought after this kind of happiness, health and long life, wealth, and numerous children. But it was to God that they looked for all these. They believed confidently that they would flourish like the trees in the sanctuary and bring forth fruit in their old age. For this reason the religious man clung with all his heart to God, in the full expectation that he would shield him in all danger and bring him to a good end. On the other hand, the high and the rich mocked this faith of "the upright heart." They thought they knew better. There was no God to look down from heaven and watch over the fate of mortals. Therefore the religious man called them "wicked." They pursued their evil ways in secret and committed all kinds of wickedness. Both parties thus equally relied on the result—a genuinely Judean feature. Each side watched with equal zeal the fate of the other, which was bound to bring the truth to light. Protestants and Catholics adopted a somewhat similar attitude during the Reformation era. They too watched the kind of death that overtook friends and foes. Thus, as sometimes happens when a foreign power holds sway in a country, when ruin overwhelms the powerful, the "righteous" rejoice. Unfortunately, however, it most frequently happens that the faithful worshiper of Yahweh perishes miserably, and in addition to his other sorrows he has to bear the scorn of the "wicked." "He committed his cause to Yahweh; let him deliver him, let him rescue him, for he delights in him" (Ps 22:8). That is why we find so frequently in the complaint songs sickness and scorn conjoined. The psalmists are tortured by this scorn, because they cannot deny that it seems to be justified. They are deeply distressed to see that actual conditions so frequently contradict their religious faith. In their prayers, therefore, they wrestle not only for their happiness and even for their lives, but also for God and his cause.

Again and again we hear of slanders against the psalmist. In his wretchedness he is cast out by all. Even among his closest friends he finds no sympathy; even his own parents will have nothing to do with him; everyone treats him like a heinous sinner and only waits for his death. In order to understand this we must take several considerations into account. Vile gossip and slander are the special vices of small communities where people live close together and busy themselves with each other's affairs. In ancient times, it must have been quite common for the friends of the sick to desert and disown them. It was the dread of illness that made people do so. Parallels are found in the treatment meted out to lepers in the East, and in the fear of the mentally afflicted that is found within our own cultures in the modern era. In Judaism this tendency was increased by the belief in divine retribution. Even religious people, who had perhaps been disciples of the suffering psalmist till now, began to doubt his integrity when he fell ill or suffered misfortune, and to suspect that he was in reality a wicked man, whose sins God has exposed by sending these sufferings upon him. He could not possibly be a good person. He must be a wicked person, a criminal, indicated as such by God himself.

Such was the lot of Job, whose friends exhorted him to repentance, instead of comforting him in his misery. Similarly we find the psalmist bewailing his sufferings and complaining about the mockery of his enemies and the slanders of his friends.

Along with this we hear the complaint about the aloofness of God, the hiding of his face. "My God, my God, why have you forsaken me?" (Ps 22:1). Thus the psalmist bewails both his external lot and his abandonment by God. To be convinced of God's grace while sickness overwhelmed him was very difficult for the sufferer in ancient days. He was sure, rather, that his evil condition was the sign of God's anger, or at least of God's deserting him. The opposite was also true: God's grace and deliverance from trouble were inseparably connected. The Israelite believer could only find inward assurance in a favorable external situation. Occasionally, however, we hear in these complaint songs such true notes of piety as to enable us to believe that the one heartfelt desire of the singer was, after all, the nearness of God:[25]

> As a hart longs for flowing streams,
>   so longs my soul for you, O God.
> My soul thirsts for God,
>   for the living God.
> When shall I come and behold
>   the face of God? (Ps 42:1-2)

These lines show us that, in the psalmist's mind, the distance and nearness of God are still literally associated with the thought of temple worship. Living far from Zion and its magnificent celebrations, dwelling among a country of strangers hostile both to him and his religion, he feels that this local distance is symbolic of his distance from God. We see here a religion that has almost attained to spirituality but which cannot yet completely dispense with visible symbols.

On the whole, these complaint songs are very monotonous. Again and again we come upon the same feelings, thoughts, expressions, and metaphors. This is due to the manner in which this literary type arose. These songs are all based on temple formulations. True, the material is touched by personal emotion, but one cannot say the emotion pervades it. The individual element appears, but it is still far from being prominent. It is confined to a definite circle of feelings and forms of expression. The poets of the complaint songs never even mention their own names. We must, therefore, be cautious about using phrases like "the freedom of the individual," "the place of the individual in religion," as if they had definite meaning.[26] Most peculiar of all are the complaints of Jeremiah, in which personal experiences of the prophet's calling are coupled with the complaint style of poetry. His enemies are the people who refuse to believe his message, and who accuse him of lack of patriotism because of his prophecies of destruction. Similar self-reliance characterizes the complaints of Job. Here too it is a sick person who utters the prayers, but the complaints take a wider range since the poet is thinking not only of himself but also of the sufferings of all humanity and voices his world pain in the moving words:

> Man that is born of a woman
> is of few days, and full of trouble. (Job 14:1)

The Book of Job finds a problem here, but we shall deal with that later.

The culminating point of the complaint song is the prayer or petition. This is the purpose, implicit or explicit, of all complaint songs. The complaint and the prayer alternate with each other, but the arrangement is loose. The content of the prayer corresponds to that of the complaint. "Save me from my distress; heal my sickness; let my foes be ashamed; do not give me over to their scorn, but keep your word to your servant. Bring me again to Zion that I may behold your temple. Judge the wicked." The prayer is marked by passionate urgency, as if it would take God by storm. That other prayer, "Father, not as I will, but as you will" (Mark 14:36), is on quite a different level. The petitioner in the complaint song claims to know what God must do. He seeks to move God to fulfill his will, and his passion reaches its climax in his prayer for vengeance against his adversary. The idea and ideal of forgiving the adversary are utterly absent. With burning anger, and at times with coarse expressions, he prays for destruction upon his enemies. Even a man like Jeremiah prayed this way. The so-called imprecatory psalms contain little else than such curses. The psalmist utters these prayers quite frankly, without any thought of concealment, for his enemies are Yahweh's enemies as well. "Do I not hate them who hate you, O Yahweh?" (Ps 139:21). He is convinced that there is nothing unjust in such prayers, for his enemies have richly deserved destruction. Let the evil they have done or purposed return upon their own head.

The psalmist occasionally sums up all his desires in one comprehensive figure of speech. He hopes after his recovery to make a pilgrimage to Jerusalem—then he will have attained his heart's desire: healing and nearness to God. And still another thought emerges: the temple is a refuge. No one can hurt the person whom Yahweh covers with protection in his sanctuary, and in the house of the Lord he finds rest from the persecutions of the wicked.

The idea of life after death appears nowhere in the Psalter. What the psalmist desires is deliverance from his present danger. This desire is often expressed in passionate language:

> For you do not give me up to Sheol,
>> or let your godly one see the Pit. (Ps 16:10)

But this does not mean deliverance into a new life beyond death, but a new life before death, a life that to his ardent mind seems an everlasting life:

> You show me the path of life;
>> in your presence there is fullness of joy,
>> in your right hand are pleasures for evermore. (Ps 16:11)

Another concept never found in these psalms is education through suffering. The pious person does not try to bear patiently the chastisements of God; he or she seeks to be delivered from such ills. For example, Job angrily rejects the opinion of his friends that God has sent his sufferings upon him to warn and chasten him. On the other hand, this idea occurs in the psalms of thanksgiving and is quite frequent in the Proverbs.

It is common to find both complaint and petition supported by all kinds of motives in order to induce God to intervene, and by thoughts with which the psalmist comforts and soothes his troubled mind. One of the most frequent is the declaration of immovable confidence in the help of God. Complaint and petition thus pass into calm confidence and settled assurance.

> [M]any are saying of me,
>> there is no help for him God.
> But you, O Yahweh, are a shield about me,
>> my glory, and the lifter of my head. (Ps 3:2-3)

He finds it soothing to declare this confidence, and he hopes that God will not put to shame one who approaches him in this way. God cannot refuse hands that cling to him so confidently. Such trust cannot fail to move his heart. Nor can a brief, humble word of personal experience, justifying such confidence, be out of place. "Upon you was I cast from my birth" (Ps 22:10a); "Do not cast me off in the time of old age" (Ps 71:9a).

Songs of penitence and songs of innocence form important subgenres of these complaint psalms. In both the psalmist complains of his misery and prays for its removal. The difference between them is that in the former he confesses his sin, while in the latter he maintains his innocence. Both types were originally used in public worship, and Babylonian literature supplies parallels for both.

Psalms of Penitence

The authors of the songs of penitence are convinced that by their sin they have incurred God's anger, and the purpose of their psalms is to urge God to forgive them. A classical example is Psalm 60. The whole content of these psalms must be interpreted in view of their purpose, which is to incline God's heart to mercy. The psalmist, for example, reminds God of the universality of human sin, so that his own sinfulness may not appear so grievous:

> Behold, I was brought forth in iniquity,
> and in sin did my mother conceive me. (Ps 51:5)

That is to say, "For an unclean person in whom sin is inborn, you cannot demand perfection." Again, he confesses his sin with the utmost frankness, humbling himself before the Most High, emphasizing the idea:

> Toward the scorners he is scornful,
> but to the humble he shows favor. (Prov 3:34)

Those who sincerely acknowledge their sin can expect forgiveness; those who conceal it must be punished until their obstinacy is broken. But the deepest prayer in the penitential psalms is that for a new and clean heart (Ps 51:10), a prayer that stands far above all other prayers in the Psalter. Elsewhere we find prayers for external possessions, for life and prosperity, even for instruction regarding the way of righteousness and for guidance to do what is right. All these assume that humans can and should fulfill God's will. But in this profound prayer the idea emerges that goodness in humanity must be the work of God. This is the culmination of the religion of the Psalms. Here it transcends itself.

Psalms of Innocence

There is one essential feature in which the songs of innocence present a contrast to the penitential psalms. In the former the psalmist also inquires for the cause of his sufferings, but he cannot find it in himself, for there is no sin in him. The characteristic and ever recurrent feature of these poems is that the psalmist strongly asserts his innocence:

> If you try my heart, if you visit me by night,
> if you test me, you will find no wickedness in me. (Ps 17:3)

Such declarations of innocence, lofty in style, are frequent in the Book of Job; but when the author of such a song finds absolutely no reason for his misfortune in his own sin, he cries all the more loudly to God for help and pours out his passion strongly upon his adversaries. Psalms of vengeance and psalms of innocence belong together.

Today we are inclined to set a higher value on the penitential psalms, with their confessions of sin, than on the songs of innocence, with their insistence on personal righteousness. But perhaps this judgment is not altogether just and right. In the psalmists' day, it was not difficult for people in distress to speak of their sin. Babylonian prayers contain many such confessions, all of them evidently superficial and insincere. But it is more courageous for a person whose spirit is not broken by misfortune to maintain the conviction of innocence. The moral greatness to which such a person may rise is seen in Job, sublime in his defiance of misfortune.

The songs of innocence contain frequent references to divine retribution. This tenet of Israelite faith has already been mentioned, but we must now deal with it more fully.

This doctrine is not found in the oldest complaint songs. The earlier religion was satisfied with the faith that Yahweh cannot abandon his loyal servants. But eventually reflection entered more strongly into lyric poetry. The complaint song and wisdom literature—originally distinct and separate—coalesced; and it was in the latter that the doctrine of retribution was discussed. Then the religious mind, to assure itself of divine help, fell back on the base principle of divine dealing, and found refuge in the thought that God deals well by those that fear him. Ultimately, this principle became the guiding line of piety and appeared even in the religion of the Psalms.

The doctrine is usually found in the form of the blessing:

> Blessed is the man
>> who walks not in the counsel of the wicked. . . .
> He is like a tree
>> planted by streams of water. (Ps 1:1, 3; see Ps 128)

Occasionally a high degree of individualism is found:

> A thousand may fall at your side,
>> ten thousand at your right hand;
>> but it will not come near you. (Ps 91:7)

It even finds expression in the form of exhortation (Psalm 37). At a still later time, the suffering pious one consoled himself with the same thoughts in his complaint.

Sometimes, but only rarely, the theme is what God requires of people. This also takes the form of the blessing (Psalm 1), or a hymn to the Law (Ps 19:7-11). Psalm 1 gives a solemn exposition of the Law in a manner reminiscent of the prophets. The Psalms contain little that indicates any high estimate of the legal ceremonies, and it strongly repudiates zeal for the Law apart from morality of life. Everywhere in the Old Testament, including the prophets, the relationship between God and humanity in the Psalms is based on the Law— God commands and humans must obey, receiving in return protection and reward. Any important influence of the great legal systems, such as became clearly apparent in later Judaism, is entirely absent from the Psalms.

The doctrine of retribution has lost much of its certainty for the authors of the later complaint songs. When they see how things really are in the world, how the wicked blaspheme God and yet enjoy prosperity, they are seized with dread and ask: Is there really an avenging God? The psalmists who tackle this problem find consolation in the hope that divine judgment will ultimately fall upon the workers of wickedness (Psalms 37 and 73).

Almost all the complaint songs end on a note of triumph. Glad certainty finally fills the psalmist's heart. Out of his cry, even out of his despair, he rises to the assurance that God will aid him. This inward assurance is the answer to his prayer.

This assured confidence comes so suddenly that many psalms seem to fall into two entirely separate parts. Indeed, some modern scholars would call these parts two independent poems. Psalm 22 is an example. But this view leaves out of account the passion of Israelite prayer. It is possible, however, that the two parts, when sung originally, were separated by the announce-ment of the priestly oracle.

The usual form of the conclusion is that the psalmist makes a vow to sing a song of thanksgiving after his deliverance has come and sings this song in anticipation of it. And so the complaint, which began with cries and tears, ends with thanksgiving and praise.

We saw previously that the state religion oscillated between two extremes: sorrow and joy, the complaint and the eschatological poem. The same is true of the personal religion in the Psalms. Complaint song and thanksgiving song are found side by side.

The songs of thanksgiving are full of exultation. The whole situation has changed. The former sufferer, now basking in the sunshine of happiness, tri-umphantly tells friends of former griefs and recounts how God heard his or her cry. This former sufferer is seen by others, with joy and pride, as proof that God does not abandon faithful worshipers. While the complaint songs of the individual are sung in privacy, the songs of thanksgiving are meant to be heard by all. The most sacred duty of the person to whom deliverance has come is to give the glory to God, and to testify aloud of God's goodness so that all the world may hear.

The songs of thanksgiving are an exact contrast to the complaint songs—the flipside of the coin—and thus they interpret each other. To take one example, the singer complains: "I am swallowed by the pit"; he prays, "Lord, save my life from the pit"; he concludes with the vow, "I will praise you, when you have raised me from the pit." On other hand, the man who has been delivered opens his song by recounting his distress and his deliverance. "I had been swallowed up by Sheol, but you saved my life from the pit." And the song concludes with "I bless you that you have raised me from the pit." This comparison is another proof that the prayer of deliverance from death does not envisage a life after death, but help in the midst of the present danger.

This alternation between the complaint song and the thanksgiving song covers the entire religious life. In need, a person calls on God; when happiness returns, God is praised. The glowing passion of the Israelite mind, of which we have repeatedly spoken, explains why the religion is full of such contrasts.

All this emphasizes the value we attach to the exceptions. Some passages in the complaint songs declare the psalmist's confidence in God. The tone is that of calm assurance. The tumult has been stilled and quiet confidence fills the heart:

> Yahweh is my light and my salvation;
>   whom shall I fear?
> Yahweh is the stronghold of my life;
>   of whom shall I be afraid? (Ps 27:1)

The poems in which these two moods find voice simultaneously are true to life and touch us deeply. Examples are Psalms 3, 123, and 130. It is a majestic picture that the author of the splendid verses in Psalms 43 and 44 unveils, combining deep grief, gnawing pain, powerful pleading, remembrance of a happier past, with confident certainty. Especially beautiful is a poem like Psalm 121, in which the poet reads off his varying emotions. In a few psalms, the complaint and petition have completely ceased and only confidence is expressed. "Yahweh is my shepherd, I shall not want" (Ps 23:1). These songs of trust, in which the passionate, ardent Israelite has disciplined his heart's restlessness to peace, are to us the finest individual poetry in the Psalter.

But perhaps the finest verse in all the Psalms is that in which a poet, after a painful debate with his own heart concerning the prosperity of the wicked and his own sufferings, has found the grace to say:

Whom have I in heaven but you?
    And there is nothing upon earth that I desire besides you.
My flesh and my heart may fail,
        but God is the strength of my heart and my portion for ever.
    (Ps 73:25-26)

CONCLUSION

This is a mere outline of the religion of the Psalms that I have been able to give. Only some specially frequent notes of this religion and a few simple aspects of it have been commented upon. The contents of the Psalms are far richer and more copious. Especially in the later period, when the poetic genres became more and more literary, a great deal of mixture took place and the structure became more complicated. The poet's joy in his deliverance is tinged by the recollection of his need, and he now reflects the complaint song he sang in his distress (Jonah 2:5). Or the complaint song adopts hymn material and exhibits the strong contrast between human sorrow and God's glory as a means for opening the heart of God (Ps 22:3-5). Or it describes how transitory human life is (a complaint motif) in order to highlight God's eternity (Ps 103:15-17). Other examples of mixture are found in the liturgy, where passages of varied character are conjoined for use in the sanctuary. In this way the religion became richer as time passed.

Ultimately, naïve religion was invaded by a rational reflection that finally destroyed it. That is what we have in Psalm 119 and in the noncanonical *Psalms of Solomon*.[27]

I have tried to provide in as unbiased a manner as I could the results of my studies in the Psalms. While I have not concealed the weak points in the religion, I have tried to bring out its strength. Such a study may justifiably be concluded by an impartial and understanding verdict on the value of the Psalms, and I should like to indicate briefly the opinion I have formed. On the one hand, it is utterly impossible for us to use the entire Psalter in Christian worship, although earlier times may have so used it. The modern mind has found in it so much that is alien and even repellent that we have long been compelled to make selections for use in church and school and home. On the other hand, we should be careful not to go too far in this direction. We must remember that the Psalter is not a contemporary book and therefore cannot possibly voice modern thoughts and feelings. The layperson who seeks religious edification in this book will do well simply to pass over what is unintelligible and strange. Further experience of life will perhaps cast a different light upon it. Whoever earnestly studies these poems will not fail to find many passages that give perfect expression to true religion, and generations still to come will humbly bend the knee on this holy ground and learn from the Israelite psalmists how to pray.

NOTES

[Editor's Note: This was originally delivered as a lecture at the Association for Contemporary Christianity (Bund für Gegenwartschristentum), Eisenach, Germany, October 4, 1921. Only notes 1 and 13 are Gunkel's.]

1. I have already hinted at such a study in my *Reden und Aufsätze* and in the article "Psalmen" in *RGG²*; and I shall return to it at greater length in my *Einleitung in die Psalmen* (see below, note 2 for the English trans.).

[2.] For the author's book-length analysis of Israel's *poetic forms and tradition* (completed a decade later than the original publication of this article), see Hermann Gunkel and Joachim Begrich, *An Introduction to Psalms: The Genres of the Religious Lyric of Israel*, trans. J. D. Nogalski, MLBS (Macon, Ga.: Mercer Univ. Press, 1998; German ed. 1933).

For treatments of the *poetic genres* that specifically build on Gunkel's work (even when sometimes disagreeing with his conclusions), see Sigmund Mowinckel, *The Psalms in Israel's Worship*, 2 vols., trans. D. R. Ap-Thomas (Nashville: Abingdon, 1962); Claus Westermann, *Praise and Lament in the Psalms*, trans. K. Crim and R. N. Soulen (Atlanta: John Knox, 1981); Erhard S. Gerstenberger, "The Lyrical Literature," in *The Hebrew Bible and Its Modern Interpreters* (Philadelphia: Fortress Press; Chico, Calif.: Scholars Press, 1985) 409–44; Gerstenberger, *Psalms; Part 1, with an Introduction to Cultic Poetry*, FOTL 14 (Grand Rapids: Eerdmans, 1988); Hans-Joachim Kraus, *Psalms 1–59*, *Psalms 60–150*, trans. H. C. Oswald, CC (Minneapolis: Augsburg, 1988–89); and Gerstenberger, *Psalms; Part 2*, FOTL 15 (Grand Rapids: Eerdmans, 2001).

[3.] For form-critical and theological analyses of the Israelite *hymn*, see Gunkel and Begrich, *An Introduction to Psalms*, 22–65; Mowinckel, *The Psalms in Israel's Worship*, 1.81–192; Klaus Koch, *The Growth of the Biblical Tradition: The Form-Critical Method*, trans. S. M. Cupitt (London: Adam & Charles Black, 1969) 159–70; Harvey H. Guthrie Jr., *Israel's Sacred Songs: A Study of Dominant Themes* (New York: Seabury, 1978) 59–117; Claus Westermann, *Praise and Lament in the Psalms*, 15–165; Walter Brueggemann, *The Message of the Psalms: A Theological Commentary* (Minneapolis: Augsburg, 1984) 25–49; idem, *Israel's Praise: Doxology against Idolatry and Ideology* (Philadelphia: Fortress Press, 1988); Patrick D. Miller, Jr., *Interpreting the Psalms* (Philadelphia: Fortress Press, 1986) 68–78; idem, *They Cried to the Lord: The Form and Theology of Biblical Prayer* (Minneapolis: Fortress Press,

1994) 204–32; Gerstenberger, *Psalms; Part 1*, 16–19. See Psalms 8, 19, 24, 47, 68, 93, 96, 104, 105, 145–150.

[4.] Since Gunkel died when the discoveries at Ugarit were just being made, he was not aware of the Ugaritic descriptions of Baal is a "rider on the clouds" (see Ps 68:4; Isa 19:1), who is manifested in the storm. See T. H. Gaster, "Psalm 29," *JQR* 37 (1946) 54–67; Frank Moore Cross, "Notes on a Canaanite Psalm in the Old Testament," *BASOR* 117 (1950) 19–21; F. C. Fensham, "Psalm 29 and Ugarit," *OTWP* (1963) 84–99; Peter C. Craigie, "Psalm XXIX in the Hebrew Poetic Tradition," *VT* 22 (1972) 143–51; Frank Moore Cross, *Canaanite Myth and Hebrew Epic* (Cambridge: Harvard Univ. Press, 1973) 147–94.

The Akkadian texts also provide counter-examples to Gunkel's point. Kraus notes, for example, that Marduk is praised in terms of storms, earthquakes, and floods (*Psalms 1–59*, 347):

> The word that causes the heavens above to quake;
>   the word that makes the earth below to shake;
>   the word that brings the Anunnaki down to ruin . . .
> His word makes the heavens quake, makes the earth shake . . .
>   the Lord's word is a rising flash flood that beclouds the countenance;
>   the word of Marduk is a flood that catches hold of the dam.
> His word, it sweeps away huge lotus trees [?];
>   his word is a storm, it saddles all things with burdens [?].
> The word of Enlil storms about without an eye seeing it.

In other words, rather than a distinctive element of Israelite religion (per Gunkel), the depictions of Yahweh in terms of storm, thunder, lightning, and earthquake are right in line with contemporary Near Eastern theologies.

[5.] See Rolf Knierim, "On the Theology of Psalm 19," in *The Task of Old Testament Theology: Substance, Method, and Cases* (Grand Rapids: Eerdmans, 1995) 322–50.

[6.] For form-critical and theological analyses of the Israelite *communal complaint song*, see Gunkel and Begrich, *Introduction to Psalms*, 82–98; Mowinckel, *The Psalms in Israel's Worship*, 1.193–224; Guthrie, *Israel's Sacred Songs*, 118–45; Westermann, *Praise and Lament in the Psalms*, 165–280; Brueggemann, *The Message of the Psalms*, 51–58, 67–77; idem, *Interpreting the Psalms*, 48–63; Miller, *They Cried to the Lord*, 55–79; and Gerstenberger, *Psalms; Part 1*, 10–14. See Psalms 44, 60, 74, 79, 80, 83, 85, 89.

[7.] For an analysis of the meaning of *rich and poor* in the ancient Mediterranean, see Bruce J. Malina, "Wealth and Poverty in the New Testament and Its World," *Int* 41 (1987) 354–67; and T. R. Hobbs, "Reflections on the Poor and the Old Testament," *ExpT* 100 (1989) 291–94.

[8.] For form-critical and theological analyses of the *communal thanks-giving song*, see: Gunkel and Begrich, *Introduction to Psalms*, 240–47; Mowinckel, *The Psalms in Israel's Worship*, 2.26–30; Guthrie, *Israel's Sacred Songs*, 147–57; Brueggemann, *The Message of the Psalms*, 134–40; Miller, *They Cried to the Lord*, 203–4; and Gerstenberger, *Psalms; Part 1*, 14–16. See Psalms 66, 67, 124, 129.

[9.] "Eschatological psalms" is not one of Gunkel's most helpful form-critical designations. Some of these might be identified as hymns, while others are prophetic liturgies, Zion songs, or Yahweh-enthronement psalms. On the general point, Brueggemann comments, "The scholarly debate has tended to divide, either following Gunkel in an eschatological interpretation, or Mowinckel in a cultic reading. But what needs to be seen afresh is that good liturgical activity which evokes and receives God is the gift of a new word (new creation) and is always eschatological in the sense that it subverts the old world now being superseded by the new world generated in the liturgical process. The eschatological and cultic dimensions must be held together or both will be misunderstood" (*The Message of the Psalms*, 181–82).

[10.] On the interpretation of *Psalm 82 and its mythological imagery*, see Julian Morgenstern, "The Mythological Background of Psalm 82," *HUCA* 14 (1939) 29–126; Roger T. O'Callaghan, "A Note on the Canaanite Background of Psalm 82," *CBQ* 15 (1953) 311–14; Otto Eissfeldt, "El and Yahweh," *JSS* 1 (1956) 25–37; Gerald Cooke, "The Sons of (the) God(s)," *ZAW* 76 (1964) 22–47; J. J. M. Roberts, "The Davidic Origin of the Zion Tradition," *JBL* 92 (1973) 339–44; Cross, *Canaanite Myth and Hebrew Epic*, 186–90; E. Theodore Mullen, *The Divine Council in Canaanite and Early Hebrew Literature*, HSM 24 (Chico, Calif.: Scholars, 1980) 228–31; and Miller, *Interpreting the Psalms*, 120–24.

[11.] It seems as though Gunkel is attempting to "rescue" the purity of Israel's religion by separating its mythology as only a poetic device; in light of all the comparative material from the ancient Near East, this is no longer tenable. See Theodor H. Gaster, *Thespis: Ritual, Myth, and Drama in the Ancient Near East*, rev. ed. (Garden City, N.Y.: Doubleday, 1961) 442–66; Mowinckel, *The Psalms in Israel's Worship*, 1.140–69; John Rogerson, *Myth in Old Testament Interpretation*, BZAW 134 (Berlin: de Gruyter, 1974); Robert A. Oden Jr., "Interpreting Biblical Myths," in *The Bible Without Theology: The Theological Tradition and Alternatives to It*, NVBS (San Francisco: Harper & Row, 1987) 40–91; and *idem*, "Myth and Mythology (OT)," in *ABD* 4.956–60.

[12.] For form-critical and theological analyses of the *royal psalms*, see Gunkel and Begrich, *An Introduction to Psalms*, 99–120; Keith R. Crim, *The Royal Psalms* (Richmond: John Knox, 1962); Mowinckel, *The Psalms in Israel's Worship*, 1.42–80; J. H. Eaton, *Kingship and the Psalms*, SBT 2/32 (London: SCM, 1976); Guthrie, *Israel's Sacred Songs*, 98–106; Hans-Joachim Kraus, *Theol-*

ogy of the Psalms, trans. K. Crim, CC (Minneapolis: Augsburg, 1986) 107–23. For a unique perspective, see Gerstenberger, *Psalms; Part 1*, 19. Note also Sigmund Mowinckel, *He That Cometh: The Messiah Concept in the Old Testament and Later Judaism*, trans. G. W. Anderson (Nashville: Abingdon, 1956). See Psalms 2, 18, 20, 21, 45, 72, 89, 101, 110, 132, and 144.

13. Friedrich Schiller, *The Bride of Messina; or, The Enemy Brothers, A Tragedy with Choruses*, trans. C. E. Passage (New York: Ungar, 1962).

[14.] On Israelite *royal ideology*, see: Aubrey R. Johnson, *Sacral Kingship in Ancient Israel*, 2nd ed. (Cardiff: Univ. of Wales Press, 1967); Tomoo Ishida, *The Royal Dynasties in Ancient Israel: A Study on the Formation and Development of Royal-Dynastic Ideology*, BZAW 142 (Berlin: de Gruyter, 1977); Gösta W. Ahlström, *Royal Administration and National Religion in Ancient Palestine*, SHANE 1 (Leiden: Brill, 1982); and Keith W. Whitelam, "Israelite Kingship: The Royal Ideology and Its Opponents," in *The World of Ancient Israel: Sociological, Anthropological and Political Perspectives*, ed. R. E. Clements (Cambridge: Cambridge Univ. Press, 1989) 119–39.

[15.] See Gerhard von Rad, "The Royal Ritual in Judah," in *The Problem of the Hexateuch and Other Essays*, trans. E. W. T. Dicken (New York: McGraw-Hill, 1966) 222–31.

[16.] For form-critical and theological analyses of the Israelite *individual complaint song*, see Gunkel and Begrich, *An Introduction to Psalms*, 121–98; Mowinckel, *The Psalms in Israel's Worship*, 2.1–25; Gerstenberger, "Jeremiah's Complaints: Observations on Jeremiah 15:10-21," *JBL* 82 (1963) 393–408; *Psalms; Part 1*, 11–14; Koch, *The Growth of the Biblical Tradition*, 171–82; Guthrie, *Israel's Sacred Songs*, 118–45; Westermann, *Praise and Lament in the Psalms*, 165–280; Brueggemann, "The Formfulness of Grief," *Int* 31 (1977) 263–75; idem, *The Message of the Psalms*, 58–67; and Miller, *They Cried to the Lord*, 79–86. It was Gerstenberger who articulated the important distinction between a lament (dealing with grief over unalterable loss, such as death and destruction) and complaint (dealing with the cries for help in times of need, such as sickness, danger, and other desperate circumstances). Unfortunately, many interpreters (and translators) have not caught on to the significance of this insight. See especially Psalms 3, 4, 5, 6, 7, 11, 12, 13, 17, 22, 26, 27, 28, 31, 35, 38, 39, 42–43, 51, 54, 55, 56, 57, 59, 61, 63, 64, 65, 66, 68, 69, 70, 71, 86, 88, 102, 109, 120, 130, 140, 141, 142, 143.

[17.] See Mowinckel, *The Psalms in Israel's Worship*, 1.42–46.

[18.] On *suffering and healing* see: Erhard S. Gerstenberger and Wolfgang Schrage, *Suffering*, trans. J. E. Steeley, Biblical Encounter Series (Nashville: Abingdon, 1977); John J. Pilch, *Healing in the New Testament: Insights from Medical and Mediterranean Anthropology* (Minneapolis: Fortress Press, 2000); Mary Douglas, "The Healing Rite," *Man* 5 (1970) 302–8.

[19.] See the foundational essay by Gunkel's colleague and son-in-law on *"the priestly oracle of salvation"*: Joachim Begrich, "Das priestliche Heilsorakel," *ZAW* 52 (1934) 81–92; reprinted in Begrich, *Gesammelte Studien zum Alten Testament*, ThBü 21 (Munich: Kaiser, 1964) 217–31; and Edgar W. Conrad, "Second Isaiah and the Priestly Oracle of Salvation," *ZAW* 73 (1981) 234–46.

[20.] On *cursing and the evil eye*, see Mowinckel, *The Psalms in Israel's Worship*, 2.1–8; Miller, *They Cried to the Lord*, 153–73; John H. Elliott, "The Evil Eye in the First Testament: The Ecology and Culture of a Pervasive Belief," in *The Bible and the Politics of Exegesis: Essays in Honor of Norman K. Gottwald on His Sixty-Fifth Birthday*, ed. D. Jobling et al. (Cleveland, Ohio: Pilgrim, 1991) 147–59, 332–36; and *idem, The Fear of the Leer: The Evil Eye in the Bible and Antiquity* (Minneapolis: Fortress Press, forthcoming).

[21.] For form-critical and theological analyses of the Israelite *individual thanksgiving song*, see Gunkel and Begrich, *An Introduction to Psalms*, 199–221; Mowinckel, *The Psalms in Israel's Worship*, 2.31–43; Gerstenberger, *Psalms; Part 1*, 14–16; Brueggemann, *The Message of the Psalms*, 123–34; and Miller, *They Cried to the Lord*, 178–203. See especially Psalms 30, 32, 34, 40, 67, 75, 92, 103, 107, 116, 118, 136, 137, 138.

[22.] Note the continuing discussion of *factions and parties* in ancient Israel in: Morton Smith, *Palestinian Parties and Politics that Shaped the Old Testament* (New York: Columbia Univ. Press, 1971); and Bernhard Lang, *Monotheism and the Prophetic Minority: An Essay in Biblical History and Sociology*, SWBA 1 (Sheffield: Almond, 1983) 13–59.

[23.] On *death and the underworld*, see Nicholas J. Tromp, *Primitive Conceptions of Death and the Nether World in the Old Testament*, BibOr 21 (Rome: Pontifical Biblical Institute Press, 1969); and Theodore J. Lewis, *Cults of the Dead in Ancient Israel and Ugarit*, HSM 39 (Atlanta: Scholars, 1989); and *idem*, "Dead, Abode of the," in *ABD* 2.101–5.

[24.] The topic of the *enemies in the Psalms* has been widely treated. See, e.g., Harris Birkeland, *The Evildoers in the Book of Psalms*, Norske Videnskaps-Akademi: Historisk Klasse. Avhandlinger, 1955, 2 (Oslo: Dybwad, 1955); Erhard S. Gerstenberger, "Enemies and Evildoers in the Psalms," *Horizons in Biblical Theology* 5.1 (1983) 61–77; Hans-Joachim Kraus, *Theology of the Psalms*, K. Crim, trans., CC (Minneapolis: Augsburg, 1985) 125–36; Erhard S. Gerstenberger, "Enemies and Evildoers in the Psalms," *Horizons in Biblical Theology* 5.1 (1983) 61–77; and T. R. Hobbs and P. K. Jackson, "The Enemies in the Psalms," *BTB* 21 (1991) 22–29.

[25.] Concerning *God's absence/presence, distance/nearness*, see Samuel Terrien, *The Elusive Presence: Toward a New Biblical Theology* (New York: Harper & Row, 1978); and Walter Brueggemann, *Theology of the Old Testament: Testimony, Dispute, Advocacy* (Minneapolis: Fortress Press, 1996) 333–58, 567–77.

[26.] On *the individual and the group* in the ancient Mediterranean and cross-cultural perspective, see, e.g., Mowinckel, *The Psalms in Israel's Worship*, 1.42–46 and 2.126–45; Harry C. Triandis, "Cross-Cultural Studies in Individualism and Collectivism," in *Nebraska Symposium on Motivation 1989*, ed. J. J. Berman (Lincoln: Univ. of Nebraska Press, 1990) 41–133; Bruce J. Malina, *The New Testament World: Insights from Cultural Anthropology*, 3rd ed. (Louisville: Westminster John Knox, 2001) 58–80; *idem*, "The Mediterranean Self: A Social Psychological Model," in *The Social World of Jesus and the Gospels* (London: Routledge, 1996) 67–96; and K. C. Hanson, "Sin, Purification, and Group Process," in *Problems in Biblical Theology: Essays in Honor of Rolf Knierim*, ed. H. T. C. Sun et al. (Grand Rapids: Eerdmans, 1997) 167–91.

[27.] For the text of the *Psalms of Solomon*, see the translation by R. B. Wright in *OTP* (1985) 2.639–70.

A Select Bibliography on the Psalms

Brueggemann, Walter. *The Message of the Psalms: A Theological Commentary*. Minneapolis: Augsburg, 1984.

———. *Israel's Praise: Doxology against Idolatry and Ideology*. Philadelphia: Fortress Press, 1988.

Gerstenberger, Erhard S. *Psalms, Part 1; with an Introduction to Cultic Poetry*. FOTL 14. Grand Rapids: Eerdmans, 1988.

———. *Psalms, Part 2; Lamentations*. FOTL 15. Grand Rapids: Eerdmans, 2001.

Gunkel, Hermann. *Introduction to Psalms: The Genres of the Religious Lyric of Israel*, completed by Joachim Begrich, translated by J. D. Nogalski. MLBS. Macon, Ga.: Mercer Univ. Press, 1998.

Kraus, Hans-Joachim. *Psalms: A Commentary*, translated by H. C. Oswald. 2 vols. CC. Minneapolis: Augsburg, 1988–89.

———. *Theology of the Psalms*, translated by K. Crim. CC. Minneapolis: Augsburg, 1986.

Miller, Patrick D., Jr. *Interpreting the Psalms*. Philadelphia: Fortress Press, 1986.

———. *They Cried to the Lord: The Form and Theology of Biblical Prayer*. Minneapolis: Fortress Press, 1994.

Mowinckel, Sigmund. *The Psalms in Israel's Worship*, translated by D. R. Ap-Thomas. 2 vols. Nashville: Abingdon, 1962.

Westermann, Claus. *Praise and Lament in the Psalms*, translated by K. R. Crim and R. N. Soulen. Atlanta: John Knox, 1981.

Wilson, Gerald H. *The Editing of the Hebrew Psalter*. SBLDS 76. Chico, Calif.: Scholars, 1985.

Bibliography

The Works of Hermann Gunkel in English

I. Books

The Folktale in the Old Testament, translated by M. D. Rutter. HTIBS. Sheffield: Almond, 1987. (German ed. 1921.)

Genesis, translated by M. E. Biddle. MLBS. Macon, Ga.: Mercer Univ. Press, 1997. (German 3rd ed. 1910.)

The History of Religion and Old Testament Criticism. London: Williams & Norgate, 1910.

The Influence of the Holy Spirit: The Popular View of the Apostolic Age and the Teaching of the Apostle Paul, translated by R. A. Harrisville and P. A. Quanbeck II. Philadelphia: Fortress Press, 1979. (German ed. 1888.)

Introduction to the Psalms: The Genres of the Religious Lyric of Israel, completed by Joachim Begrich, translated by J. D. Nogalski. MLBS. Macon, Ga.: Mercer Univ. Press, 1998. (German ed. 1933.)

Israel and Babylon: The Influence of Babylon on the Religion of Israel, translated by E. S. B. Philadelphia: McVey, 1904. (German ed. 1903.)

The Legends of Genesis: The Biblical Saga and History, translated by W. H. Carruth. Chicago: Open Court, 1901; reprint with Introduction by W. F. Albright, New York: Schocken, 1964. (German ed. 1901.)

The Psalms: A Form-Critical Introduction, Introduction by James Muilenburg, translated by T. M. Horner. FBBS 19. Philadelphia: Fortress Press, 1967. (German ed. 1927.)

The Stories of Genesis, translated by J. J. Scullion, edited by W. R. Scott. Vallejo, Calif.: BIBAL, 1994. (German ed. 1910.)

What Remains of the Old Testament and Other Essays, Introduction by James Moffatt, translated by A. K. Dallas. London: George Allen & Unwin; New York: Macmillan, 1928.

II. Articles

"The Close of Micah: A Prophetical Liturgy." In *What Remains of the Old Testament and Other Essays*, 115–49. ("Der Micha-Schluss." *ZS* 2 [1924] 145–83.)

"Elisha: The Successor of Elijah." *ExpT* 41 (1929/30) 182–86.

"Fundamental Problems of Hebrew Literary History." In *What Remains*, 57–68. ("Grundprobleme der israelitische Literaturgeschichte." *DLZ* 27 [1906] cols. 1797–1800, 1861–66.)

"The 'Historical Movement' in the Study of Religion." *ExpT* 38 (1926/27) 532–36.

"The Israelite Prophecy from the Time of Amos." In *Twentieth Century Theology in the Making*. Vol. 1: *Themes of Biblical Theology*, translated by R. A. Wilson, edited by J. Pelikan, 48–75. New York: Harper & Row, 1969. (*RGG*², 1927–32.)

"Jacob." In *What Remains*, 151–86. ("Jakob." *PJ* 176 [1919]).

"The Poetry of the Psalms: Its Literary History and Its Application to the Dating of the Psalms." In *Old Testament Essays*, edited by D. C. Simpson, 118–42. London: Griffin, 1927.

"Psalm 1: An Interpretation." *BibWor* 21 (1903) 120–23.

"Psalm 8: An Interpretation." *BibWor* 21 (1903) 206–9.

"Psalm 19:1-6: An Interpretation." *BibWor* 21 (1903) 281–83.

"Psalm 24: An Interpretation." *BibWor* 21 (1903) 366–70.

"Psalm 42 and 43: An Interpretation." *BibWor* 21 (1903) 433–49.

"Psalm 46: An Interpretation." *BibWor* 21 (1903) 28–31.

"Psalm 103: An Interpretation." *BibWor* 22 (1904) 209–15.

"Psalm 137: An Interpretation." *BibWor* 22 (1904) 290–93.

"Psalm 149: An Interpretation." *BibWor* 22 (1904) 363–66.

"The Religio-Historical Interpretation of the New Testament." *Mon* 3 (1903) 398–455. (*Zum religionsgeschichtlichen Verständnis des Neuen Testaments*. FRLANT 1. Göttingen: Vandenhoeck & Ruprecht, 1903.)

"The Religion of the Psalms." In *What Remains*, 69–114. (*ChrW* 36 [1922] nos. 1, 2, 5, 6, 7.)

"The Secret Experiences of the Prophets." *Expos* (1924) 356–66, 427–35; (1925) 23–32.

"The Two Accounts of Hagar (Genesis xvi. and xxi., 8-21)." *Mon* 10 (1900) 321–42.

"What is Left of the Old Testament?" In *What Remains*, 13–56. (*DR* 41 [1914]).

Hermann Gunkel's Major Works

Ausgewählte Psalmen. Göttingen: Vandenhoeck & Ruprecht, 1904.

Einleitung in die Psalmen: Die Gattungen der religösen Lyrik Israels. Completed by Joachim Begrich. HAT. Göttingen: Vandenhoeck & Ruprecht, 1933.

Genesis übersetzt und erklärt. HAT. Göttingen: Vandenhoeck & Ruprecht, 1st ed. 1901; 3rd ed. 1910.

Israel und Babylonien: Die Einfluss Babyloniens auf die israelitische Religion. Göttingen: Vandenhoeck & Ruprecht, 1903.

Das Märchen im Alten Testament. Relgionsgeschichtliche Volksbücher. Tübingen: Mohr/Siebeck, 1921.

I Peter. *Der Schriften des Neuen Testaments.* 1906. 3rd ed. Göttingen: Vandenhoeck & Ruprecht, 1917–18.

Die Prophet Esra (IV. Esra). Tübingen: Mohr/Siebeck, 1900.

Die Propheten. Göttingen: Vandenhoeck & Ruprecht, 1917.

Die Psalmen. HAT. Göttingen: Vandenhoeck & Ruprecht, 1929.

Reden und Aufsätze. Göttingen: Vandenhoeck & Ruprecht, 1913.

Schöpfung und Chaos in Urzeit und Endzeit: Eine Religionsgeschichtliche Untersuchung über Gen. 1 und Ap. Joh. 12. Göttingen: Vandenhoeck & Ruprecht, 1895.

Die Wirkungen des heiligen Geistes nach der populären Anschauung der apostolischen Zeit und der Lehre des Apostels Paulus. Göttingen: Vandenhoeck & Ruprecht, 1888.

Assessments of Gunkel's Work

Baumgartner, Walther. "Hermann Gunkel." *Neue Zürcher Zeitung* 489/499. Reprinted in: *idem, Zum Alten Testament und seiner Umwelt: Ausgewälte Aufsätze,* 371–78. Leiden: Brill, 1959.

———. "Zum 100: Geburtstag von Hermann Gunkel." In *Congress Volume: Bonn, 1962,* 1–18. VTSup 9. Leiden: Brill, 1963.

Bovon, François. "Hermann Gunkel: Historian of Religion and Exegete of Literary Genres." In *Exegesis: Problems of Method and Exercises in Reading.* Edited by F. Bovon and G. Rouiller. Translated by D. G. Miller. Pittsburgh Theological Monograph Series 21. Pittsburgh: Pickwick, 1978 (French ed. 1975).

Childs, Brevard S. "Review of Werner Klatt, *Hermann Gunkel.*" *JBL* 88 (1969) 508–9.

Galling, Kurt. "Hermann Gunkel." *Zeitschrift für Mission und Religionswissenschaft* (1932) 257–74.

Humbert, Paul. "Hermann Gunkel, un maétre des études hébraiques. Nécrologie." *Revue de Théologie et Philosophie* (1932) 5–19.

Klatt, Werner. "Die 'Eigentümlichkeit' der israelitischen Religion in der Sicht von Hermann Gunkel." *Evangelische Theologie* 28 (1968) 153–60.

———. *Hermann Gunkel: Zu seiner Theologie der Religionsgeschichte und zur Entstehung der formgeschichtlichen Methode.* FRLANT 100. Göttingen: Vandenhoeck & Rupprecht, 1969.

Nicholson, Ernest W. "Hermann Gunkel as a Pioneer of Modern Old Testament Study." Forward to Hermann Gunkel, *Genesis*, translated by M. E. Biddle. MLBS. Macon, Ga.: Mercer Univ. Press, 1997.

Oden, Robert A., Jr. "Intellectual History and the Study of the Bible." In *The Future of Biblical Studies: The Hebrew Scriptures*, edited by R. E. Friedman and H. G. M. Williamson, 1–18. Semeia Studies. Atlanta: Scholars, 1987.

Rollmann, H. "Zwei Briefe Hermann Gunkels an Adolf Jülicher zur religionsgeschichtlichen und formgeschichtlichen Methode." *ZTK* 78 (1981) 276–88.

Schmidt, Hans. "In Memoriam Hermann Gunkel." *TBl* 11 (1932) 97–103.

Scullion, J. J. "Gunkel, Johannes Heinrich Hermann." In *Dictionary of Biblical Interpretation*, edited by J. H. Hayes, 1.472–73. Nashville: Abingdon, 1999.

Smend, Rudolf. "Gunkel, Hermann." In *Deutsche Alttestamentler in drei Jahrhunderten*, 160–72. Göttingen: Vandenhoeck & Ruprecht, 1989.

Index of Modern Authors

Editor's Note: Dates have been supplied for authors of earlier generations in order to provide historical context.

Index of Ancient Sources